"*The Telling Room* spins [a] hila_____ ull of Castilian-size detours, it is a tr_____ sonal memoir rolled into one hugely likable book. It is also a classic example of how the tale of getting the tale can, in the right hands, be storytelling gold."
—*The Boston Globe*

"You do not have to be interested in Spain, or even in cheese, to be blown away by [*The Telling Room*]. This fascinating nonfiction book ostensibly is about a Spanish cheesemaker, but it really is about the power of myth— how we use stories to sustain and define us, and how we tell and retell our stories until they become our truth. . . . It's wise and funny and almost as thrilling as the subtitle suggests." —Minneapolis *Star-Tribune*

"It's a testament to Paterniti's powers that he's able to squeeze a saga about a beautiful country and an unforgettable man from a (delicious) hunk of curdled fat." —*Entertainment Weekly* (Grade: A)

"Breathtakingly cinematic . . . reads like Bill Buford's *Heat*, conveying the passions of both author and subject, but with David Foster Wallace's gift for digression." —*Tampa Bay Times*

"Paterniti dives deeply into Spain's political history, the pleasures of craft, and the motives and methods of storytelling itself." —*Harper's*

"An entertaining olio of anecdotes, fables, lore, facts, gossip and family legends ... By absorbing and being accepted among the eighty souls of Guzmán, [Paterniti] gains access to their feuds and fears and stories, especially the one about the curds and whey that put them on the map." —*Bloomberg*

"The list of writers I would read even if they were to write about a piece of cheese has always been short, but it includes Michael Paterniti. He has proved here that if you love something enough, and pay a passionate-enough attention to it, the whole world can become present in it. That's true of both the cheese and the book."
—JOHN JEREMIAH SULLIVAN, author of *Pulphead*

"Lovely [and] rollicking ... Paterniti writes with charm and verve, providing cultural context with discursive footnotes that mimic Ambrosio's own circuitous style. He leads the reader down his own twisting path to a deeper understanding of why we need the Ambrosios of the world: They are the storytellers whose magic makes reality bearable." —*BookPage*

"Full of drama . . . A great product is a nice thing to have, but a good product with a great back story is a blessing beyond riches."—*Los Angeles Times*

"For my money, Paterniti is one of the most expansive and joyful writers around—big-hearted and humane and funny. This book is a wild and amazing ride." —GEORGE SAUNDERS, author of *Tenth of December*

"Yes, *The Telling Room* is about a cheese, Páramo de Guzmán, but it is also a book about the way Americans live now, what we eat and how our food is produced (farmers market fetishists and artisanal eggheads, take note). It is about stories and their tellers, truth and lies, facts and illusions." —*Newsday*

"Extraordinary . . . Paterniti is one of the best contemporary nonfiction writers whose words I have consumed. . . . Pyrotechnic writing, an unforgettable central character, fascinating asides (rendered mostly as footnotes) and plenty of insights into Paterniti's mind." —*The Dallas Morning News*

"Few writers can write about the taste of food with Paterniti's vibrancy and precision. . . . [He] is a master of finding and telling great stories (the finding, for most writers, often being as difficult as the telling) that appear to be about something small, such as cheese, but are actually about something far larger—in this case, the whole of human existence. . . . As much as *The Telling Room* is about a Spaniard's quest to create a cheese that embodies all the love and pain and joy he's ever known, it's also the story of a writer's quest to channel that obsession into the perfect story." —*Esquire*

"If you love food and love reading about food, you can't do better than this beautiful, passionate book. I finished it and wanted to fly immediately to Spain and eat everything in sight."
—MARCUS SAMUELSSON, author of *Yes, Chef*

"Paterniti's writing sings, whether he's talking about how food activates memory, or the joys of watching his children grow. It's the first biography of a cheese that might just bring a tear to your eye." —NPR

"Paterniti immerses you in an immersion-friendly milieu of sun-baked highland plateaus, argumentative village rustics and beguiling old ways. . . . A wonderful pretext for a book . . . Ambrosio is a heck of a teller, a natural ham . . . whose fits of emotion and loquacity are delightfully barmy. . . . I'm glad Paterniti dared to take cheese-sign prose to the outer limits." —*The New York Times Book Review*

"Besides being a great story, *The Telling Room* is also about the way stories shape our perception of reality. . . . I'm not quite sure what to call this book. It's not easily categorized. It exists in the ether, somewhere between memoir, 'new journalism,' slow-food manifesto, a brief history of Spain, small town mystery, and Don Quixote remix. At its heart, it is a story about idealism versus practicality, and the difficulty of building a life worth living. Besides all those super deep/profound things, it's just an amazingly well-crafted story. We should all admire Michael Paterniti—first for bringing us this story, and second for telling it the way it's supposed to be told."
—*The Christian Science Monitor*

"Much as Molinos regales Paterniti with his rich voice, Paterniti entertains us by retelling this saga of a man who successfully recovers his family's cheese recipe, whose childhood friend betrays him by stealing the business, and who half-heartedly seeks revenge for the betrayal . . . Paterniti's zestful storytelling carries us along on a delightful journey through a village rich with the traditions of food and family." —*Publishers Weekly* (starred review)

"A beguiling, multifaceted narrative larded with delightful culinary, historical, political, psychological and literary layers . . . Paterniti gracefully unravels how tradition, culture and a sense of place affect the human heart, while simultaneously wrestling with the joys and boundaries of storytelling and journalism. . . . Enriched by Paterniti's singular art of storytelling, this is a deeply satisfying voyage across a remarkable landscape into the mysteries and joys of the human heart." —*Kirkus Reviews* (starred review)

"Elegant, strange, funny, and insightful, *The Telling Room* is a marvelous tale and a joyful read, a trip into a world peopled by some of the most remarkable characters—and yes, cheese—in memory."
—Susan Orlean, author of *The Orchid Thief*

"Michael Paterniti is one of the best living practitioners of the art of literary journalism, able to fully elucidate and humanize the everyday and the epic. In his hands, every subject, every moment of personal or global upheaval, is treated with the same curiosity, respect, empathy, and clear-eyed wisdom."
—Dave Eggers, author of *A Hologram for the King*

ALSO BY MICHAEL PATERNITI

Driving Mr. Albert

THE TELLING ROOM

DIAL PRESS TRADE PAPERBACKS
NEW YORK

THE TELLING ROOM

A TALE OF LOVE, BETRAYAL, REVENGE, AND THE WORLD'S GREATEST PIECE OF CHEESE

MICHAEL PATERNITI

2014 Dial Press Trade Paperback Edition

Copyright © 2013 by Michael Paterniti

Published in the United States by Dial Press Trade Paperbacks, an imprint of Random House, a division of Random House LLC, a Penguin Random House Company, New York.

DIAL PRESS and the HOUSE colophon are registered trademarks of Random House LLC.

Originally published in hardcover in the United States by The Dial Press, an imprint of Random House, a division of Random House LLC, in 2013.

Map and illustrations on pages v, 1, 91, 245, and 317 copyright © 2013 by Benjamin Busch. Used by permission. Photos on page xiii and 177 copyright © 2013 by Gerry Hadden. Used by permission.

Library of Congress Cataloging-in-Publication Data
Paterniti, Michael.
The Telling Room : a tale of love, betrayal, revenge, and the world's greatest piece of cheese / Michael Paterniti.
pages cm
ISBN 978-0-385-33701-4
eBook ISBN 978-0-8129-9454-4
1. Cheesemakers—Spain—Guzmán—Biography.
2. Cheesemaking—Spain—Guzmán—History.
3. Guzmán (Spain)—Biography.
4. Paterniti, Michael—Travel—Spain—Guzmán. I. Title.
SF274.S7P37 2013
637'.3092—dc23 [B] 2013001430

Printed in the United States of America on acid-free paper

www.dialpress.com

2 4 6 8 9 7 5 3 1

Book design by Susan Turner

For Marianne and Richard,
my mom and dad,
with love, awe, and gratitude.

Let us be confident:
There will be no truth
In anything we think.

—ANTONIO MACHADO

CONTENTS

I.

II.

III.

IV.

I

*Imagination magnifies small objects
with fantastic exaggeration
until they fill our soul . . .*

Blaise Pascal, *Human Happiness*

1

1991

"It sat silently, hoarding its secrets."

THIS PARTICULAR STORY BEGINS IN THE DUSKY HOLLOWS OF 1991, remembered as a rotten year through and through by almost everybody living, dead, or unborn. I'm sure there were a few who had it good, maybe even made millions off other people's misfortune, but for the rest of us, there wasn't a glimmer. January dawned with tracers over Baghdad, the Gulf War. It was a bad year for Saddam Hussein and the Israeli farmer (Scud missiles, weak harvest), the Politburo of the Soviet Union (dissolved), and the sawmills of British Columbia (rising stumpage fees, etc.). An estimated one hundred and fifty thousand people died in a Bangladeshi cyclone. The IRA launched a mortar attack on 10 Downing Street, shattering the windows and scorching the wall of the room where Prime Minister John Major was meeting with his Cabinet ("I think we'd better start again, somewhere else," said the prime minister). In the Philippines, Mount Pinatubo erupted, ejecting 30 billion metric tons of magma and aerosols, draping a thick layer of sulfuric acid over the earth, cooling temperatures while torching the ozone layer.

It was a brutal year for the ozone layer.

Here in America, it was no better: the rise of Jack Kevorkian, Magic Johnson's HIV diagnosis, Donald Trump's dwindling empire. Rape, mass murder, and masturbation.* The country slopped along in a recession, and meanwhile, I wasn't feeling so good myself.

To kick things off, I got dumped in January. I was twenty-six years old, making about $5,000 a year, pretax. I lived in a two-bedroom apartment in Ann Arbor, Michigan, with my roommate, Miles, both of us graduate students in the creative writing program for fiction, a.k.a. Storytelling School. We each had a futon and a stereo—and everything else (two couches, black-and-white TV, waffle iron) we'd foraged from piles in front of houses on Big Trash Day.

That year, I toted around a book entitled *The Great Depression of 1990,* one bought on remainder for a dollar, and that predicted absolute global meltdown . . . *in 1990.* But I, for one, wasn't going to look like an idiot if it hit a year or two late. The advantage I had over most everyone else in the world was my lack of participation in the economy, except to issue policy statements, from the couch, before our blizzardy TV screen of black-and-white pixels. The eleven o'clock news brought us Detroit anchorman Bill Bonds and all the bad acid and strange perversions of the year—the William Kennedy Smith trial, the Clarence Thomas hearings, the Rodney King beating—all delivered from beneath his superb toupee, woven it seemed with fine Incan silver.

Nineteen-ninety-one was the year we were to graduate, and as the months progressed toward that spring rite of passage, a funny thing happened: We, the storytellers, could not get our stories published—*anywhere.* We typed in fits of Kerouacian ecstasy, swaddled our stories in manila envelopes, sent them out to small journals across the country. The rejections came back in our own self-addressed envelopes, like homing pigeons.

So we stewed in our obscurity—and futility. We were Artists. We

---

* Mike Tyson, Jeffrey Dahmer, Pee-wee Herman.

worked as course assistants and teachers of Creative Writing 101, reading Wallace Stevens poems to the uvulas of the yawning undergrad horde, moving ourselves to inspiration while the class spoke among itself. We kept office hours in a holding pen with sixteen other teachers, and then went and drank cheap beer at Old Town Tavern, swapping lines from our rejection letters. As it began to dawn on us that the end of our cosseted academic ride was near, the tension ratcheted so high that we started spending extra time with the only people who were consistently more miserable than we were: the poets.

In pictures from our graduation, we—my posse and I—look so innocent, like kids really, kids with full heads of hair and skinny bodies and a glint of fear in our eyes, gazing out at the savage world and our futures. You can almost see our brains at work in those photos, now just hours away from the cruelest epiphany: Those preciously imagined short story collections and novels, copied and bound lovingly at Kinko's, called *The Shape of Grief* or *What the Helix Said*,* qualified us for, well, almost . . . exactly . . . *nothing.*

Which is what led me to a local deli, a place called Zingerman's, to see if they needed an extra sandwich-maker on weekends. This was Zingerman's before it did $44 million in annual sales and possessed a half million customers, but it was already an Ann Arbor legend, a fabled arcade of fantastic food, a classic, slightly cramped New York–style deli in the Midwest, with a tin ceiling, black-and-white tiled floor, and the yummiest delicacies from around the world. The shelves overflowed with bottles of Italian lemonade, exotic marmalade spreads, and tapenades. The brothy smell of matzo ball soup permeated the place. On Saturday mornings, before Michigan football games, people thronged, forming a line down Kingsley Street. The sandwiches cost

---

* Mine was entitled *Augie Twinkle's Lament*, and detailed—some might say excruciatingly—the progress of a minor league pitcher to his final game on the mound, where, after being shelled, he exits over the center-field fence, discarding his uniform, piece by piece, in grief-stricken striptease. From there, left only in his codpiece, he goes on a laundry-stealing binge . . . and the rest, you'll have to trust me, is heartrending, humorous, and deeply compelling.

twice as much as anywhere else, and whenever we splurged as students, we'd go there and stand in the long line, the longer the better actually, just to prolong the experience. Then we'd order from colorful chalkboards hung from the ceiling, detailing a cornucopia of sandwiches with names like "Gemini Rocks the House," "Who's Greenberg Anyway?," and "The Ferber Experience," each made on homemade farm bread or grilled challah or Jewish rye, stuffed with Amish chicken breast or peppered ham or homemade pastrami, with Wisconsin muenster or Switzerland Swiss or Manchester creamy cheddar, and topped with applewood-smoked bacon or organic sunflower sprouts or honey mustard.

In the days before the rise of gourmand culture, before our obsession with purity and pesticides, before the most fetishistic of us could sit over plates of Humboldt Fog expounding on our favorite truffles or estate-bottled olive oil, Zingerman's preached a new way of thinking about food: Eat the best, and eat homemade. Why choke down oversalted, processed chicken soup when you might slurp Zingerman's rich stock, with its tender carrots and hint of rosemary? Why suffer any old chocolate when you might indulge in handcrafted, chocolate-covered clementines from some picturesque village in northern Italy, treats that exploded in your mouth, the citrus flooding in tingles across the tongue with the melted cocoa spreading beneath it, lifting and wrapping the clementine once again, but differently now, in the sweetest chocolate-orange cradle of sensory pleasure? Judging by the towering shelves of rare, five-star products from around the world—the quinces and capers, the salamis and spoonfruits, the sixteen-year-old balsamic vinegar and Finnish black licorice—the quest for higher and higher gustatory ecstasies never ceased.

If Zingerman's preached a new way of thinking about food, it was by practicing the old ways, by trying to make latkes as they'd been made a hundred years ago, by returning to traditional recipes. The idea was to deepen the experience of eating by giving customers a sense of culinary history and geography, to ask questions like: *Why* are bagels round?

To my mind, such inquiry and excellence deserved me, and even if I was only going to build sandwiches, I would beam my own excellence in perfect slathers of mayo and mustard. After all, I needed a job, and the food and the karma were so good at Zingerman's, it felt like a place I could make home for a while.

So one June day found me hiking up the steep stairs to the office above the deli and presenting myself as the answer to Zingerman's problems, whatever its problems were. I came armed with my résumé bearing the proud monogram MFA, and within three minutes, two of them spent waiting, one of the deli mistresses set me straight.

"We don't have anything right now," she said, as seven phones rang at once, and turned back to business.

A few days later, the deli called. They wanted to see me regarding a special opportunity. I beelined back to the office and stood before the deli woman again. "I noticed you've done some proofreading," she said casually, her eyes skimming my résumé to jog specifics. "Ari writes all the newsletters himself, and we could use someone to check it each month." It wasn't for sure, my new boss cautioned. And it might be four to six hours a month. We could try one first. To see how it went.

I thought I heard something like eight dollars an hour. "Done," I said.

I left with a folder clutched tightly under my arm and a new *sproing* in my step. The newsletter, the monthly newsletter! It sat in stacks in the store. Everyone from the ebullient hard-core gourmands to the morose doctoral students read it while waiting in line, especially because it contained a menu and you couldn't read the chalkboards from a mile away. But it was more than that: It was part foodie bible, part travelogue, in which Ari brought to stirring life his global search for goodies as he played out the thrilling Indiana Jones lead. From a business point of view, the newsletter had always been a bit of marketing genius, and now it had become Ari's trademark, one his followers craved reading as much as their latest *New Yorker* issues.

The Ari in question was Ari Weinzweig, co-owner of the Zingerman universe and a man of panache, chutzpah, and wide-roaming palate. Once he'd been a University of Michigan history major and collector of anarchist literature; now he was caught in a daily downpour of money from the clouds of patrons at his doorstep. Ari was tall, handsome, with dark ringlets of hair, the overeducated man's Jeff Goldblum. Everybody seemed to want a word. He was ARI, gourmet argonaut, the Sherlock Holmes of nosh and niblets.* I'd seen him once or twice in the deli, wearing spandex shorts, just in from a run. He was always trailed by a gaggle of pretty people. Long, lean, hypnotic, the magic man of food—AHHHH-REEE.

And so, naturally, the newsletter was a revved-up reflection of Ari's peregrinations, and as such was never meant to be literature. His was a breezy, conversational style, full of exclamations (*This is the best!*) and enthusiasms (*You gotta try it!*), a pleated high-school pep squad for his personal pantry. His greatest strength was a knack for making you hungry. Back at my apartment, even as I imagined Ari up in first class on a flight to St. Petersburg in search of the world's best beluga caviar, I dug a couple of pencils from the drawer, then pulled the folder from my backpack, placed it on the desk, and began perusing the pages. On first read, it was good, if a bit rustic. There was the occasional clunker, but that was to be expected. I made some marks, deleted a few words, added a suggestion. I got up and fixed a grilled cheese. Sat back down. Made more notes. Were we being a little *too* effusive about the Jewish noodle kugel? Couldn't we add a more savory detail re: the sour-cream coffee cake? What about expanding our adjective horizon beyond "tasty" and "delicious"?

By late afternoon, I'd completely rewritten the thing. Ari's style was now more . . . *Cheeveresque.* I couldn't wait for him to return from St. Petersburg, or wherever, so I could entirely rewrite his next newsletter about beluga caviar. I put the folder aside, revisited it once more

---

* In a *New York Times* article from the Business section on May 3, 2007, about the populist rise of Zingerman's, Michael Ruhlman, a food industry expert and writer, summed up the deli's success over the decades like this: "There's not a lot the consumer can do, really, to get Iberian ham, but Ari can."

late that night while eating cold noodles. Yes. Perfect. Bill Bonds came on: Boris Yeltsin was standing on top of a tank in front of the Kremlin; the Soviet regime had been toppled.

Things were looking up.

Back at the deli a few days later, reaction to the revolution—my first edit—was surprisingly muted. "I think we're trying to keep Ari's voice intact," said my boss, handing back my edit. *Maybe we should let Ari be the judge of that,* I wanted to say. But really, I needed the job. So I gathered the pages into the folder again and, home at my desk, armed with a plump red eraser, brought him back to life. I added more exclamations. In the margins, I wrote: "Wouldn't this be a good place for a 'delicious'?" I reminded myself that I was thrilled not only to get paid for reading but also to be reading anything besides lit-crit books that quoted heavily from Lukács's theory of reification.

During a time when microwave popcorn passed for dinner, the subject of fine food also offered a vicarious thrill. While I couldn't afford to eat well, I could certainly *aspire* to. So I read with an enthusiasm that matched Ari's on the page. I could taste the pickles and smoked fish. I could hear the cow moo and the butter churn. I was drawn deeper and deeper into his savory world, though I never forgot my place as foot servant. The truth is, Ari Weinzweig never would have recognized me if we'd smacked into each other before the loaves of rye.

That, however, didn't dampen my enthusiasm about our next order of business together: the October newsletter, which was Zingerman's second annual celebration of Spanish food. The deli was working in concert with the Spanish tourist board and artisanal food makers there, and sometime earlier that year, Ari had eaten his way across the country in search of delectables. Something about the evocation of warm sun, sangria, and gluttony just as the low ceiling of gray lake clouds closed over Michigan for the next half year struck a chord, and while *my* only visit to Spain had come on a chilly European jaunt during my junior year abroad in London—there were Uzi'd *policia* in the streets of Madrid ten years after Franco's death

and an elaborate night trying to find Salvador Dalí on the Costa
Brava*—the country flashed back now through Ari's prose.

That October newsletter was his aria, his masterpiece, his opus.
The writing seemed to come from a different man. The passion was
unbridled. *¡Vaya!* He sang the praises of Spanish olives and Rías
Baixas wine, Salamancan ham and a host of cheeses that included
Manchegos, Cabrales, Majoreros. I tightened and added a few
"delicious"es. I padded an entry about sherry, lightened another about
olive oil. I turned the page—and suddenly, from nowhere, came an
entry that needed no intervention whatsoever. It was about a special
cheese Ari had hunted down, and it appeared under the heading
"New and Amazing," three paragraphs buried among six type-packed,
oversized pages—crammed between a primer on Sephardic Jewish
cooking and an ad for a paella-making clinic.

"Though I've saved this one for last," wrote Ari, "don't let me
mislead you. This is really an outstanding piece of cheese . . . so anon-
ymous I discovered it by chance in London. It's also the most expensive cheese we've ever sold. Makes me a little nervous just putting it on
the counter."

The item went on to describe how this piece of "sublime" cheese
was made in Castile, in the north-central part of the country, and
how, when Ari had visited the cheesemaker himself, the Spaniard had
shared vivid memories of his grandmother making the very same
cheese and imploring him to keep the tradition alive. When asked by
Ari how he justified making such an expensive cheese, the man had
said, "Because it's made with love."

But there was more: Each day this cheesemaker collected fresh

---

* We ended up at Dalí's seaside villa in Cadaqués, where a friend and I crept to the
door at midnight to hear the artist's favorite music, *Tristan and Isolde,* at full volume. When our knocking went unheeded, we retreated to Dalí's high garden wall
and drank two bottles of wine, which, along with high winds and a bevy of bats,
fanned the flames of that haunted night until, terrified, we leaped at some sound
and, entirely misjudging the drop, ended up sprained and bloody, limping miles
before we found our backpacker hostel again.

milk from "his flock of one hundred Churra sheep." The milk was poured into vats, stirred, and after it had coagulated, the curd was hand-cut into tiny pieces "in order to expel as much liquid as possible." Each wheel of the cheese was then pressed to rid it of any remaining moisture and transported to a nearby cave. After the first aging, the cheese was submerged in extra-virgin olive oil and aged again, for at least a year. The stuff of his job—the minutiae, the care, the importance of time—happened to sound a lot like the job of a writer.

"It's rich, dense, intense," sang Ari, "a bit like Manchego, but with its own distinct set of flavors and character."

There was something about all of it, not just the perfection of Ari's prose, but the story he told—the village cheesemaker, the ancient family recipe, the old-fashioned process by which the cheese was born, the idiosyncratic tin in which it was packaged—that I couldn't stop thinking about, even as I went on to contend with misplaced modifiers in a passage about marzipan. It occurred to me that there we were, living through cursed 1991, in a crushing recession—when the national dialogue centered around whether Clarence Thomas had uttered the question "Who has put pubic hair on my Coke?"—and along came this outrageous, overpriced, presumptuous little cheese, almost angelic in its naïveté, fabulist in character, seemingly made by an incorruptible artiste who, with an apparent straight face, had stated that its high price tag came because it was "made with love."

Was this for real?

I went to the deli. At $22* a pound for the cheese, I had no intention of buying any. I'd come, however odd it sounds, to gaze upon it. Thus I timed my visit for in-between rushes. I picked up the finished newsletter at the door and stood for a while, reading as if the words were not only brand-new to me but the most fascinating thing I'd ever had occasion to trip over. I watched a few other nicely dressed

---

* Twenty-two dollars equaling eight chili dogs, or seven falafels, or five bibimbaps, i.e., a week's worth of dinners.

people—quilted jackets, colorful scarves—reading it, taking pleasure in their pleasure. Then I dove in, jostling through holes in the line, moving across the black-and-white-checked floor until I found myself face-to-face with the cheeses behind the nursery glass: There were the Manchego and Cabrales, Mahón and Garrotxa . . . and there was *my* cheese. It seemed to hover there, apart in its own mystical world. It came in its white tin with black etching that read PÁRAMO DE GUZMÁN. The package, which was almost oval in shape, bore the emblem of a gold medal for supreme excellence above all other cheeses, an honor from some agricultural fair, it appeared. And perched there in the display, before a pyramid of the tins, was a piece cut into three wedges. Unlike its paler Manchego and Mahón brethren, it possessed an over-all caramel hue. It may sound strange to call a cheese soulful, but that's what this cheese seemed to be, just by sight. It had traveled so far to be here, and from so long ago. I let myself fantasize about what it might taste like, as I could only fantasize about a gourmandizing, dandy's life in which I might pen the words ". . . discovered it by chance in London."

And this is when an odd shift occurred inside: That little hand-made cheese in the tin, and its brash lack of cynicism in a rotten year, gave me a strange kind of hope. I sensed the presence of purity and transcendence. I felt I knew this cheese somehow, or would. It sat si-lently, hoarding its secrets. How long would it wait to speak?

A long time, as it turned out. But when it did, the cheese had a lot to say. Unlike that day in 1991, when I felt so pressed to leave the deli in order to put the finishing touches on another one of my overheated homing pigeons of prose, it became nearly impossible for me to walk away.

2

THE OFFERING

"Ambrosio Molinos, it's your time to kick ass!"

ONCE UPON A TIME, IN THE VAST, EMPTY HIGHLANDS OF THE Central Plateau of Spain . . . in the kingdom of Castile . . . in a village on a hill . . . on a bed in a house where the summer temperature hovered at one hundred degrees . . . a woman named Purificación lay writhing in labor. For hours the baby's soon-to-be father had come and gone from the dark bedroom as the woman, sylphed in shadows, rode the wave of each contraction. "Anyone here yet?" said the man, smiling, sipping a cold drink. His wife, a woman of owlish beauty and a certain refinement, said to the midwife, "Get that donkey's ass away from me!"

Eventually, the baby was born—in the same room, on the same bed, beneath the same roof as his great-grandfather—making him the youngest of three boys belonging to the husband and wife. He had almond-shaped eyes, a body as hefty as a bag of oats, and, even then, lungs that never quit, emitting a loud, gravelly cry. He was not to be overlooked. He ate more than his brothers; slept less. And he had inordinate passion. From the beginning, he endeared himself to his parents by loving them as hard as he could, with an exquisite kind of ardor. When he learned to walk, he followed them everywhere; when he could speak, he spoke to them.

Incessantly.

While basking in his mother's love, he came to idolize his father. But it wasn't just that: From the start, he wanted to *be* his father, an immensely likeable, tough-minded farmer—of big ears and strong, curled fingers the reddish color of the earth here—who had a story for any occasion, a punch line for every dull moment. Each morning, his father zipped himself into his *mulo,* his blue farmer's jumpsuit, put on his black beret, and, whistling contentedly, strode the eighth of a mile to the barn along a dirt path that looked down on the high flatlands of Castile, those harsh, empty steppes that make up Spain's Meseta and that bring scouring gales and then burning sun. Living half a mile above sea level, the Castilians often described their weather as nine months of winter and three months of hell.

This was 1950s Spain, bitter times to be a farmer, bitter times to be a Spaniard. In the second decade of Franco's dictatorship, poverty was a fact of life; there was little food or electricity in the hinterlands.*
Meanwhile, people were migrating in droves away from the semiarid Meseta to the big industrial cities—Bilbao, Barcelona, Valencia—while those left behind farmed the land mostly as they had for centuries, plowing, planting, and threshing by hand. Even the language of the fields was antiquated. Sometimes the boy's father would greet a friend by proffering a hand with an old salutation that translated as "Hey, shake the shovel."

---

* "Country, religion, family—this is our eat and drink," Franco says in stumbling English in a newsreel from the time when it's estimated that there were as many as 200,000 deaths in Spain due to hunger. Franco, who himself was a strange kind of cipher (depending on accounts, a homicidal kleptomaniac or the father of new Spain), became enamored of a cockamamie scheme to feed Spain's population of 30 million with sandwiches made of dolphin meat to be pulled from local waters. It wasn't until 1959, when economic control was wrested from Falangist ideologues, that fortunes changed and the seeds of the "Spanish Miracle," a period of intense growth, were sown.

The village in which they lived bore the name of the Guzmán family, prominent nobles (statesmen, generals, viceroys) instrumental in the workings of the kingdom of León beginning in the twelfth century. Sometime along the way, a Leonese monarch had bequeathed the Guzmáns 3,000 hectares in the Duero River region for a retreat. In the 1700s, Cristóbal Guzmán built the castle—known in the village as the *palacio*—over the span of sixty years, as an exact replica (if seventeen times smaller) of the family's castle in León. Around it, the village flourished, populated at its height by thousands of inhabitants whose patronage sustained restaurants and bars, barbershops and several markets. Though the father—and his father, and his father's father, and so on—had lived his entire life in the village, it was unclear how deep the family roots ran in the region, even as they flourished. At the height of the family's influence, they'd come to own the palace. But by the 1950s, the family was in the process of diminishment, losing more of their field hands to the city as they sold off more of their land. The father had an uncanny knack for making the worst of times seem like the best of times. No matter what the crisis, he remained undaunted in his happiness, singing and drinking his homemade wine. He played cards at crowded tables and told story after story, some about his youthful indiscretions, meeting girls in the fields for the old *chaca chaca,* some about his days in Morocco with the Spanish army, where the troops seemed to spend more time changing punctured truck tires than anything else. One he loved to tell had occurred when he was younger, when Castile was being heavily bombed by planes during the Civil War. Whenever the church bells tolled a warning, everyone ran and hid in the caves that pocked the countryside here. Except for him and his friends. They would jump on their motorbikes and, beneath the roar of fighter planes, leaning low over the handlebars, they would gun the twenty miles to the nearby city of Aranda de Duero, where they found all the restaurants and bars abandoned, with food and drink still on the tables. The perfect *comida:* a partial *chuleta* and freshly poured red wine, a piece of fish and cerveza, a half-eaten flan with digestif. All the better if there was some cheese on the table, for he adored cheese. They went from establishment to establishment until the bombing ceased, and with the first signs of a return to normalcy fled again, zigzagging back up the hill to home.

And so it was after this man—the happy-whistling guzzler of life, the father-farmer-gadfly—that his baby was named: *Ambrosio,* suggesting the food of the gods, but meaning "immortal." After a time, the villagers called father and son "los dos Ambrosios," the two Ambrosios, which later was shortened to "los Ambrosios," such was the power of their stamp on each other and the town. If you were talking to one of the Ambrosios, it was understood that you were talking to both of the Ambrosios, and all the ancestral Ambrosios, too, even poor great-grandfather, whose ashes were kept in a porcelain vessel in the downstairs dining room, partly in memoriam and partly to make them laugh, as they did, at the misspelled inscription on the jar: *Anbrosio.*

For a certain kind of boy, the kind that the younger Ambrosio happened to be—a bit rough, mischievous, full of irrepressible joy and physical energy—Guzmán was a wonderland of ruins and hiding places, broad fields and indentations called *barcos,* perfect for ambush. The main street wound upward, snaking between the stone homes, past the church to the palace, past *caseta* and pig barn, out into a whole other infinite world above—what was called *arriba* here, a polar cap of fertile soil. In this landscape, Ambrosio ran feral with the local kids, playing *la talusa* and *linka.* Even in school, he dreamed of his afternoon freedom, when he'd be at play again, or hanging out at one of the natural springs or fountains (where the people did their wash, collected their water, filled tanks for irrigation). He celebrated the village's annual fiesta by keeping himself awake for as long as he could over the course of five September days: to be chased by the exploding bull—a man dressed in a costume with Roman candles for horns—and watch the fireworks and sing *jotas* and dance with the grown-ups.

He bore witness to the wonders of the outside world, on those occasions when they penetrated. Sometime in the sixties, Gypsies brought the first moving pictures to town, projecting them on the side of the *palacio,* old black-and-white films from the thirties. Another time, a magician named Barbache the Seal-man balanced an enormous hand plow on his nose. If he'd sneezed, he would have chopped himself in half.

Above all, there was the *bodega*.

This region of Castile is littered with *bodegas,* handmade caves dating back to a time before refrigeration. In Aranda de Duero, the Bodega de las Ánimas, built in the fifteenth century, is a maze of three hundred caves, equaling seven miles of underground tunnel, in which seven million bottles of wine are produced each year. In Guzmán, there existed two dozen or so caves, located in the hill that marked the village's northern boundary. Some of the *bodegas* here were said to date back as far as the Roman occupation of Spain, just before the birth of Christ. Each autumn, the fruits of the harvest were brought to the caves and stored—bushels of grain, vegetables, and, in particular, cheese and wine, the latter transported in casks made from cured goat carcasses—to be accessed during the long winter and spring. Legend had it that a man would sit in a room built above the cave and itemize what went down into the cellars. This room became known as *el contador,* or the counting room.

As all the families in the village built or inherited *bodegas,* they also added these counting rooms, sometimes sculpting a foyer and perhaps stairs that led up to a cramped, cozy space that included a fireplace. Soon, people gathered at the *contador* to share meals around a table and pass the time. And as the centuries unfolded, as refrigeration techniques improved and the caves came to serve a purpose less utilitarian than social, the room took on the other definition of *contar,* "to tell." The *contador,* then, became a "telling room," or a room in which stories were told. It was the place where, on cold winter nights or endless summer days, villagers traded their histories and secrets and dreams. If one had an important revelation, or needed the intimate company of friends, one might head to the telling room, and over wine and chorizo, unfolding in the wonderfully digressive way of Castilian conversation, the story would out. On weekends, casual gatherings might last an entire day and night, with stories wandering from details of the recent harvest to the dramas of village life to perhaps, finally, the war stories of the past, all accompanied by copious wine. In this way, the *bodega,* with its telling room, became a mystical state of mind as much as a physical place. It was here where the young Ambrosio first fell under the trance of his father telling stories.

Something about those stories chimed loudly inside the mind of the boy, something he could never have articulated at first, but that insisted itself over time. It was a feeling of wonder, an aliveness that came in the timeless hush and clamor of the telling room, in the presence of his father narrating stories. Young Ambrosio was transfixed. He would listen for hours, and then think about the tales afterward, haunted by some weave of detail his father had spun. As garrulous as the boy was, he had the same Pavlovian response to any story being told: He would shut up and listen in a state of mesmerized joy.

Ambrosio possessed no interest in school, and yet his mother had dreams that maybe one day he'd become a doctor. Like his brothers, he was sent to Catholic boarding school at a young age, about fifty miles away in the Castilian capital of Burgos. His real education, though, came in the streets and fields of home, watching the ways of the farmers, collecting the stories that filled the airspace of life here. He spent more and more time out beyond the clustered houses of the village, in that unbroken landscape stretching for miles, a patchwork of vineyards and wheat fields, walking with his father or the old men. The Meseta was littered with stories, too, there like stones to pick up. What occurred in the vineyard known as Matajudío—or Jew Killer Vineyard? What was the strange collection of perfectly round rocks, like pterodactyl eggs, doing embedded in the earth in the Barco de Palomas? Or the broken stars of bone fragments in the High Field?

So he listened, and as he traveled his patch of the earth, he asked himself over and over, *What happened here?* Even as a child, Ambrosio took the lead of his forebears: He spoke to ghosts.

EVENTUALLY, AMBROSIO ENTERED A new kind of restlessness, wandering in search of stories and storytellers, peers with whom he could align himself for life. He started down the hill, in the neighboring village of Quintanamanvirgo, where people seemed more inward and shifty. The village was known by those in Guzmán as *el pueblo de los toros,* because it was said the inhabitants hid in the dark of their alcoves like cowardly bulls when released into the bright center of a bullring. But those people had a story, too, about a secret tunnel that ran through the mesa, joining them to the spirit world.

Another village, Roa, lay beyond—larger and more raucous, self-assured if not prideful, with a multitude of stores and bars and, most important, a flock of young people like himself. It was here that Ambrosio first heard a story, "The Asses of Roa," which he himself later perfected.*

---

* This would have been in the days before the Civil War, when there lived in Roa a priest of such arrogant demeanor that he would never allow himself to be seen without his collar. If confronted with bad behavior—excessive drinking, children fighting in the street—he badgered people with his Bible. Catching sight of him from afar, the townspeople dodged into alleys to avoid His Holiness. In short, he was a priggish, pious bore whose biggest problem was that he'd never been laid.

Now, one day came word of a man suddenly dying in a nearby village, perhaps six miles away. The priest was needed at once to administer the last rites. The priest owned no horse of his own, so he began knocking on doors: the right-hand neighbor's mare needed new shoes; the left-hand neighbor's stallion was already in the fields; and on and on. Finally the priest found a man who had a donkey—and who was only too glad to be of assistance. "May the Lord have mercy on you," the priest said, clambering aboard, making the sign of the cross. And off he rode at breakneck speed.

Not long into his ride, his holiest thoughts were penetrated by a faint braying sound. With slight annoyance, he ignored it. Still, as he rode the braying intensified and became a strange, frantic chorus. Irked now, forcibly distracted from his prayers, he peered behind and to his alarm discovered a pack of donkeys in hot pursuit. The villagers along the road saw a vision they'd never forget—a wild pack of male donkeys chasing a female in heat, the priest with an expression of

And finally, the outer ring of Ambrosio's universe became the metropolis of Aranda de Duero, his father's wartime watering hole, where his best friend, Julián, lived. They'd met at nine years of age, playing basketball for their separate boarding schools. On the court that day Ambrosio was assigned to cover Julián, who was tall and thin, with brown hair. The kid had gangly legs, long arms, and spindly fingers, hands exactly like Ambrosio's—and a body exactly like his, for that matter. They both had big knees. If their *baloncesto* careers were short-lived, something more lasting took root that day. In the changing room, Ambrosio heard a familiar singsong accent, and being congenitally extroverted, he sought out the opposing team and said, "Which one of you is from Aranda?"

Shy and introverted, Julián blushed and raised his hand. "I am," he said. "Why?"

"Because I'm from Guzmán," said Ambrosio.

It turned out that Ambrosio's cousin Nacho was Julián's best friend. Julián named others in his group of friends, and Ambrosio said, "Those are friends of mine, too."

"If you're Nacho's cousin, then why don't I know you?" asked Julián, and a memory clicked for Ambrosio. A family gathering, a Communion party a few years earlier, when they were all of six. "You were smoking cigarettes in the stairwell, and I smoked with you," Ambrosio said. And that had been it.

A beautiful beginning.

---

alarm. The priest did the only thing he could do: He urged his mare on at a greater clip even as the male donkeys became more aggressive, bumping up hard against one another. Finally, one was able to launch himself forward, attaching to the haunch of the lady burro, landing with either hoof in the priest's pockets, pinning him there, in the middle of what soon became donkey in flagrante.

Those who saw the unholy act say that had the priest's garment been less well made, he might have escaped with fewer injuries. As it was, the priest rode on, head whiplashing, pretending that none of it was happening, making the sign of the cross. By the time the priest arrived, the sick man had miraculously recovered, and the priest took to his bed, some say so traumatized he never returned to Roa—or its asses—again.

If Julián was outwardly more serious, Ambrosio appreciated his stealthy bemusement at life, his sidelong smile and sly humor. And Julián loved Ambrosio's shock-at-all-cost abandon, the impulse that led him, time after time, to be expelled from the Catholic schools he attended. Ambrosio was the ringleader and carnival-maker; Julián became his happy conspirator.

They walked the streets yelling silly things at passersby. They hunted in the fields, not great shots like Ambrosio's brother Angel, but good enough to kill the occasional rabbit. One day they felled a wild boar and shared it with friends at the *bodega,* as Ambrosio played his guitar and sang. They took any excuse to be together. At dances and parties—for soon their focus was on women and wine—they might catch each other's eye over the heads of others and communicate telepathically: a pursed smile, a cocked eyebrow, a wink said it all.

As time passed, Julián became more intense about his studies, practicing to be a lawyer in Valladolid, while Ambrosio gave up his studies altogether. And yet they became closer still. They regularly visited each other's homes, a particularly intimate act in Spain, where one's social life is lived in the streets, bars, and *bodegas.* Accordingly, Julián was considered a part of Ambrosio's family, as Ambrosio was considered a part of Julián's. For all of their differences, they grew to be the same tall height, sprouted identical beards, bought motorcycles. They wore baggy shirts and jeans with wide, elephant cuffs. While Julián possessed a contained handsomeness—lantern-jawed, broad-shouldered, implacable, but with shy brown eyes that suggested deeper vulnerabilities—Ambrosio was all outward energy, an open invitation of comic expressions. Their devotion to each other was unwavering, cemented by Julián's sweet attentiveness and Ambrosio's extroverted mythologizing of their friendship.

Later, Julián would be there when Ambrosio met his wife; and Ambrosio was there when Julián met his. They attended each other's weddings. Julián had a standing invitation to eat at Ambrosio's house every Wednesday. And often, as young men, they sat on a Sunday afternoon, up at the *bodega,* in the telling room, staring out across the vast tablelands, sharing red wine. To Ambrosio's mind, Julián was a master storyteller, even better than he, and he reveled in his friend's ability to weave a yarn, his recall for detail and syntax. As they'd shared so much together, and because they spoke a secret kind of shorthand language, there was nothing in these moments they needed to keep from each other. While their interests became the foundation of conversation—the system for growing the best grapes, say, or a particular misadventure in the fields—the real stories that animated their lives, the deepest dreams and fears and feelings of men, are what became their bond.

As AMBROSIO REACHED HIS teenage years, the modern world, as it existed beyond the primitive dreamscape of Guzmán, began to move more quickly: mechanizing, industrializing, mass producing. In the end, a village like Guzmán offered little to hold its inhabitants except the rhythms of habit and nostalgia. With her husband's blessing, the matriarch, Purificación Molinos—for Molinos was their last name—had sent her children far and wide for their education. Roberto, the oldest, was smart and studious, and over time he developed his own artistic sensibility and became a photographer in Madrid. The second son, Angel, studied engineering, while his fluency with people led him to a successful career working for an energy company that took him to Buenos Aires. And then came the third son of Purificación Molinos, the would-be doctor, the ribald heretic, the untamed horse who was Ambrosio. He was kicked out of school in Burgos, where he rebelled against the priests, and was sent to Madrid, where he rebelled again. Living with relatives, he left the house each day for school but never made it, stopping off at bars and pool halls, sharing stories and drinks, showing no interest in books or in making good.

It was now 1972, three years before Franco's demise. Ambrosio was seventeen, a man in size if not maturity walking the barrios of Madrid, killing days, pausing before trees to look up into their branches at their living blossoms and dying leaves, among the dirt and exhaust fumes, if only because they brought back memories of Guzmán. November came and his uncle appeared at the door one evening, saying that he'd come to bring Ambrosio home. A blizzard descended, huge white snow-moths inundating the road. Nothing was discernible. Up the national highway to Aranda, through Roa, and on to Quintanamanvirgo—he was lost, and he still had no idea why he was headed back to Guzmán.

When Ambrosio burst through the downstairs door to the house and climbed the stairs three at a time, with that hulking, prodigal body of his, he rushed past his mother to his father, who lay in bed, pale and motionless, covered in oozing sores. Everything about the room—the stench of putrefying flesh, the lack of light—seemed like a death chamber. As a salve, Purificación had taken a cream made of sheep's milk and rubbed it on her husband's sores, a folk remedy practiced in Guzmán. But it hadn't helped. It had made things worse. Ambrosio's father descended into delirium. His bones were losing calcium and had literally started to bend. He could no longer stand.

"When I saw him," Ambrosio would remember, "I knew that I was never going back to the city, that this was my moment to shoulder the load. I heard a voice that said, *Ambrosio Molinos, it's your time to kick ass!*"

For months the doctor made house calls, confounded by his father's illness, expecting him to die by week's end, but for months Ambrosio's father dimly struggled. He was only forty-five years old; until now, it had never occurred to his son that death might separate them at so early an age. The rugged farmer, salt of the earth, his idol: He couldn't imagine a day in the fields, around the dinner table, up at the *bodega,* in the telling room, without his father. The old man had shown him everything: how to wake early and work, how to fix a tractor, how to swear with panache. He'd shown him how a grape grows, and, in that moment when the purple clusters are flooded with sugar on the vine, how to harvest them. He'd taught his son how to make and drink wine, because wine had to be drunk carefully, with joy. But it was more than that, more than the constant tutorials and stories, the easy joking and shared rituals. His father had all along been silently teaching him to be an Old Castilian by being one himself, guided by a chivalrous code long past. He'd taught him how to listen to the earth, how to speak to the animals, how to love and look after your kind with ferocity.

Ambrosio, the son, took to carrying talismans of his father now, wearing the old man's black beret, conscripting his walking stick. And then there was his mother, who would soon be a widow, who kept on with her daily routine of running the house while wearing a brave face, washing the breakfast dishes that clattered in the sink, making shopping trips, preparing the *comida,* sweeping and polishing and watching the news. Sometimes he might find her sitting before the bleak headlines of that year—plane crash on Ibiza, killing a hundred; train accident near Seville, killing seventy-six—in a catatonic state. The pain he felt for her was unbearable. But at least she had church, and her God there. Ambrosio's God was the wind rushing over the Meseta, and the silence of stars at night. To the voice that came from the ether, urging him to "kick ass," Ambrosio eventually spoke back, offering a trade: my life for my father's. And then he waited.

IN THE MEANTIME, THERE was work to be done. Come morning he rose in darkness, went to the kitchen, ground some coffee, brewed and drank it. Fully awake, he walked in his father's footsteps, pulling on his boots, zipping into his blue *mulo,* emerging into the cool morning air, dogs running loose beside him as if borne along by a stream, in that high, thin atmosphere laced with the scent of loam and faint pig shit. He made his way to the barn, below which spread the sweeping *coterro,* the elevated farmland of Castile.

This was an age-old ritual practiced by the Molinos clan, to see what one's hands could turn of this patch of earth. Planting or nurturing in the spring (*trigo, uvas, habas*—wheat, grapes, beans), watering against the horrific dragon-fire of the summer sun, timing the harvest in those September days before the frost came to kill everything: The farmer's life was days of repetition, of wary watching (not just the crops in the field, but weather forecasts and other farmers and the rise and fall of prices), of constant mending (tractors and sheep pens, rotors and ripped sweaters), of eternal hope and leveling reality. One took one's solace in the little things.

"There's immeasurable glory in riding a tractor," Ambrosio would say. "You start by taking a lap around the fields, smelling the aroma, admiring the colors, day after day, until one morning everything smells ready, as if it's opened and unfurled, and you ask the wheat, *Is it time?* And the wheat says, *Yes, friend, it's time.* And then you know to begin the harvest."

By the time of that first harvest, a second doctor had diagnosed the senior Ambrosio with a disease transmitted by livestock. Brucellosis, or Bang's disease, is characterized by fevers and excessive sweating that smells like wet hay, followed by intense joint and muscle pain and eventually, if left untreated, the erosion of vertebrae, the loss of vision, and a breakdown of the autoimmune system. Made of unpasteurized sheep's milk, the cream meant to heal his wounds had nearly killed him. And if that wasn't enough, cancer was metastasizing in his stomach. A course of treatment was settled on, and over the slow passage of months, he recuperated, could sit upright, then stand with a wobble, then walk again, Lazarus-like. The first time his father stepped from the house under his own power, Ambrosio felt an overwhelming sense of relief. But why had he been spared? And what could Ambrosio offer the universe in return for the miracle?

3

THE TELLING ROOM

"Into this drama we now descended . . ."

IN THE RUSH OF MY OWN LIFE, THE CHEESE FADED FOR A WHILE—until it asserted itself again, with an exclamation point.

After Storytelling School—and my part-time proofreading stint at Zingerman's—I worked for a few years as an editor, for a literary journal and then a glossy outdoor magazine, where it occurred to me that turmoil in Tibet or wild isolation in Patagonia might hold interest equal to Foucault and Sartre. The boon of the job was that I saw stories of all shapes and sizes. Soon I began writing them myself, for different magazines. I traveled on assignment, yo-yoing out into the world, revolving back. I spanned Asia, took a road trip across America, saw Kilimanjaro. I published a book, interviewed the president (Bill Clinton), went to Cuba, where in one of the stranger moments, I found myself embraced and lifted off the ground by Fidel Castro, who smelled like soap. I paid quarterly taxes, and after a string of slightly better apartments, called home an old Victorian that I shared with my wife, Sara, a writer herself who'd graduated from the same Storytelling School and now did the same work as I. Most days

I woke, slurped cereal, and went straight to my office in the attic.
When it came time for a break, I might have stepped out onto my
front porch at eleven, yawning wide, in my buckskin-colored L.L.
Bean slippers and baggy pajama bottoms, to get the mail, which I'm
sure set our neighbors' tongues wagging. If they thought of me as a
crackpot stoner or woolly Hugh Hefner wannabe, I thought of myself
as living a rich, secret life of stories. I sallied forth, temporarily occupied whatever foreign country, then came home in the back of an
airport taxi with a mess of scribbled notebooks, trying to find the narrative line in all the facts and quotes. I'd finish one story in a hotel
room as I started reporting the next.

Perhaps my gallivanting was less gourmet than Ari's had been,
but ten years from my deli days, I was living a life I'd dimly imagined.
I said yes to everything, and every place—then found myself in a
backpacker's hotel in Burma, a five-star in Ho Chi Minh City, a *tukel*
in Sudan, awakened by the muezzin's call in Jakarta, or the cries of a
pig in Irian Jaya as the poor beast was shot through the heart with an
arrow by a man wearing only a penis gourd. On the phone with my
editors, I found myself muttering Ari-like proclamations: "I met the
most fascinating snake charmer in the bazaar at Marrakech." Or:
"Whale meat, not so bad." Meanwhile, I was accused of being
monosyllabic—or worse, "evasive"—in describing the details of my
work to friends and family. I often shied from the great American
question: What do you *do?* After all, was I really expected to say with
a straight face that I was a collector of stories? That I hunted and
gathered them—and then tried to write them down? Wasn't it enough
that when they were done, people could read them? Or not? At least
I could mutely point to words on a page as proof I'd been up to something.

There.

As exhilarating as this all was, I was driven by the freelancer's
absolute fear of stasis. I became the spun dreidel, dizzy and alive and
overadrenalized. And then two momentous things occurred: First—
and we'll return to this—I received a call from a magazine to visit a

chef in Spain, a Catalan who, they said, was reinventing food by mixing science and taste. And second, just days after the new millennium, my wife gave birth to our first son.

While volumes have been written about New Mother, there's this to say about New Father: As a species, he's an instant cliché. Gazing upon his progeny, he touches his own mortality. Then a couple of springs pop permanently loose in his head. Even as he acknowledges that there have been billions of fathers before him, and *blah, blah, blah* (camcorder out now, filming Baby), no one, ever, has felt this kind of powerful, blinding paternal love. One moment blushing from fits of overt pride, then trying to show some restraint and circumspection, New Father will go glottal, scrotal, and ballistic on someone driving twenty-seven in a twenty-five-mile-an-hour zone when Baby is astronauted in the backseat. He'll crawl on all fours, hand-sweeping the house for tiny beads, crumblets, and quarters, to save Baby from choking. Nothing is rational, for never has he felt this finite, looking upon the infinite. Never has he considered the shape of his legacy—his accomplishments, his bank account, his spiritual life—but now, considering it, he wonders how it all got to be in such a shambles.

Our baby's name was Leo. He had a dreamy sort of expression and an overbite. He looked as if he were always contemplating something byzantine, and, watching him watch the world, we tried to intuit what he was telling us. He seemed to be telling us so much: We bought a new car, with air bags, at his request. I cleaned the garage, so I could park the car, for him. *What's that? The back porch is looking a little deshabille?* I cleaned the back porch—and then half-started on everything else we'd neglected for years.

Soon I was emptying closet after closet, donating to Goodwill all the clothes I'd first come by years earlier at . . . Goodwill. I threw out old cassette tapes of bands that wouldn't interest Baby, bands like Joy Division or Jesus and Mary Chain. Bach was good for Baby; early Cure, circa *Pornography,* not. I abandoned my plans to buy drums, closed the wood cabinet that held the dartboard. And in this act of editing down my former life, I ruthlessly discarded old files from every epoch—labeled "Real Estate Ideas," "Greenland," and "Other Possibilities," one that was entirely empty. During this housecleaning, I came upon a folder labeled "Stuff," with the now-yellowed shred of that old Zingerman's newsletter, about that expensive Spanish cheese called Páramo de Guzmán.

It felt like so long ago—and then just yesterday. Here now, on my knees in the office, holding the parchment with Leo's cry rising up from the lower rooms of the house, something dawned on me: My life was over. My new life had just begun, but my life was over. I found myself asking a simple question: Did that mean all of the old vows and dreams were over, too?

The cheese was named after its village—Guzmán. At the very least, before recycling the scrap, I wanted to know where that village was. It was a weekday in midwinter (How do I remember this? A pattern of kaleidoscopic ice on the window, and a naïve thought: *Spain must be really warm*), and I went to the atlas, but the town didn't appear on what seemed to be a pretty detailed map of the country. So I went directly out and bought a Michelin map (this being the unimaginable days before Google Earth), drove home, and then flipped it open, watching it accordion over half of my office floor, a scroll dotted with unknown places, places where, at this very moment, old men were probably taking their *café* with brandy. I spent a long time hovering over it, squinting at village after village, like a jeweler in search of clarity. *Where was Guzmán?* I started at Madrid, and with my finger I wipered my way north, up through the kingdom of Castile, touching on nearly every town, letting the names play through my mind—La Horra (The Free One), Iglesiarrubia (Blond Church), Fria (Cold), Zarza (Bramble), Pinafuente (Pine Fountain), Pozal de Gallinas (Bucket of Hens)—until, finally, to the west of Aranda de Duero, there it was: Guzmán, a tiny bubble floating in all that emptiness. Besides cheese, I couldn't begin to imagine what one might find there.

Contrary to what the retroactive translations above would lead you to believe, the sum total of my Spanish education came from old sitcom episodes of *Chico and the Man*. Having verified the existence of Guzmán, I found myself calling my friend Carlos, a high-school Spanish teacher who lived down the street. Carlos had been born of Colombian parents, and grown up bilingual. When he arrived, I gave him the whole backstory—the deli, the cheese, the dream I had of eating it. I showed him the map. I was unshaven, hadn't been sleeping much, enslaved to Baby. Unfazed, he suggested we call the international operator and ask for any listed number for Guzmán, which we did.

There seemed to be only one, for the bar. So Carlos punched out a dozen digits or so. While it rang, he cleared his throat. And then someone answered. Carlos's eyebrows shot up, and he introduced himself by saying, Hello, good afternoon, he was calling from America and was hoping to speak to the man who made the famous cheese, Páramo de Guzmán. I could hear a woman's voice in response from across the room, exploding, lacking all romance, jamming short, staccato paragraphs down his ear canal. Carlos listened closely, murmuring *"Sí, sí,"* then her voice broke off altogether, even as he offered a halfhearted goodbye. The entirety of their conversation had lasted about twenty seconds.

"What happened?" I asked.

"She hung up," said Carlos.

"But did she seem friendly?"

"I wouldn't say that."

"What did she say about the cheese?"

"She said it's not made there anymore. Or she said, 'The *man* doesn't make it anymore.' And then she hung up."

"The man? Did she say anything else?"

Taking in my disappointment, Carlos said, "Sorry, man."

Another little death. I felt as I'd once felt at fifth-grade catechism when, out of the blue and even as I stood there dreamily at recess staring at clouds, Joe Ursone indiscriminately roundhoused me. One minute I was swaying in awe before the possibility of the universe, channeling universal love, religious zealot that I momentarily was, and the next I was in a slo-mo crumple, clenched over with that sudden, prickly radiation of pain from my jaw, eyes welling with tears, swearing revenge.*

Ari's words echoed: "Rich, dense, intense . . . sublime . . . discovered it by chance in London . . . made with love." What was so crazy about believing in purity—and then going to find it?

A STORY IS TIME itself, boxed and compressed. It is the briefest entertainment and simulacrum of real life, which is big and messy and requires a strange kind of endurance. The story is stylized for that flash of laughter and pain, thwarted desire and odd consummation, while life waterfalls with it—all of it—every day: prodigious, cloying, in decay. And when the story is finally over—even if the protagonist survives a spray of gunfire and goes on living—it's over. Meanwhile, life carries on, river-swift.

As, of course, did mine.

I made plans to see the iconoclastic Spanish chef for my magazine story, but it was the cheese I couldn't let go of. It rang now in my head as a question: *Man makes world-famous delicacy from ancient family recipe, then just stops. Why?* It didn't seem like the end of a story, but the beginning of one. I rang Carlos.

"Do you think we could call the woman at the bar again?"

Carlos hesitated. "You think that's a good idea?"

A few minutes later we were in my attic office, Carlos dialing the number. This time a man answered. If he was a bit gruff, at least he

---

* Truth is, I plotted for years how I was going to jump Joe Ursone when he least expected it. I would get him in an alley somewhere, with a crowbar to the knees. I would attain a black belt in jujitsu without him knowing, feign fear in his presence, fake-cower, then rearrange his face. I would be, like, all *whassup?,* then knee him in the groin. Actually, not really having a stomach for violence, I wished for an older brother who could just do it for me, but as luck had it, mine were all younger, my revenge nothing more than a phantasm of revenge, these imagined acts committed repeatedly in my mind.

didn't hang up. Our cheesemaker wasn't there, he said, but since we'd called during a quiet moment, he was willing to give us a number. He acted as if he was doing us a favor, one that might have been a violation of local etiquette. Carlos asked why the cheese was no longer made in the village. *"Una historia difícil"*—a difficult story—said the man with a sigh that signaled the totality of what he had to say about it.

Now we had a number. Carlos dialed again. A woman answered. Carlos explained that we were from the United States, and that we were looking for a man who kept cheese in a cave, a cheese called Páramo de Guzmán. The woman listened. Then, after a long hesitation, she said we'd called the wrong number. "The cheese wasn't made by her husband . . ." Carlos began translating, even as she was finishing her sentence: ". . . anymore."

Had she just said *anymore*? She'd said *anymore*! The cheese wasn't made by her husband *anymore*.

Carlos asked if there was a good time to call back, to talk to her husband. She said he was traveling. She seemed so uncertain. Carlos asked for his name, and that much she allowed.

"My husband is Ambrosio," she said.

Ambrosio. The name beamed up, bounced off a satellite, and fell to our ears. Ambrosio, the Maker of the Divine Cheese.

Over the ensuing weeks, whenever I could get Carlos over, we called that same number. Mostly the phone just rang. But then one night a man answered. He spoke in such a forceful baritone that Carlos, not expecting a voice at all, literally had his head snap back.

"A ver," Ambrosio said, as if to say: Yes, you have my attention, now what do you want? The words were almost a growl, the grinding of tectonic plates.

What *did* I want?

I stammered for a moment. I wanted to say, *Hola,* my name is Miguel Ricardo, and as a grad student in Ann Arbor, a place in the middle west of our great country of Indians and Cowboys and Pilgrims, I'd come upon his *queso* at a *tienda* named Zingerman's Deli. Because I'd been a man of meager means and had not actually consumed his cheese, its *story* was as important to me as the thing itself. I had struggled for years to find myself as a writer, and had, until that time, failed miserably—but then the story of his cheese had struck some deeper chord. Perhaps what I'd seen in his cheese was the reflection of an artist who'd taken the rocky, eccentric path, and my slowly drowning self had been buoyed.

Carlos was waiting for me to speak, and finally said, "What do you *want*?"

"Tell him I'd like to meet him," I said. "I plan to be in Spain this summer when the baby's a little older."

He conveyed this to Ambrosio, who was nothing if not decisive, whose voice could be heard making a basoonlike proclamation. On that April day, he said he could meet us on the third Sunday of August in the village.

"Where in the village?" asked Carlos.

"You'll find me," said Ambrosio. And then the line clicked dead.

So, ON TO SPAIN it was, to visit the Catalan chef—and this Ambrosio. Because the trip coincided with Carlos's summer vacation from teaching, and because I beseeched him until he relented, he became my Sancho Panza. We then convinced our wives to come along, tantalizing them with visions of the Mediterranean coast and a stay in the beach town of Roses, a couple of hours north of Barcelona, near the Catalan chef's Michelin-three-star restaurant.

The chef was a short man named Ferran, with frantic hair and quick, thin lips. He was a voyager in the kitchen, exploring faraway planets. The food was like nothing I'd seen, or eaten: white spoons filled with green jelly and topped with what seemed to be caviar; mesospheric formations in yellow and pink; a plate that, by my best estimation, was covered with orange worms.

The chef said things like: "There's more emotion, more feeling, in a piece of ruby-red grapefruit with a little sprinkle of salt on it than in a big piece of fish." Or: "The important thing is the miniskirt, not what color it is." In the kitchen he worked hand in hand with chemists and biologists, inventors and engineers; his cooking utensils were doctor's syringes, forceps, hammers, blowtorches, and fine sewing needles.

A few seasons after discovering the "foams"—what he called "air"—that had made him an international superstar he more or less stopped serving them, frenetically moving on to the next discovery: asparagus ice cream, apple caviar, cotton-candy cuttlefish. "If you want new emotions, and really big emotions," he said, "you need new techniques."

He was a man obsessed, sleeping little, moving at the speed of our digitized world, headlong into a fantastical future. It was exhausting to try to keep up.

In our free time Carlos and I went back to our German-run hotel, which seemed more cathouse than auberge, with shiny pillows and ceiling mirrors and a shower stall through which you could watch a bather from the bed, all of which absolutely delighted our eight-month-old Leo. Constellated on the beach in front of the hotel was a whole galaxy of overripe, topless European bathers and lingam-hugging Speedos that made us feel acutely American. And yet the combination of sun, sea, wine, and fine food was a potent antidote to the life we'd just left behind—the frenzied now-now-now of deadlines and credit-card bills, a life led by reflex and stopgap.

On that Sunday—the third in August—Carlos and I flew to Madrid. The flight was a short one, and when I gazed up from my magazine, a radical landscape revealed itself below. Rather than the verdant, tropical, palm-laden one of Catalonia, here was Spain's Meseta, which appeared like Mars, its red, lifeless dirt stretching the horizon. Here was a vast sea of nothingness floating on top of huge limestone plates, all the more spectacular for its stubborn refusal to reveal life. Along the surface of the crater, one imagined a desiccating heat, a hint of smoke, and the skeletal remains of a hundred spaghetti-Western film crews.

Madrid appeared finally, as a distant mirage out the window of the circling plane, a flash of glass and metal, a jumble of sandstones and lurid reds, and then we were on the ground. At the car rental desk we

procured a shiny compact, and when we stepped from the airport's ter-
rarium we were met with a blast of heat so stiff and all-consuming it
felt like, well, the burp of Hades after a green-chile relleno.*

O, Castile in August was a heat greater than that of tanning beds
and Finnish saunas, equatorial sands and the orange, overfried skin of
reckless eastern Europeans on vacation. It was so hot that the tires on
automobiles actually melted while driving the road north, the road
known as National Highway One, the main-trunk highway that ran
up the gut of the country, through Burgos, the capital of the province,
and onward to Basque country, to San Sebastian and the Atlantic
Ocean. We had the windows up, air-conditioning cranked, and, still,
it felt as if we manned a lunar module heading into the sun.

The Meseta is comprised of two tiers, bisected in part by the Sierra de Guadarrama, a barren, jagged escalation with all the charm
and invitation of the Funeral Mountains rising from Death Valley.
The British writer Richard Ford, whose 1846 masterpiece, *A Hand-
book for Travelers in Spain,* sounded a starting gun for English tour-
ists, claimed the country was one huge mountain of "dreary and harsh
character, yet not without a certain desolate sublimity." (Madrid itself
is Europe's highest capital, if you don't count Andorra la Vella—and
really, who counts Andorra la Vella?)

Geologically speaking, we were traversing one of the world's most
intriguing hinterlands, the country littered with rock dating back to
the Ediacaran. And grinding north up the Guadarrama, we drove
toward the sky, it seemed, until we split the last, ear-popping *puerto,*
or mountain pass, and saw there below us, like something from those
Bible movies, the great expanse of the upper Meseta, the silted land

---

* Too much? Perhaps, but in the throes of story-making—an act that, by its nature,
is hyperbolic, exculpatory, and biased even when tamped down and allegedly made
objective—the storyteller can't always be bound by the *quality* of simile, rather
thrills to the music of "burp" and "relleno" a few words apart. Until his editor
comes along. And then the storyteller adds a footnote like this one, to acknowledge
his too-muchedness, to calm with self-consciousness, to create the smokescreen of
restraint and perspicacity that really allows him to continue piling it on.

glinting with flecks of red, gold, and green as we hovered momentarily between two worlds, ghosts rising from the *páramo* below in
siroccos that swept from the northwest, the direction of all significant
weather here. In that moment, it wouldn't have been particularly surprising to have seen the entire flow of history illuminate that stage:
megaraptors skittering after prey followed by savage packs of prehu-
mans;* the Romans building their roads and the Visigoths plotting
and conniving; and, after them, the marauding Moors and marauding conquistadores, pillaging in the name of Allah, God, or chivalry;
and then the huge, undulating flocks of sheep, whose wool became
the source of Spain's wealth in the fifteenth and sixteenth centuries,
spurring grand imperialistic designs that brought galleons to the New
World . . . and so on.

Into this drama we now descended, the road melting in black goo
beneath the vicious eye of the sun. Roadblocks were set up on the highway because, as we'd find out later, Basque separatists had, in rapid
succession, blown up a mayor, shot a police officer, and detonated a car
bomb in the capital. Diverging from the national highway at Aranda de
Duero, then heading west, the road went from four lanes to two—and
finally from two to one-and-a-half, which is when we found ourselves
lost. The village of Guzmán may as well not have existed at all. There
were no signs for it. So we started asking directions—seven times in all.
After a while we just left the windows down, allowing in all that sun
and swelter as we rode a swerving incline through browned vineyards,
barley fields, and sunflowers, hundreds upon thousands of them, heads
tilted like so many furry satellite dishes to the mother source.

---

* In March of 2008, a human jaw, dated at 1.2 million years old, was found in a
limestone cave in the Sierra de Atapuerca, near the city of Burgos, making it the
oldest discovery of human bones in Europe. Contrary to expert theory holding that
hominids, early precursors of human beings, entered Europe from the east, perhaps through the Caucasus region, the revelation suggested the possibility that they
may have simultaneously entered Europe through the Iberian Peninsula from Africa. At the very least, it was proof that the Meseta had been the site of some of the
continent's earliest visitors.

We turned right, then left, another right, and again. We looped back to the crossroad that looked like a facsimile of the other crossroad where we'd just been—stone buildings like all the others except for an awning and a sign that read BAR—then we looped out in the opposite direction, back into the fields again, until we were returned to another pile of identical pale stone.

Was this a joke?

Finally, three old men perched on a bench, each sporting a black beret, pointed us down a road that ran among acacia trees, then upward toward another jumble of pale-angled edifices. By the time we passed the first building of the village, we seemed to be driving out of town.

"Was that it?" Carlos asked, jerking his head around to catch one last look.

Our first visit to Guzmán was over in less than twenty seconds.

AFTER NEARLY RUNNING DOWN a sheep, a cat, and a cavorting hen and then reversing direction, I carefully guided the car back into the village, gliding down past the first barn and the second, past a large, newish home on the left (that of the baker, as I'd later find out) and then a hivelike cluster of older stone homes that signaled the heart of the village itself. Guzmán, improbable Pleistocene city on the hill! Or: just more imploding Castilian rock. The village was a warren of these homes, a collection of cul-de-sacs and tight alleys that broke off between houses, leading, one imagined, to more of the same, or perhaps some secret altar. The whole place seemed chipped and faded. Next to intact houses were half houses that seemed to have been cracked open like eggs. It was startling to see a crushed roof, broken beams, the early afternoon sun filtering down on an abandoned pair of leather shoes, strewn books, someone's bloomers.

With our car windows down, Guzmán smelled salty, an almost sulfuric whiff with a slight bouquet of manure, but as we moved through the alleys, that scent was erased by one of simmering broths

and stews. Somewhere inside all these locked-up fortresses, people
were cooking.*

The road carried us into a square where to our right loomed the
imposing north wall of the town's *palacio*. Just ahead, the road wish-
boned into two extremely tight openings, sluices contained by stone
walls with no more breadth, it seemed, than the exact width of our
car.† Now we crawled—through a thin alley, which spilled into another little square, and there before us loomed the church, built in
solid, unadorned Romanesque, an oversized rectangle, its bell tower
rising at least six stories. Like every other structure in the village, it
was bound shut. Even on a Sunday, in a country where they took
their Catholicism with the same passion they reserved for bullfighting and football, there was no evidence that the church had ever been
in use.‡

---

* Or more accurately, they were cooking the *comida,* the big sacramental midday
meal. The sharing of food was so essential to this country that the Spaniards had
long ago added two meals to the normal three a day in order to make five. There
were the preliminary meals, *desayuno* (breakfast) and *almuerzo* (late-morning
snack), the aforementioned *comida* in the early afternoon, and then the latter meals
of the day, *merienda* (late-afternoon snack) and *cena* (dinner).

† Somehow the cramped, jagged openings retroactively explained the obsession of
the rental car employee who'd led us to our vehicle at Barajas Airport and then
circled it repeatedly with her clipboard in hand, jotting down all the scratches and
dents, which were numerous. It was probably a cottage industry: The fine print I
hadn't read detailed hundreds of additional euros in penalties for sandpapering
one's car against the rough walls of villages like this one.

‡ I'd later find out that on a typical Sunday the priest traveled from village to village and Mass to Mass, returning for an 11:00 A.M. service in Guzmán, after which
he retired to his home, or rather the home of a local widow, for his Sunday meal.
Depending on whom you asked—his friends or enemies—the priest either rented
a room in that house and was mothered respectfully, or, contrarily, was said to
enjoy a more controversial hospitality. If the latter, a long precedent existed in
Spanish history for priests participating in worldly pleasures, dating back to the
thirteenth century, when concubinage was, according to one history book, "accepted practice among the supposedly celibate clergy." As it was, the book claimed
that "the sons of a priest could even inherit his property."

We trawled on, the road doglegging left. The total distance from the first building to the last, from beginning to end through the cubist maze, might have been two hundred yards, past *palacio* and church to the sudden sight of the bar—the same bar we'd telephoned, now shuttered, too, its faded awning rolled up, a chain locked across a metal door. Ambrosio had said we'd find him, but here we were on the third Sunday in August, having burned an unconscionable amount of fossil fuel to arrive at an absolute ghost town.

The car drifted of its own accord, and something serendipitous occurred. A last sharp left appeared before we were ejected out of Guzmán and back into the fields, and I took it—or the car did, for it was now unclear who was steering whom—wiggling past one more derelict home, then switchbacking up a small hill, on a dirt track that lifted us over the red-tile rooftops, a little higher, until hobbit dwellings of some sort appeared before us, each with a thick wooden door. Before one of these sat a group of people, *actual humans,* drinking wine at a stone table. A group of tanned, lined faces, maybe six or seven of them. The palette of their clothing was the same as the earth itself—beiges, duns, and umbers—yet they seemed to have been expecting us. Before we'd even sat ourselves down at their invitation, an old man with a face of parchment thrust a strange object into my hands. It appeared to be a glass decanter with a spout, something from the bong genus, sloshing with red liquid. Were these guys, average age of seventy-five, doing exotic hits?

The device was called a *porrón,* and during George Orwell's Civil War sojourn here he refused to drink from it, as it reminded him of a bed bottle. Yet the old man instructed us on its wonders: Of Catalan origin, the *porrón* had been co-opted long ago by the rest of the country for communal drinking, the perfect reliquary for the most holy of Spanish libations, wine. Carlos nodded his head while I sat there smiling like an organ-grinder's monkey, my soon-to-be-familiar pose in this place. According to the unwritten rules of the land, it was an egregious violation of etiquette to suck on the spout with your mouth. Rather, you held the *porrón* aloft and sent the wine arcing down your open gullet. It was an art form, really. One of the old men—he wore a black beret and a sweater despite the heat—showed us how. He thrust the *porrón* skyward as he simultaneously tilted it. The wine came tumbling even as he spoke, and just before it reached his mouth, he paused, drew back his lips, and snatched the ruby goodness out of the air. When the *porrón* came to me, I made the fatal mistake of all first-timers: I tilted it tentatively, which created a lack of downward pressure, and a limp rivulet flowed through the glass nozzle, missing my lower lip but leaving a jagged red line down the front of my shirt, as if I'd been shot. When everyone laughed, I knew that this was actually happening, that we had indeed arrived.

We chatted amiably for a while—about the weather (*mucho calor*) and the caves in the hill (*muy antiguas*)—and then, since it wasn't exactly every day that a couple of stray *americanos* appeared around here in the kiln of August, we told them that we'd come to eat the cheese of a man named Ambrosio. At the name, a few nodded their heads in recognition and a few shook their heads with what seemed to be disappointment. The sweatered old man pointed to the next cave over. "There," he said, "is the *bodega* of Ambrosio."

THE ENTRANCE WAS A weathered oaken door, thick, cross-hatched, and centuries-old. Standing now ten paces from our new friends, I hesitated before knocking. Though I'd had months to imagine this meeting, it crossed my mind that it would have been nice to have prepared an opening statement of some sort. Which is when the door suddenly swung open before us.

"*Venga,*" said a booming voice. Come this way. This was the man on the phone, the cheesemaker himself: *the* Ambrosio![*] A bulky form

---

[*] Am-*bro*-zee-*oh*. The tongue not so much tripping or tapping, but the mouth starting with intimations of *ham,* then making itself bigger, wider, in order to birth the *bro,* a reflexive smile on the third syllable—*zee*—then open again to appease the exclamation of that primordial *oh!*

filled the frame, head slightly stooped to fit the opening, then he moved back to make way for us. Through the door to the *bodega* was a narrow entryway with worn stone steps leading down into a murk from which gusts of refreshing, cool cave air emanated; to the right were a few more worn steps climbing to a small room. We followed the man's broad back as our eyes adjusted from bright sunlight. Inside it was dark, with a fireplace full of ashes and a tangle of dried grapevines. In the streamlets of light filtering through the shutters, a long, wood-plank table materialized, at which another man of about seventy-five was sitting on a bench. "My father," said Ambrosio, grinning. Another *porrón* appeared on the table, and before we sat he offered it to me, which I accepted, expertly drizzling red wine once more on my shirt. Then he produced a plate of chorizo.

Though I hadn't a clue what he said at first, his voice echoed in that cramped room like shock waves. I'd expected him to be much older, his father's age maybe, had envisioned him in his own black beret, maybe even with a cane, small and humped and slightly deaf, but no, here he was, resolving before my eyes into a strapping specimen of ample, Falstaffian belly, in his mid-forties, with a full head of thick, parted hair and mournful eyes. He possessed a broad face, close-set eyes, and a prominent nose, the full effect of which left the impression of a surprising handsomeness. He was dressed in dusty work boots, and the cuffs of his pants were dirty, too. But he also sported an elegant collared shirt with thin navy pinstripes and a pocket embroidered with his monogram, AM.

The cheesemaker sat heavily on a chair at the head of the table, offering us the bench across from his father. Lined along the shelves were empty sardine tins, a bottle full of cloudy liquor bobbing with waterlogged cherries, a tin of Colombian coffee. A pack of Camels lay on the table, and Ambrosio drew a cigarette and lit it. He inquired about our travels. He lifted the *porrón,* his head wreathed by smoke, placed the cigarette in an ashtray, and sucked the equivalent of a glass of wine from the air while I told him the tale of how I'd first learned of his cheese during the days of my deli proofreading, how I'd gone on to become a journalist, and when I realized that I'd be in Spain on assignment, I'd decided to see if I could find him and his cheese. I instinctively pulled a tape recorder from my pocket as if showing my credentials and asked if I could record our conversation.

Ambrosio listened to me intently, replacing the *porrón* before him on the table, and then spoke, as if picking up in the middle of a conversation we'd been having. Or delivering a familiar speech that came as a non sequitur. "The problem with the world," he said, "is that no one knows how to shit anymore."

Had we misheard? He'd used a form of the word *cagar*: to shit. There wasn't a flicker of a smile.

"This is very important," he said, wagging a finger. "It's the most important thing. To shit well, you have to eat well. I was born here in 1955, and as a child, I lived an old kind of life. Not like people living in Madrid or Tokyo or New York. It was a way of life that meant you raised chickens from the egg, you had a good relationship with your dog, you held your animals and prepared the animals for your table by giving them your love. It was the end of an era when everything was natural. There were no mad cows, there was no such thing as preservatives here. We ate in an ancient way."

He stressed that he still tried to eat in an ancient way, and "the act" was nothing to be afraid of. When the feeling struck, especially in the fields, it was natural to unbuckle and squat, and to do so with friends was, well, edifying, equalizing, true. He painted a picture of what it meant to *cagar* on a place he called Mon Virgo. His father sat nodding his head, but it was unclear whether this was, in fact, the delirium of fatigue, because soon he let himself droop on the table and fell to light snoring.

"You start by eating good beans and a good lettuce salad with olive oil and tender lamb chop or fresh rabbit," Ambrosio explained. "Everything is accompanied by a good piece of wheat bread and a good wine and good friends and, at the end, a sip of brandy. Oh how happy you are—and your body's happy! And it begins to digest. You ask, *Now?* And your body says, *In a half hour.* And so, eventually, your intestines tell you: This is the moment! You can't lie, it's an honest moment. If you go to a meeting or work on the computer or drive your car, you're going to miss one of the best events of your life. You're surrounded by the wonderful aromas of the earth—the sage and chamomile—and you can see the village and your home and your entire life down here below Mon Virgo. In this moment you could say to your friends, 'Look where we are! Look at how incredible this is! Look how happy!' It's as if you're seeing God in this moment."

Carlos translated with a Gettysburg Address kind of seriousness, while I subtly raised my eyebrows, as if to say: *Are you kidding me?*

But Ambrosio was dead serious. He rose from the table and drew back the shutter that opened to the east, revealing yet another little old man, who stood there blinking and startled in his beret. Had he been eavesdropping? *"Tomás,"* Ambrosio bellowed, as if expecting him. "He's a cheesemaker, too!" he said. He returned to the table, uncorked another bottle of wine, filled the *porrón,* and offered it to Tomás, who grabbed hold and downed a quarter of its contents.

Ambrosio pointed in the direction of a celestial mass, a mesa that rose out of the burnt earth a few miles from Guzmán. "That's Mon Virgo," he said. He allowed that, over the years, he and his friends had dug holes all through the fields—while out hunting, walking, harvesting—and that Mon Virgo really was the five-star. "It's the most perfect place on earth to take a shit," he said.

I wondered for a moment just who Ambrosio thought I might be, what he saw in me. I mean, he now knew from the skimpiest of banter that I was an American journalist, and he knew, too, that I'd come, like others in another time, for his cheese. But did he see me as yet another person from the modern world in need of this sideways proselytizing, this one-way lecturing? In his telling room that day, I was left wondering: What man tries to convert you by sharing the details of his private bodily matters?

Ambrosio asked Tomás in, but Tomás seemed content to stand beside the window and listen in. Ambrosio left the shutter open, returned to the table. He popped disks of chorizo into his mouth, then took more wine from the *porrón* and passed it along for us to dribble on our shirts yet again. Watching us do so, he took pity, found two small glasses and set them before us, filling them. "I can tell you exactly when the end came," he said. "It was a day in the seventies when my friends and I were here at the *bodega* having a meal, and we had a can that read 'York Ham.' And, of course, we were all very curious.* Was it ham made in Yorkshire? Or New York? The can didn't say. So we opened it. And there was something in there, something dead, a color between white and pink. It looked like a tongue. No one was willing to try it, until finally my friend did and nearly got sick. I was next. It was my first industrial product," Ambrosio said, "and there was nothing positive about it."

I sat there letting the words wash over me, having a slight out-of-body experience in that hand-dug burrow. I ate some version of that crap all the time! There'd hardly been an Easter from my childhood that hadn't starred a red-boiled rugby ball of pig from God knows where. And now that he mentioned it, even slathered with mustard, that porcine spectacle *had* been disgusting. "Pigs need to eat beautiful acorns," Ambrosio said, and then he talked about the importance of slowing down to eat well. He talked about how the impersonal machinery of modernity had destroyed the values and sensitivities, the tenderness and powerful connection that came from living close to the earth. The more he talked, the more I realized that perhaps I hadn't ever known what I really yearned for, what he made

---

* The Castilian takes his or her pig as seriously as his religion—and most Castilian kitchens harbor at least one rather large pig leg, often set on a stand, the pig's elegant hoof held aloft, to offer an easier means of slicing from the plump shank. Here where vegetables are scarce—or, it seems, scarcely eaten—there are times when ham (gorgeous, fantastic ham!) is the starter, the vegetable, and the main dish, all in one. The names of the best pig farms are known in the same way that the French know certain vineyards, the Japanese grades of sushi. In shopwindows all over Spain hang hog legs, each with a little plastic receptacle, like a little white umbrella, there to catch leaking grease. At holidays these legs are given as gifts of the highest order and can cost up to $500 apiece. One of the most famous hams—Joselito brand, from near Salamanca—comes from pigs that scrounge through the mountains for acorns, truffles, and grass. And like the inevitability of red wine among friends, the offering of some porcine product is also one of the most basic acts of hospitality in Spain.

me yearn for. He was webbed to the here and now, sunk into it, while I seemed to spend a great deal of time racing through airports, a processed cream-cheese bagel in hand, trying to reach the future. Now I sat noticing everything, infused with mindfulness: the pallor of light, the still life of the smooth-glass *porrón* on the wood-grooved table, the oversized man sitting in his shadow, occasionally revealed at angles or by the rumble or raggedness in his voice or the various ways he simply lit a cigarette between big fingers (now with show, now as an afterthought, now with the slinky, fumbling desperation of an addict).

Outside, the light oozed over the fields. At the table, with glass in hand, I found myself gulping wine enthusiastically, like everyone else there. I'd come to think of red wine as something that required age and oaky gravitas, polished wood paneling and shelves of first-edition hardbacks, the perfect pour for cold winter evenings, but this was the perfect pour for *now*—cool and effervescent. Ambrosio allowed that the family harvested their own grapes each fall and made their own wine, a wine free of middlemen, a new wine newly sipped. Nothing had been lost in the translation. There was no need to let it breathe, either: it was already breathing. And it was delicious.

He rose one last time and disappeared down the stairs for a while, then returned with three more bottles, setting them with a satisfying thud on the table, the fine film of limestone dust on each calling to mind that dark entrance we'd seen when we'd first entered, the one leading down into the earth. Was it possible that, along with a cache of wine bottles, the cheese sat waiting thirty feet below us in the naturally air-conditioned chambers of Roman ingenuity?

I waited for a lull—which only took place when Ambrosio drank, it seemed—and opened my mouth to speak. "Can he tell us the story of his cheese?" I asked Carlos to ask Ambrosio.

After Carlos's translation, there seemed to be a second of shocked silence—had I violated some unwritten protocol?—and then came a palpable exhalation from Tomás, who instantly disappeared from the window with a "*Venga*" and the flourish of a wave. Ambrosio's father cleared his throat, grimaced as he stood up, then walked stiffly with his cane to the door. Ambrosio watched them go, his expression unreadable.

There was silence and some uncomfortable shifting (mine). With the three of us alone in the telling room, Carlos and I watched his face transform with the difficulty of what he would say next. He wiped the back of his hand across pursed lips and looked up with those sad eyes. For such a handsome man, his face somehow contained in its lines and loosening flesh both a life of hard-lived mirth and strange tragedy.

In the vortex of this silence, I imagined the strain of a song. The story itself spoke, calling out for a teller and a hero. It craved a dramatic ending, even if the truth needed tweaking or the lead needed revising. It had us, these strangers from across the ocean, listening intently. At last Ambrosio's words breached the surface, unsure at first and then gaining the strength of a slow-breaking roller. The story burst forth then, over the next eight hours—through the evening and into early morning, with a pause only for dinner.

By the time it was over, I, too, wanted revenge.

4

PÁRAMO DE GUZMÁN

"I shit in the milk of God."

Aᴀ fter spending his youth in Catholic schools, Ambrosio had come to despise priests and organized religion almost as much as he did ham in a can and city life.* And yet he believed in a spirit, or Creator, to whom he spoke almost daily—and who sometimes spoke back to him. He listened to the howl of the wind and the groan of the earth, the bleat of sheep and the call of the wheat. If he was patient, the voices sometimes told him what to do next. So he'd waited years to make good on the offering he'd promised that voice from the ether—had it been Death itself?—in exchange for his father's life.

In the meantime, the gearwheels of the universe worked in mysteri-

---

* In truth, Ambrosio was a variety of heretic, and historically, heretics did not fare well in Spain. Or at least that's how the story went: From the carnage of the fifteenth- and sixteenth-century Inquisition, during which thousands upon thousands of alleged unbelievers were tortured and burned at the stake, rose what was known as the Black Legend—an exaggerated mash-up of horror stories that pinned the Spanish, and in particular the Castilians, with a nasty reputation that endured for centuries. One British writer of the time described them as "a filthie

ous ways. During his father's illness, Ambrosio had girded himself for the unimaginable, and when the son went to the fields alone without his father, he declared himself a farmer, accepting the weight that comes with the cycle of life on the Meseta. For better or worse, he'd been consecrated into the ranks of a history that connected him to the first Castilian farmer and the tacit code of his people: chivalry, faith, honor. He'd stepped into the absence left by the senior Ambrosio—and his father had consequently, against all odds, lived. Had risen from beneath wool blankets, body untwisting to life. And then *los Ambrosios* resumed their lives, though eventually in reversed roles, the son in charge where his father once had been.

As much as Ambrosio saw himself carrying forward the old traditions—even as a young man he possessed a certain grandiosity—he was walking into a relatively new world on the Meseta. Not ten years

---

heape of the most loathsome, infected, and slavish people that ever yet lived on earth." He then went on to itemize "theyr filthy, monstrous and abominable luxurie, theyr lustfull and inhumaine deflouring of theyr wives and daughters, matchless and sodomiticall ravishing of young boys." Maybe it was a bit of Protestant-on-Catholic vengeance by the British, thought largely to be the primary propagators of the Black Legend, or maybe the legend did reflect the actual fervor of the faithful, partly played out in the grand pageantry of the auto-da-fé, a religious rite in which unrepentant heretics were flame-broiled before huge crowds in village squares. Perhaps, though, this was merely a sign of routinely barbarous times, with two religious superpowers in a heated global land grab: England was in the throes of its own brutal religious reformation, and more generally none of Europe's seafaring imperialists—the French in Senegal, the Portuguese in Brazil, and so on—were winning humanitarian awards for good deeds on distant shores. In defense of the Spaniards, many scholars believe that, comparatively speaking at that time, Spain possessed the most equitable colonial legal system in Europe, and at least theoretically operated under a royal decree, issued by Isabella I, calling for native peoples to be treated with dignity.

Interestingly, a couple of centuries later, during the Civil War of the 1930s, as Franco's Nationalists did battle against the Republicans, the Black Legend was invoked again—as a narrative tool used to blackball the pro-Franco Castilians as having been born of conniving and bloodthirsty stock. However, this time, the Nationalists caught on to the effect of a good story, especially a tawdry one, firing back with their own bit of narrative rehab known to Spanish historians as the White Legend, which lauded the virtues of the Inquisition, reglorified the honor and courage that brought the Spanish to the New World, and in the process fanned the ferocious brand of regional pride that continues to this day.

earlier, in the 1960s, the mechanization of Spanish agriculture had finally, if glacially, reached Guzmán, too, with the arrival of the first tractors.* Meanwhile, the once-robust Molinos empire was now a lesser collection of broken-up parcels, some of them miles apart. There was a vineyard below the village on an L-shaped tract of land, another by the road to Quintanamanvirgo, a third tucked in near the hills. Their wheat- and hayfields could be found in every direction from town, *arriba,* on the high plain above, or on the *coterro,* the lands below.

Like the other farmers in town, Ambrosio rose early each morning, scuttling between fields, visiting his grapes, soybeans, and wheat. He collected water at the *fuente,* irrigated, spread manure. His brothers were off, ascending into their successful careers in the big cities, and here he was, living his father's life, living his grandfather's life—and the life of other Molinos patriarchs before—in what was known as the *tierras de pan llevar* (the bread-carrying lands) of Old Castile. He might be down at the bar; in a crowd with Pinto, Carlos, and Abel, Antonio, Teo, and Cristian, discussing weather patterns and grain prices; or up at the *bodega* plotting rotations and new seeds (this year, sunflowers; the next, hay). Endurance was one part of being a farmer, as was hope. And because of the harshness and unpredictability of the climate,† one's dignity was derived less from results than

---

* Only about a half-century behind the times, however.

† Hail, locusts, lack of rain—these were the main culprits in the Duero region, named for the river just south of Guzmán. From the time of the earliest records, in the late medieval period, fully a quarter of the harvests were significantly affected by *granizo,* or hail, alone. The severity of storms and droughts, plagues and unforeseen events such as frost, flood, and fire, could also be seen in church records detailing *rogativas,* the religious processions tied to agricultural life that were brought to Spain by the Romans. One can picture these medieval moments as they are related for us: thousands bearing statues of the Virgin marching into the fields, kneeling and beating the dusty earth while frantically calling out to God for rain. In fact the rituals remain, though they're limited now to holidays and fiestas: In Guzmán a statue of the Virgin Mary is taken from the hermitage and processed through town while the villagers sing and dance, conjuring the same mania of faith their forebears displayed in calling on their Creator for a bountiful harvest.

from hard work. Could you survive the bad years, the catastrophic, the penurious? What if the bad years lasted decades, as they had during the thirties and forties, upending everything, leaving people only with the by-product of their backbreaking labor, referred to during that time simply as El Hambre, or The Hunger?

As hard as he worked, however—and despite the fact that farmers could turn inward and superstitious under the weight of their anxieties—Ambrosio never had a problem with merriment, welcoming any *porrón* of wine, any plate of food, any fiesta or gathering of friends. And Julián, his treasured *majo,* could often be found by his side. They fit so easily together that their friendship became a photo album of dances and youthful drunks, meals at the *bodega* and vacation double dates. Ambrosio had met a girl, Asunción, from Julián's town, Aranda, and began courting her as Julián began courting his wife. Eventually Ambrosio married, had a daughter, then a son, and another son. Julián had his own daughter. They would meet on Sundays, sharing *porrones,* discussing their good times and bad. "He's my blood brother," Ambrosio said. Remembering those rich hours spent in repose, he described them as "some of the best of my life."

All the while, he was aware of owing the universe, to the extent that he sometimes grew panicky. A parent himself now, he was reminded of the primordial bond between father and son. And he knew, of course, that time was the great undoer. So how could one slow *that* beast? In some bygone era, he'd have placated the gods, and their death-greed, by trekking up Mon Virgo and putting the flashing blade to the neck of a beautiful lamb or a succulent pig. In this era, he might have been at church each day, saying the rosary. But since that wasn't possible, he could only wait.

Until there came that fine summer evening, twilight in the offing, dust rising off the earth, sky a Tyrian purple the color of the grapes. Out in the fields together, he and his father had missed their *merienda,* the late-day snack before dinner. They were starving, talking about food. Ambrosio's father craved some wine, which was typical, and a little piece of something. It was nothing more than a passing statement: *Some cheese would be fine.* It would have ended there. Or more likely it would have ended with the father and son knocking off work, heading up to the *bodega* with a block of Manchego from the refrigerator, filling the *porrón,* and then sitting back and telling stories before the *cena.* But it may have been that sky, illumined with stained-glass light, or it may have been the sound of his father's voice, with its tenor of youth—whatever the spark, the idea entered Ambrosio's mind fully formed.

Once there'd been a time when families had made their own cheese, as they'd made their own wine.* Ambrosio had a memory of eating his family's cheese as a child, and even now could conjure its sharp tang and the images associated with it: his mother's kitchen, with its gas fires and simmering pots of milk, and the *bodega* shelves, where it was stored—in each case, surrounded by people, warmth, the past. As he understood it, the family cheese had been made for so long there'd never been a written recipe.

Then came the Civil War, mass killing, societal rupture, dictatorship, The Hunger. The government began rationing food; people scrounged for what little could be had. Soon droves abandoned the countryside for the cities, trading fieldwork for factory shifts, killing rural life. With less and less land, and fewer hired hands, the Molinos family found its batches of cheese diminishing, until that time in the 1950s, when Ambrosio was a boy, when they agreed to stop making it. It was another luxury they couldn't afford anymore.

But standing in that twilight field with his hungry father, Ambrosio Molinos had a revelation: *why?* Why had they stopped making it? Or

---

* And, as with their wine, the families argued in a good-natured way about whose cheese tasted best. In fact, in addition to the cleanliness of one's home, the quality of one's homemade food was a Castilian bragging right. In the past, it had been even more than that. For instance, when the Molinos family had owned huge tracts of land and commanded a small army of labor, up to sixty people during the harvest, they were responsible for feeding their hired hands with a steady supply of wine and cheese. Often the delectability of that fare became a deciding factor in the quality of your workforce: that is, everyone wanted to work for good food, and if your food was really good, you had your pick of the best workers.

why couldn't they make it again? That very same cheese. He had no clue how to do it, but it was something his father craved. And his father was still standing here, alive and able to crave it. And here was Ambrosio the son, breathing and alive and able to give it. And to the son's great, backward-reaching brain—the fantastically impractical dream device between his two ears—the thought arrived as if by directive. There were no *what if*s or *let's see*s, just that Iberian blast of confidence (the same that set Spanish galleons sailing to the New World): *we will*.

We will . . . commit an act of sheer folly, with money we do not have, with time we can ill afford, with equipment we no longer possess, all in the name of resurrecting a cheese for which we have no recipe. *We will* . . . rise early in the morning and work late into the night, scribbling notes, racking our brains, acting on hunches, trusting fate. *We will* . . . give everything of ourselves to this cheese, so that we may become bigger than any rational thing that stands in our way.

And with this line of thought, with this altruism and bravado, Ambrosio had his offering. He would make the family cheese again. So his father could eat.

THE REASON PURIFICACIÓN MOLINOS de las Heras never touched a glass of wine was that the sight of blood-red liquid brought back that distant afternoon when her beloved *abuelo* had drowned in a vat of fermenting grapes. "Drowned" was not exactly the proper word for what had become of her grandfather—"desiccated" was more apt—and the vat was a stone cistern, measuring fifteen feet deep and twenty across, housed in a stone *caseta* that was used expressly for winemaking. After the grapes had been picked in the vineyards and destemmed, they were dumped from straw baskets into the cistern and crushed by foot or with large wooden paddles, and then punched down and stirred three or four times a day into a must, or juice. Yeast was added, catalyzing a fierce chemical reaction. Sugars transformed to alcohol, releasing clouds of carbon dioxide that hovered over the foaming must like a storm front.

In those days much time was devoted—and still is—to everything having to do with the grapes. In the spring the vines were clipped, tied, and tended to. With the appearance of the first hard green bulbs in summer, a grower's life became one of vigilance and prayer: against fungus and drought, plagues and storms. The men watched the skies, looking for ragged clouds on the horizon, for signs and comings.* They watched the green bulbs grow, become fleshy and pendulous, and then one day near the end of August turn purple. Until this time the grapes were bitter, but when the sugars of the vine were released into the fruit itself, the crucial decision of when to harvest came down to one man's intuition about late-season storms and a willingness to gamble for the perfect wine.

Purificación Molinos de las Heras grew up eighteen miles from Guzmán, in the lower lands of La Aguilera, just outside of Aranda. Later, after marrying, she'd moved directly to the other side of Mon Virgo, exchanging one small village for another, but it seemed like a different country in Guzmán, up there on the hill over the *coterro,* beneath the bell tower of the limestone church, strange and charmed, if equally full of death. She was the middle child of five brothers and sisters, nicknamed Puri (pronounced pure-*ee*). Even as a girl, she possessed a dignified beauty, her acumen glinting behind wide-set eyes. Her displeasure was a wincing grimace; her joy was a laugh that, as she aged, came in a girlish register higher than her voice. She was at once warm and a bit apart—aloof, some said—but most of all, she was sensitive. From the beginning, church was a place to reclaim one's faith in humankind.

Her grandfather had been relatively young for a grandfather—and able. The fields had a way of breaking a person; by fifty, if injury hadn't already curtailed the body, there came a slow resignation to the new, more able-bodied generation. But he was as active as ever, involved in every last decision, up on the gangplanks that crisscrossed the bubbling stew of fruit skin and guts, punching down the must.

---

* In Guzmán, however, homemade rockets were often fired into hovering clouds with the hope of disrupting an approaching rain.

Working alone, he must have slipped, leaned too close for inspection or reached out with his paddle only to have found no bottom. Then he was in the air, suspended above the grape slurry.

The mixture was like quicksand. Perhaps he might have been able to stay afloat for a moment, or even touch bottom, but because he was now down in the clouds rather than above them on the gangplank, and because the relentless fermentation process wouldn't end until the last of the sugar had been converted to alcohol, he stood no chance. His turgid realization probably occurred the moment he lost his footing and lasted until he was asphyxiated. Then the grapes ate his body. He was found slopped in the must, as if he'd been dealt an unexpected blow by some invisible hand.

Puri initially absorbed the event through the despondency of her own mother. She noticed how the townspeople, with their red-rimmed eyes, consoled her. She deduced that her *abuelo* wasn't coming back, and because theirs had been that special grandfather-granddaughter bond, she felt that she'd been eaten by grapes, too. The irony of the incident came years later, from a totally different perspective of time, when the children of Purificación Molinos de las Heras joked in her absence that dying in a vat of wine would be the most perfect death. But to the citizens of La Aguilera, her grandfather's passing was an occupational hazard, really. Her people, like everyone in this part of Spain, were grape people. Making wine was a way of life for them. Accidents happened.*

With her move to the village, Puri inherited a wine-loving husband and his vineyards. She inherited streets that ran uphill and a tall villa, across from *la ermita,* the hermitage, that demanded much of her attention. Despite her almost aristocratic bearing, she was a farmer's wife, and so her place was in the home, preparing food, cleaning, tending to the children.

It was in those early days that she'd been put in charge of making

---

* For her family, church also could be counted as an occupational hazard: Her other grandfather was thrown thirty feet to the ground while in the act of ringing the bells one day before Mass. He survived the fall.

the family cheese—and then, at some point during Ambrosio's childhood, she'd stopped. Years later, when her son came to her in hopes
that she might remember the recipe, she was fuzzy on the details. One
thing she would never forget, however, was its taste.* Although it was
a *queso tipico,* what the Castilians called a "house cheese"—which
meant it had always been there, on a board set on the kitchen table, to
be sliced and nibbled on at all hours—the Molinos cheese, as she recalled it, was much stronger than Manchego, almost piquant, with an
earthy vein and nearly overwhelming tang. She remembered that the
cheese was often heated slightly before it was served, to soften it and
let it perspire, in order to release its flavors. The cheese had been like
the first of all cheeses,† a mistake, an improvisation, a reflex, and then,
under the watchful eye of the Molinos matriarch—depending on the
era, it could have been Candida, Felipa, or Tomasa—a fine evolution.
It was a hard cheese—hard to cut, hard to categorize—the kind that
forced you to savor each bite. So powerful was this cheese that even

---

* If any supernatural trait could be assigned to members of the Molinos family (or
if Ambrosio assigned it to them), it may well have been this: Their senses of both
taste and smell were acute. Once, on a trip to Argentina to visit his brother Angel,
Ambrosio walked into an old silo, one unused for decades, and, inhaling, pro-
ceeded to give a history of everything that had been stored there over the course of
a century, to the dumbfounded amazement of the owner: wheat, garbanzos,
cheese. . . . As for that faraway look on Ambrosio's face when he was sipping a
good wine, I came to realize that it was less theater than a secondary gaze down
through the portal of time, at the end of which was another visage, his own, in the
rapture of that first time drinking and tasting beautiful wine. And so the Ambrosio of the Present sat, wine in hand, considering the Ambrosio of the Past, trying to
find affinities between two moments connected by taste, as if memory were the
conduit between sucks of wine.

† The first human encounter with cheese may have occurred between 8000 and
3000 B.C. with the domestication of sheep, when an Arab trader, carrying milk in a
pouch made from calf's stomach, tarried through the hot day, slept through the
night, and, when craving a drink the next morning, discovered that by some mysterious chemical reaction his milk had transformed into cheese curds, which he ate,
and found salty and delicious. Later, the Romans made hard, molded cheese to feed
their legionnaires, called *formaticum,* a word that gave birth to offshoots in other
languages: *fromage, fromaggio, formatge, fourmaj,* and *furmo.* The original Latin
for cheese, *caseus,* in turn, gave rise to the Spanish *queso* and the English *cheese.*

the members of the Molinos family could eat only a few slices at a time.

Making it again soon became Ambrosio's overriding obsession. He purchased a dozen or so Churra sheep,* a hardy Iberian breed whose grazing habits had, in part, laid the Meseta bare. Space was cleared in the *caseta,* pens were repaired, cobwebs swept away, windows washed, floors cleaned, feed bins built. Besides the dogs and cats, the mice and moles, it had been years since honest-to-goodness farm animals had abided here. In that shadowy, nearly forgotten place came new blades of light, freshly mown hay, the happy, daily whistling of Ambrosio. The sheep huddled there, bumping bodies, masticating in wonder, Jesus-faced and smelling of Rasta wool. The idea was to let the sheep graze freely by day over the expanse of the Meseta under the watchful eyes of some local shepherds, to gather and milk them by hand at the barn and then transport the milk in canisters a quarter mile up the rough, rocky road to a small building that had once been a horse stall across from Ambrosio's childhood home. The stall soon looked like the lab of a mad scientist, strewn with ladles and measuring spoons, knives and triers, cheesecloth and wax, molds and presses, vats and thermometers.

Ambrosio also implored their old family friend Tomás to share his wisdom, which he gladly did. First there was the matter of the milk, for all good cheese begins with good milk, not just fresh and full but carrying with it a resonance of the earth and air where it's made. Ambrosio kept a detailed journal, marking the locations where the sheep grazed and what they ate. For instance, if the sheep munched on thyme and chamomile, common herbs found especially in the *barcos* below town, that taste came through in the milk—which then created pleasant hints in the cheese. Conversely, if the sheep grazed on weeds and dirty shoots, the cheese-milk might result in a bland or even sour product.

---

* Sheep's milk, being slightly sweeter than cow's milk, lends its cheeses a nuttiness, as well as a burnt caramel undertone. Often sheep's milk cheeses smell of lanolin or wet wool.

Simultaneous with Ambrosio's effort to control the quality of milk—to ensure that the sheep were expressing uniformly thick and creamy *leche* with a faint bloom of flowers and caramel—he focused his attention on the bigger experiment in the horse-stall lab. Behind the weathered door was a world of fire and boiling liquid. All cheeses, from blue to Gruyère, from those sporting pale, bloomy rinds to those with orange overcoats, are created equal, or at least adhere to the same three basic principles in their creation: the conversion of milk to curds by the introduction of rennet and the expulsion of water, or whey; the demineralization of what's known as the "casein," the predominant protein in milk; and the addition of salt to a nascent, ripening *queso*. And while all cheese is a solid born of liquid,* each also contains varying degrees of water, acid, and salt content, which affect the ripening process and determine in part the bouquet, texture, and flavor of each individual cheese.†

In Ambrosio's stall, the milk was poured from canister to vat, at which time he added the rennet, a natural coagulating agent of enzymes,‡ which had the effect of gathering casein molecules together just as planets formed from molecular clouds. Next, the thickening broth was cut into floating blocks with a cheese harp, then heated to temperatures over 100 degrees Fahrenheit, and stirred, further dividing the fat from the liquid, the curds from the whey. These growing milk planets—known in Spanish as *la cuajada* and in English as

---

* Writes Clifton Fadiman: "A cheese may disappoint. It may be dull, it may be naive, it may be oversophisticated. Yet it remains cheese, milk's leap toward immortality."

† In a famous quip attributed to Charles de Gaulle, the former president of France said of his nation, "One can't impose unity out of the blue on a country that has 265 different kinds of cheese."

‡ Bought in a little village near Santander, Ambrosio's rennet was the kind often used in artisanal cheeses, pure and organic, harvested from the inner mucosa of the fourth stomach chamber of suckling calves, dried, cleaned, cut into small pieces, and soaked in wine before being deployed in the coagulation process, which turned the milk into a moist gel.

"micelles"—clumped or, in cheesemaker jargon, "knitted" into blocks and glops of curd, and were separated out by draining the whey.

For Ambrosio, cheesemaking was both beautiful and primal: the milking and hauling, the pouring and harping, the careful progression of heating that depended on the right flame, all of it down to the work of one's callused hands, leading after a number of months to some unknown destination, some new birth, some revelation rising out of the physical. It was an act of faith, really. The curds were pressed by hand, Ambrosio leaning his substantial weight down, applying the full force of his person to evacuate the last of the water, after which they were salted and placed in braided molds called *espartos*. This was the most hopeful moment, when the curds were formed into the shape of a four-pound wheel. It was the moment when, exhausted, Ambrosio could let himself hope, *Perhaps this is it. Perhaps we've arrived.* The molds were removed to the family *bodega,* carried down to the cave thirty feet under the earth, where over time the cheese further ripened and began to transmogrify into a version of that hard Castilian *queso tipico.* But would it be *the* version, the legendary Molinos original?

The truth was that countless variables existed within a narrow bandwidth. It was like painting. You started with three primary colors—red, yellow, and blue—but the possibilities they offered ranged from Goya to Picasso, in a palette as wide as the thin, spectral light off the purple ice in a faraway galaxy to the blazing sunflowers in the fields out your back door. Being a farmer, Ambrosio had acquired an almost geological patience, accustomed as he was to toiling in an unforgiving environment. He enjoyed the intellectual exercise of making cheese and, surely, the process of creation, which stirred deep emotion. But even if his attention span had been known to flit here and there with a butterfly's cursive redundancy, he considered the cheese his own personal mission. The grail was at hand, and Ambrosio rode forth with a kind of superhuman zeal. Faced with setbacks—a bad batch when all signs had pointed to a great one, or technical breakdowns—he dove into the work again, in the name of the cheese.

At first he kept his cheesemaking a secret. Guzmán, being a typical Spanish village, was rife with gossip and old feuds, secret alliances and plotted vengeance. But this was hardly unusual in Castile, a kingdom known for its medieval grudges. For instance, Ambrosio's avowed enemy (though once they'd been close friends) was a woman named Emilia del Rincón; the reason for their schism—they, too, had attended each other's weddings when young—had been lost to time. Pinto, the bartender, could at any moment be at odds with almost anyone. Antonio, the local stonemason, could never figure out exactly who had it in for him, but once, after planting three olive trees before the public hall in honor of Andalusia, his birthplace, someone chopped one down as a warning that most took to mean: Welcome to Castile. *Joda su Andalucía!* (Fuck your Andalusia!)

There were feuds over field boundaries and political affiliations,* and jealousies that festered: Someone's *bodega* was situated in a better spot on the hill, someone never bought rounds at the bar or failed to invite someone else to go dove or rabbit hunting in the fall. To show anyone what mattered most was to risk your dreams. Thus the closed door to the lab was like so many others in town: You never knew exactly what lay behind. Some hid horses or chickens. Some opened onto a garden or a cat's cradle of laundry lines pinned with sheets and large, fluttering bras. Others shielded personal projects of one kind or another: Cristian had his sculptures; Abel had his metalwork inventions; Antonio had an eccentric collection of sticks and rocks.

And yet everybody had an inkling about what lay behind those closed doors. For instance, it was hard to conceal sheep as they grazed on the *riberas,* or slopes, around the village, or the large silver canisters of milk moving between the *caseta* and the stall, or the bare light spilling out on the street late at night, to form a single clean line at the edge of the door, and Ambrosio's rumbling baritone inside, plotting the

---

* Some of these dated back to the horror of the Civil War, when friends and acquaintances in the village found each other on opposite sides of the fray, a fact that led to one of Guzmán's most unsettling and closely guarded secrets, a story that would take me years to uncover and try to sort out.

next move. It became harder still to transport molds of cheese up through town to the *bodega,* where in close proximity to other *bodegas* they were unloaded and shuttled into the cave for aging.

The cave was thirteen steps down into the earth, and Ambrosio had transformed the long, thin space into a virtual cheese library. He'd built wooden shelves along the walls and stockpiled them with wheel after wheel of experimental cheese: various batches being aged for anywhere between three months and a year. Each time he returned to the cave, he spoke to the cheese the way he spoke to the sheep, asking after their health. When a new batch was ready for testing, Ambrosio, his mother, and Tomás, like a college of bishops, retired to the cave. Ambrosio then flicked open his pocketknife and carved out a few pieces, which he handed around. For this, he had a ritual. Before taking a bite, he'd ask the cheese, "Are you the one who'll remember us?"

These meetings were like salons. Each batch tasted slightly—or radically—different from the last. Some were too salty or sour; some too soft. One came as a big surprise: When the curds hadn't been pressed enough, veins of mold striped the *queso.* Almost a blue cheese: delicious and strange, but not right. Others counterfeited their way through a first bite—the right hint of caramel, the perfect trace of chamomile—but when the palate had been cleansed by wine and it was time for another piece, the charade was up, and they turned themselves in as frauds.

Each tasting called for an evaluation. Did the cheese need more salt? Had the curds been cut small enough? Was it time to move the sheep to entirely different grasslands? Did the aging process need adjustment? This went on for months, years. Over time, Ambrosio added his own innovations. He found that the cheese tasted better if soaked in olive oil, and if it sat in the dark of the cave at a consistent 50 degrees Fahrenheit for twelve months. He invented a system of turning the cheese: The first week he would turn the cheese every day; the second week, every other day; the third week, every third day . . . and so on.

Minutes, months, years—irrelevant time! How old was the kingdom of Castile itself?* No one had the courage to tell Ambrosio that
perhaps he should set a deadline. No one had the *cojones* (Ambrosio's
word) to say there is no such thing as fairy tales anymore. Making
cheese was a lot of work. Inevitably, the fields suffered and yielded
less. There were many compelling reasons to stop: his young children,
debts that might lead to the loss of more land, the heightening of disil-
lusionment. But faced with the sheer will of Ambrosio, no one expressed doubt. Not even Puri.

In increments, the slow trudge of time reveals all—and one day,
he made believers of them all. Thirteen steps down into the cave, the
latest batch—his folly or triumph—waited. The three of them gathered, and Ambrosio lifted a wheel from the shelf, then sat back on a
rickety wooden chair and drew open the cheesecloth, gazing upon the
queso. Even as he pressed in the blade of his pocketknife, before the
cheese had been fully revealed, by smell and feel alone, Ambrosio declared, "I think this is it."

And his mother said, "This must be it!"

Tomás let them eat first, for only the taste buds of a Molinos could
tell the truth.

Was it surprise that overtook Ambrosio when he realized he'd
cracked the old family recipe? Unbridled joy? No, it was the return of
that simple certainty, the same certainty that had sent armies south in
the name of God to uproot the Moors or launched a thousand Spanish
galleons, the certainty he'd felt when he first stood in that field with
his father and pledged that he would resurrect his family's cheese.

"*¡Puta madre!*" he said to the cheese. "Welcome home!"

---

* Rhetorical question, but the kingdom of Castile dates to the ninth century.
Modern-day Spain is said to have begun its germination on the day—October 19,
1469—when the nineteen-year-old Isabella of Castile, clad in ermine and white
brocade, married her eighteen-year-old first cousin, Fernando of Aragón, in the
castle at Valladolid. Soon began the thirty-five-year reign of Los Reyes Católicos,
the Catholic Monarchs. After presiding over a string of military victories, a minor
cultural renaissance, and Colombus's expedition to the New World, the monarchs
adroitly, if tenuously, unified the lands that comprise Spain today.

His mother let loose her high girlish laugh, whole notes of musical joy she couldn't control, and for someone who was only moderately prolix—which, by comparison to her son and husband, at least, made her downright taciturn—she nearly chirped with repetitive happiness: "This is it . . . *exactly*. . . . This is it . . . *exactly*. . . ."

Ambrosio took a new wedge, wrapped it in paper, and they hurried it to his father, who happened to be down at the *caseta,* inspecting a faulty thresher. He was distracted and a little ticked off—there was always something broken. When they offered him the *queso,* he accepted it with dirty fingers, the crescent moons of his nails caked with earth. Glad for the diversion but expecting nothing, he felt its weight in the palm of his hand, drew in the bouquet with flaring nostrils. Before his expectant audience, he placed a piece in his mouth and let it soften and swarm. And then he stood in silence, in a reverie, until his face transformed, or momentarily reappeared, as that of the boy he'd once been. His eyes grew wide and liquid. His mouth kept moving slowly, masticating, watering, until tears formed, breaching his lower lids.

"*Me cago en la leche de Dios,*" he said. I shit in the milk of God.

Then he asked for another piece.

ONE IMAGINES CHRISTOPHER COLUMBUS—who as a boy is said to have helped his wool-weaving father sell cheese on the side, and who ironically was first buried in Valladolid, just forty miles from the village of Guzmán—imagining his expedition to the Indies in the late 1400s. He draws up detailed plans, itemizing the number of boats, men, and barrels of salted meat and drinking water it may take. No one has ever sailed more than thirty days without resupply, and most navigators believe that to do so, especially into uncharted waters, is a suicide mission. Nonetheless, Columbus brings his plan to Queen Isabella of Spain, and with visions of a new empire she eventually backs the venture, providing him with an annual allowance of 12,000 maravedis, or roughly $1,200.

On August 3, 1492, he sets sail across the Atlantic under the Spanish flag, enduring a total of eight weeks at sea, including a re-supply in the Canary Islands. The grandiosity and insanity of the endeavor is obvious, and when the Bahamas appear on the horizon, he mistakes it for the edge of the Asian continent. After decades of dreaming this moment, of forcing it to fruition, the moment arrives in the full glare of day. He lights upon land with great certainty—and, one must imagine, some small amount of trepidation—to meet a peaceful tribe. There are palm trees, white sand, a warm breeze, and, he hopes (in vain), spices and gold. But after having the gall to sail off the map into an exotic otherworld, he's left with a question: Now what?*

If Ambrosio Molinos had gone forth in the same spirit of discovery he was left with the same question, emanating from a similar sense of excitement and accomplishment. Watching his father eat the cheese had been a spiritual moment akin to the birth of a baby. The son had set out to complete the cycle—and had. Now that he'd solved the mystery of the recipe, he consulted his notes and went back to making more batches. As those ripened and announced their readiness, Ambrosio passed the cheese to more of his friends in the village. The cheese had been made as an act of love and generosity, and Ambrosio gave it away in the same spirit.

---

* And what he can't foresee in that moment of innocence is how much of himself he is about to lose by having succeeded. Flash forward to the end: After three additional voyages, after dotting the Caribbean and mainland with temporary Spanish settlements, after subduing his enemies (in part by committing savage acts of enslavement and cruelty against the native people and hanging some of his own crew members), he is arrested, manacled, and conveyed in chains back to Spain, where he is imprisoned. No longer the boy dreamer but a broken and arthritic fifty-three-year-old man, eyes blotted by chronic conjunctivitis, he seethes with a feeling that he has been badly betrayed, and in a letter to a friend at court that details his accomplishments in the name of the crown—including laying claim to a landmass equal to that of Africa—asks him to consider "how I at the end of my days have been despoiled of my honor and my property without cause, wherein is neither justice nor mercy."

Sure enough, the virtues of this Molinos cheese were not lost on the villagers. They tried it and realized it was good. Very good. They marveled at its amazing strength, its robust nuttiness, and the way it triggered a biochemical reaction bringing back lost memories, for some version of this cheese had sat on their tables, too, as they were growing up. Ambrosio's *queso* became a conduit back to their mothers' kitchens, to childhood, to a simpler time before everyone abandoned the countryside. They discussed the phenomenon of the cheese at the bar, its magical, time-traveler's quality. They shared it at the *bodega*. They passed it along to friends in the next village down the road, who passed it along, too—from Guzmán to Quintanamanvirgo, from Roa to Aranda de Duero, the circle continuing to expand outward, to the villages whose names translate as The Free One, Blond Church, Cold, Bramble, Pine Fountain, and Bucket of Hens. The cheese lingered and haunted, and its legend soon spread throughout the region. People began showing up at all hours, knocking at Ambrosio's door, wanting to buy some, triggering a thought: Why not sell it, then?*

By this time, his family was completely implicated. His wife, Asun,†

---

* In a time before artisanal cheeses, this one benefited from what the renowned British cheesemonger Patricia Michelson later told me were the hallmarks of great small-batch cheeses: "The cheesemaker goes twenty feet rather than twenty miles for his milk," she said. "The milk gets made into cheese quickly after milking because it retains its best qualities. Cheeses made on the farm with their own milk, and milking parlor, and cheesemaking area close by can be done in two hours. Then put away for aging. That's what makes the perfect artisanal cheese."

† The two met at twenty-one when Ambrosio saw her on the street in Aranda and shouted, "Hey, *morena,* we're going to get married, so you need to be my girlfriend." The next time he saw her, he offered her half of a wild boar he'd just killed. Nevertheless, they'd married in 1978 and had a daughter, Asunción (known as Asunita, or little Asun), in 1979, and then two sons: Josué in 1982 and Enrique, or Kiké (pronounced *key-KAY*), in 1985. Asun, the wife and mother, was quick to laugh, with a gentle spirit and intelligent brown eyes. She was also the heart and soul of the family, a great cook, a calm presence, and yet full of paradox: strong and soft, wary and brave, nurturing and isolated, supportive and at times, by necessity, gently critical of her husband, the dreamer. Ambrosio's stories, his constant irreverence, and the force of his creativity—all of these things kept her close. And the

had invented a name: Páramo de Guzmán.* His sister-in-law, an artist, drew a simple sheep, and it became the first logo, painted on the
side of the horse-stall laboratory. His father helped with the sheep; his
mother, the coagulation process. His brothers invested money so Ambrosio could grow the operation into a business. Their little family
cheese, which was sold in an idiosyncratic white tin (to which the children affixed the labels), started flying out the door.

One day a cheese buyer from Madrid appeared in the village, asking to speak to the person behind this curious cheese, and the villagers
pointed him to the cave. The buyer found Ambrosio underground,
turning his dear babies, an imposing figure with a broad face and
happy-sad expression. The buyer talked to Ambrosio and realized that
when the cheesemaker opened his mouth he spoke in lyrical poems
about his family and these highlands and the purity of handmade
foods, and how the best thing about being alive on this planet came
from tasting that purity in this piece of *queso*. The buyer bought as
much cheese as Ambrosio could part with and took it home with him.

Soon Ambrosio's cheese was being sold in gourmet stores in the
capital, pushed by enthusiastic cheesemongers on their customers. It
went from Madrid to London, where it was sold at Harrods, among
other shops.† It was heady stuff, and Ambrosio was rightly proud, but

---

beauty of village life deepened for her over time, though she often admitted to
missing the bustle of Aranda. To counter Ambrosio's bohemian flair, she became
the practical sorter of bills, the left brain to her husband's right, the protector of his
more vulnerable soul.

* The *páramo* in this case being the highland plain above the village where the
sheep often grazed, also known in local parlance as *arriba*. At an elevation of approximately three thousand feet and with somewhat murky boundaries, that table
of land was divided into numerous zones according to the closest village, so the
páramo of Páramo de Guzmán might also have been known as the Páramo de Vi-
llaescusa or the Páramo de Tórtoles, and so on.

† At one of those shops, an American gourmand and deli owner named Ari was cut
a piece, and, letting it melt on his tongue, declared: "This is really an outstanding
piece of cheese . . . rich, dense, intense." He took it back to Michigan, where a slightly
fuzzy, idealistic part-time employee didn't just hear the clarion call, he proofread it.

not altogether surprised. His cheese had become a little prophet in a modern world that needed one. A man of the fields, Ambrosio Molinos began to star at agricultural fairs, where his *queso* kept winning awards, starting with second prize at the 1987 London International Cheese Show and then, in quick succession, the gold medal at the 1989 Expo Láctea, the gold Tarro at the first 1990 Spanish Cheese Challenge, and a first prize at the International Cheese Challenge. This was something a person could get used to. At the cheese show in England, a great Scottish cheesemaker, an older, heavyset lass—about his weight, actually—approached with a Scotch whisky in one hand and a lit cigar in the other and smothered him with a hug, saying, "Who could make such a beautiful thing?"

That was a kindred soul. That was a woman he could love.

And the cheese kept conquering the world. Back home, the story goes, the king of Spain, Juan Carlos himself, had occasion to try it, declared it one of the finest, and ordered more. Meanwhile, Ronald Reagan and Frank Sinatra, Queen Elizabeth and Mikhail Gorbachev and Julio Iglesias, all ate the cheese. After first tasting it, Fidel Castro ordered as much as the cheesemaker could spare.

People began to ask Ambrosio, How is this possible? Does it seem like a dream? And he made a show of considering, then answered, "No. When you put love and care and hundreds of years of history into a product like this one, you can taste all of it."

As sublime as the cheese was, demand soon outstripped supply. Ambrosio needed more sheep, more equipment, more room, more cheesemakers. He wanted to find a way to make each wheel of cheese with the same amount of consideration as the first he'd given his father, for that was his gift to the world, but his family cheese was becoming big business and Ambrosio had no experience as a businessman. He had no interest in sitting at a desk, let alone scouring profit-and-loss sheets, cash flow summaries, ratio analyses. It was a waste of his time. He was a creator, wild and free. Let others organize the puzzle around him.

IN THE YEARS THAT followed the 1975 demise of Franco's interminable dictatorship, Spain reentered the world like a sluggish, sightless mole. Having been cordoned off for so long, the country's first taste of democracy was met by high inflation spurred by rising oil prices that left the economy in tatters until the mid-1980s, at which time the deficit was reduced, oil prices dropped, tourism picked up, and foreign investment crested. By the late 1980s the country was awash in nascent capitalists making scads of money—and spending it. The entrepreneurial spirit infected everyone from shop owners to investment bankers, tendriling to places like Guzmán.

One person busy capitalizing on new opportunities, building an empire of his own, was Ambrosio's friend Julián. He lived in a nice house in Aranda, had a thriving law practice, owned a radio station, a car dealership, and a gas station. He seemed to have the Midas touch, or at least to Ambrosio. Raising families now, the two friends came and went through each other's lives, sharing meals at the *bodega,* meeting in bars, singing at village fiestas arm in arm. At thirty-five they were still very much as they had been at fifteen. They spoke in the same low register, with the same intonations, burst out with the same ribald laughter, made the same gestures. Most of all, they were, and would always be, connected by the same principles: the decency and honesty of that ideal embodied in the figure of the Old Castilian.

When Ambrosio went looking for someone with business and legal acumen to help with his cheese, he looked no further than Julián. His friend seemed to love the cheese and its symbolism almost as much as Ambrosio. Meanwhile, Julián had what no one else had: Ambrosio's everlasting trust. At first what was merely the advice of a friend over food and wine became the invaluable insight of a trusted adviser. When Ambrosio expressed concern over how he could pay for more expansion—the demand kept growing—Julián formulated a business plan. He courted investors, wrote up contracts, and, over time, brought several parties to the table that pledged nearly $2 million. When the operation outgrew its stable and *bodega* in Guzmán— and an attempt to procure the derelict palace with the idea of converting it into a factory was thwarted—Ambrosio moved the company across the fields to the edge of Roa, to an ancient stone building, which was promptly renovated. On the property they added a warehouse and hired a number of cheesemakers. They built a tasting room for visitors to sample their cheese. Every morning a truck arrived with the milk of Ambrosio's sheep—the flock of a dozen had become a hundred, and they had to supplement their milk with more from other sources—which was poured into huge vats and induced to coagulate, beginning again a cycle that would lead to the distinctive cheese known as Páramo de Guzmán, maker of memories. Trucks came and went, the cheese fluttered to all corners of the globe. The division of labor was nearly perfect: Julián helped to handle the big-picture financial logistics, while Ambrosio made sure the family cheese continued to live up to its chosen name.

Sometimes at the end of the day's work, from the top windows of his parents' villa in Guzmán, Ambrosio would gaze eight miles across the fields and see the new cheese factory. It was an enormous source of pride, that factory. And that pastoral vision, with its brushstrokes of gold-white wheat in the foreground and blue sky above, of gray stone and red-tile roof in the distance, made a beautiful painting, too.

5

THE BETRAYAL

"'He stole my soul,' Ambrosio said."

T HE GIANT—WHICH IS WHAT AMBROSIO WAS IN THAT HOT, cramped space—cleared his throat, fidgeted, looked down at his hands, and then met my gaze. He seemed to choke for a moment on a small skeleton, then swallowed hard.

"I don't know why this little cheese conquered so many," he said softly. "But if you asked me the secret, I'd say it was because we made it in our home, the old way, the way it had been made for hundreds of years. Perhaps in the United States you don't know what it's like to have old flavors, flavors from the past, from centuries before. But we live with them every day here. My children know these flavors. I don't consider myself in the middle of this conflict between old and new—I'm clearly on the side of the old. I feel that there are two ways to create nourishment in food, and in the future, there's only going to be one." His big forefinger waggled. "My mission is to make sure we don't forget the old way."

Ambrosio was rolling again, inspired by the digression,* or, as he

---

* I would soon find out that digression was a national pastime in Castile, that to get to the crux of any matter you had to listen for hours, weeks, months, years. Not a

put it, *"mi grandísima filosofía de la vida."* Anything, it seemed, to keep from having to tell the next part of the story about his cheese. But there we sat, Carlos and I, rapt as two unmoving cannonballs.

"Consider the chicken," he said. "Today we have industrialized animals. A chicken needs to be cheap to be competitive in the marketplace. So the industrial chicken has a life that lasts forty-two days between its hatching and its sacrifice. They flood the chicken with twenty-three hours of light a day so that the chicken constantly feeds, and then they give it one hour of rest. They do this for six weeks, then the chickens are put on a conveyor belt and either gassed or have their heads chopped off and are immediately dumped in scalding water, after which the dead body is sent to market.

"On the other hand, the traditional chicken used to take one and a half years from hatching to sacrifice. You would see the chicken every day and speak to her, and you would share with her certain aspects of your own life. The chicken was your friend; she understood you. You loved each other. She knew she was going to have a happy life and tried to give you her best while you gave her yours. She knew her destiny, that eventually she would make a gift of her life to feed your family. But you honored each other. The chicken lived at home with you, and you ate her at home. It was divinity, not machines."

He kept on easily in this vein for quite some time, until the heat relented a few degrees and the slightest of nighttime breezes pushed through the shutter, swishing so lazily it hardly guttered the flame he'd lit. This certainly wasn't normal conversation, I knew that—or certainly not normal *American* conversation, from the country that blithely consumed nine billion chickens a year, most of them factory made and

---

fan of annotations and footnotes, I realized I had no say in the matter. Every story here was littered with footnotes and asides. And even then, after the storyteller concluded his tale—or, rather, after you'd gathered and assembled the shards of his story from a hundred other digressions—well, you'd go to the bar and have it immediately undermined by someone else's digressive, heavily annotated account of the same thing.

McNuggetized.[*] The more he spoke the more I appreciated the relative humanity of his vision. His grand philosophy wasn't just idealistic, it was achievable, actionable, with intimations of beauty and epiphany. He was in dialogue with an inaccessible world I'd never had the occasion to live in, let alone lose touch with. Yet it was one we all felt some instinctual connection to, wasn't it? As Ambrosio's thin lips kept moving, as he boasted that he could spot a wild hare from two hundred meters, smell bad weather in the air before its arrival, discern mushrooms where there didn't seem to be any, I felt buoyed, inspired, reinvigorated. He explained that this life in the fields was all part of being "an Old Castilian," something that couldn't be taught or learned, but was genetically transferred through generations. "Either this cycle of history admits you or it doesn't," he said. "Our cheese was an emblem of this."

He allowed that, in the beginning, when the cheese was young and newly found, life had been "idyllic" and "full of great happiness." All of his expectations had been met the day his father had slipped the *queso* in his mouth and momentarily become a boy again. But add time, and the plot thickens.[†]

Ambrosio absently fiddled with a knife that he'd pried from the table where it had been stuck, the blade about six inches long and pewter

---

[*] So writes Elizabeth Kolbert in a 2009 *New Yorker* review of Jonathan Safran Foer's pro-vegan *Eating Animals:* "Broiler chickens, also known, depending on size, as fryers or roasters, typically spend their lives in windowless sheds, packed in with upward of thirty thousand other birds and generations of accumulated waste. The ammonia fumes thrown off by their rotting excrement lead to breast blisters, leg sores, and respiratory disease. Bred to produce the maximum amount of meat in the minimum amount of time, fryers often become so top-heavy that they can't support their own weight. At slaughtering time, they are shackled by their feet, hung from a conveyor belt, and dipped into an electrified bath known as 'the stunner.' "

[†] Time, the ever-fickle berserker, brings the happy ending that it eventually undoes. Add a few more days, months, years to where the dire narrative ends and new forms emerge, beads of light suddenly cling to what was once a darkness. Perhaps the forlorn boy of "Araby" eventually gets the girl; the king, once in prison, returns to seize an empire. The happy ending relies on patience—but not *too* much. Add even more time, and the story curdles: desire momentarily sated, the boy becomes insufferable; the king is made a fool of. Someone calls for everyone's head. Real life intervenes, and makes its mess of things.

colored. In the overlay of darkness, he held open his empty hand, his white palm flashing in a gesture I took to be resignation—*What can I say?*—and began to recite from Páramo de Guzmán's book of Genesis. He recounted in detail all the things he'd done to bring the cheese to fruition—milking the sheep, hauling the canisters, stirring and harping the boiling curds and whey (and such a hard cheese as his required a lot of stirring and harping to break down the protein globules). The amount of cheese at first—the number of wheels—had been just enough for an inner circle of relatives and friends. But it was true, the cheese had been too wonderful. Like its maker, it demanded an audience.

"We put so much into the cheese," said Ambrosio, "but it gave so much more."

The decision to sell and market the cheese, an idea that seemed to marry so many good things (a sublime product, a sustainable way of life, a dream realized), was, in retrospect, perhaps the biggest mistake of Ambrosio's life.* Once it had been made, there was no turning back. "The real trouble," he said, "started with the new factory."

---

* Later he would say that the happiest man was the one who did what he loved most regardless of the need or desire for money. He lionized a certain local sculptor, Santiago of Sotillo, whose work was world famous and highly sought after. According to Ambrosio, the sculptor wanted only to sculpt, and so he'd struck a deal with the people of his village. As long as they kept him fed and housed, as long as he could go to his studio and work all day, hammering at stone to make beautiful things, the village could have whatever money his work raised. Meanwhile, each day a different person brought Santiago his meals; every night he had his own roof overhead. What more could he have wanted?

Likewise, Luis, one of Ambrosio's closest friends, had a workshop in Roa, where in his free time he crafted antique keys patterned after ones he'd dug out of ruins or that had been given to him or were illustrated in picture books. His workshop was lined with the keys he'd made, fine products of craftsmanship that he often gave to friends as gifts. Those exquisite keys—of nickel and brass and gold plate, some jointed or with fantastically ornate handles—opened no doors, for the doors they might have opened were all gone. They were without use—or useless, if looked at only one way. And yet by the light of his kiln, pounding at molten pieces of metal, Luis was that portrait of the fully realized man, in Ambrosio's opinion, having momentarily escaped the soul-crushing ethos of the modern world where everything that was made had to be consumed, where the symbolic had been replaced at every turn by the disposable commodity.

For the new factory, he needed Julián most of all. "Julián's role was to advise me on financial matters and to handle all the contracts," said Ambrosio, "and being a businessman, he had relationships that, of course, I didn't." At the very least, Ambrosio realized that growing the cheese operation would require something of a quantum leap. And that leap required another infusion of cash. Friend that he was, Julián promised Ambrosio that he'd find the right investors, ones who understood and appreciated Ambrosio's philosophy, who would respect and love the cheese, too—and keep its best interests in mind. And apparently that's just what Julián did.

"The factory in Roa was housed in a very old building, maybe four hundred years old, with a perfect cellar for aging the cheese," Ambrosio said. "Julián brought in the investors and we signed the contracts to form a conglomerate. We invested in state-of-the-art equipment, like stainless-steel industrial vats for the milk. We hired more cheesemakers." Watching it all unfold, as the orders continued to pour in, Ambrosio said that he felt the "cleansing obligation of work."

A typical day at the factory might have found Ambrosio arriving early to meet with his cheesemakers, standing out by the front gate to receive canisters of milk, driving to the fields to check up on the shepherds. There he was, overseeing the boiling and harping, helping to press and cut the cheese, molding it and carrying it to the dark, cool basement. He tested new batches of "the product," acting as final quality control. He helped load the cheese into boxes, onto pallets, into trucks. He met with potential buyers, and in this act of public relations he truly excelled, because he was completely himself, the Castilian man of the earth.

There was the doing side of things, the making side, the enacting of the grand philosophy, and then there were the intricacies of the profit-and-loss sheet, of price points and wage rigidity, the nitty-gritty business of selling the cheese in a way that left the company profitable. How many times had he been thankful to have Julián there, and never more so than in the new factory? It was a blessing to worry only about making the best cheese in the world. And a blessing to be sur-rounded by family and friends: his wife, Asun, who now worked on the books; his aunt, who was the secretary. His drinking buddies, the shepherds of Guzmán, still brought the milk. He couldn't have dreamed it better.

In Ambrosio's telling, the story of the cheese sounded more and more like a fable, not just because he communicated with animals and food products—and not because the tableau of little elves working by candlelight to manufacture the charmed family treasure was roughly true—but because it was the kind of fable in which everything, espe-cially the hero, is bigger than life and thus takes on the quality of legend. Ambrosio described being at the factory one day during reno-vations when a cellar beam groaned and cracked, and the ceiling began to rain down. One worker was hit by a beam; another barely escaped the cave-in with his life. Without thinking, Ambrosio threw himself at the emergency, dragging a water hose in order to make the concrete needed to stabilize the beam, which he held in place over his head for an hour while others rushed to reinforce the ceiling. "It wasn't an act of courage," he said. "I just had to."

As someone given to tilting the most quotidian events into a Vi-king epic, I couldn't get enough. I'd spent years traveling the world for my job, hoping to meet someone like this Ambrosio, someone who happened to speak in a fascinating spool of sentences, in compelling layers of stories—someone who actually *had* a grand philosophy of life. Who was profane and holy. Who had staked his life on a code that seemed to be going the way of the most endangered animals: the loggerhead turtle, the numbat, the jackass penguin.[*]

In his cameo in Ari's newsletter at Zingerman's, Ambrosio had been nothing but a two-dimensional figure, an archetype—the Rustic Cheesemaker—but here, in person, he burst, popped, and exploded

---

[*] Guzmán, too, was the jackass penguin, barely clinging to its habitat, which, right from the start made me feel like a zoologist, there to see the living thing one last time before it vanished.

into three dimensions, burnished and blazing, Ambro the Beneficent, engaged in chivalrous acts of purity.

It's rare indeed when one's highest opinion of oneself is greeted by others as the truth, but that's exactly the mirror that reflected back on Ambrosio Molinos and his cheese. As he traveled from fair to fair, manning his booth with brio, he joked with the future president of Spain, José María Aznar, a short man Ambrosio liked immensely. When they met again, he greeted him by saying, "José María, you're *still* short!" He also met Camilo José Cela, the Nobel Prize–winning Spanish writer, a not altogether pleasant experience, as it turned out.* And with each new honor that accrued to his *queso,* more enthusiasts and gourmands were drawn to the cheese and its maker.†

But more important than praise was the fact that Ambrosio found

---

* Claiming that his goal in writing was "to touch your finger to the ulcer," Cela was known to be a man of dyspeptic temper, sharp tongue, and strange outbursts. The 1942 book that brought him early fame, *The Family of Pascual Duarte,* was condemned and banned by the Franco regime for its violence, sex, and rough language. (It was first secretly published in a garage in Burgos, but with the passage of time was widely considered to have reignited Spanish literature to the extent that the Nobel committee, upon awarding the prize in 1989, called it the most popular work in Spanish since *Don Quixote.*) A biter of nuns in his childhood and the author of such irreverent books as *Chronicle of the Extraordinary Event of Archidona's Dick,* Cela appeared on Spanish talk shows later in life, claiming he could suck a liter of water through his anus and offering to demonstrate this on air. A portly basset hound of a man who took a second wife forty years his junior after an acrimonious divorce—in a 1997 *Paris Review* interview, he claimed "she fucks me so she can tire herself out a bit"—he was known by some to have abandoned his man-of-the-people persona for a Bentley and expensive suits.

Said Ambrosio of Cela, "My friend Fermin introduced me to him at a restaurant, saying I made a ballsy cheese, and we talked about the cheese, and he recognized the name of the cheese and the tin, and he was more interested in talking to me than the people he'd arrived with. He wanted to show them that he wasn't interested in them. When Fermin said I was the owner of Páramo de Guzmán, from that point forth he listened to me attentively, which means he reacted like most people do: gauging one's worth by what one possesses rather than who one is."

† In a blog entry on his website, the American writer and town crier for all good Spanish things Gerry Dawes reflected on his first encounter with Ambrosio: "Early on during my travels in the Ribera del Duero, I met Ambrosio Molinos, an aficionado of great regional food, a gourmand of repute, and one of the great arti-

himself at the forefront of a minor movement. In England, Spanish food products had mostly been ignored, but by the late eighties a Spanish renaissance was afoot, led by importers such as Monika Linton, whose company, Brindisa, was housed in a warehouse next to Southwark Cathedral on the south bank of the Thames. "One of her first products was a cheese in a tin," reads a 1994 article from *The Independent,* "which she lit upon at the Food Fair. The brainchild of Ambrosio Molinos, it was a rich cheese rather like Parmesan, packed in olive oil in a beautiful tin."

The article went on to quote Linton. " 'Because it was such an eccentric cheese, it opened quite a few doors for me. There were a couple of important restaurants and department stores in London prepared to try it. But no one really managed to sell it, partly because it was expensive,' she says. It failed to make any money but worked as a marketing experiment, because it opened doors."

It opened doors—that's all Ambrosio cared about. Doors to past memories, to one's parents, friends, and children. Yes—it was a globalizing force pushing backward against a world on the verge of globalization. But also, it was a visionary's cheese: It cut to the heart of how he felt a human being should eat. "I'd much rather drink wine made by somebody who's serving it to me, because I'm drinking that

---

san cheese makers of Castile. . . . It was the Pérez Pascuas brothers, the exceptional wine making family of the nearby village of Pedrosa, who introduced me to the stout, jovial Ambrosio, who came over to Pedrosa to eat wild boar with us and brought his guitar and one of his wonderful Burgos cheeses with him. Ambrosio has a quick and easy laugh, an incredible sense of humor, and always seemed to be in good spirits. We soon became fast friends because of a common interest in wine, regional cuisine, and his penchant for scandalous jokes. . . . Ambrosio loves to eat as much as anyone I have ever met. He relishes the intellectual aspects of gastronomy as well and can talk for hours about the art of eating, then on occasion after dinner, can spend another hilarious hour on the scatological joys of eliminating what he eats. He is a hefty man. One hot summer day, when I stopped by his home in Roa . . . I encountered Ambrosio shirtless, having a casual lunch with his family. When I kidded him about putting on weight, he clutched a roll of fat at his midsection, and told me, 'That's not me, that's my shirt.' "

person," said Ambrosio. "I'm becoming impregnated by that person's being, their love."*

Thus he saw his mission as one of disseminating that cheese-love far and wide, and, perhaps blinded by all the fine, glorious things that redounded from the cheese, he happened to miss certain business realities, reflected by the line in the article that said, *partly because it was expensive. . . . It failed to make any money.*

The year was now 1991. One day the secretary, his aunt, took him aside. We have money problems, she said bluntly.†

Money problems? It seemed preposterous. Here they were, making one of the most coveted cheeses in the world. For every order that went out, three more came back over the transom. And now there were . . . *money problems?*

It was hard to calculate the meaning of this news, but after the disbelief, Ambrosio claimed his body was seized with an unsettling sensation—a need to move. He propelled his large frame three steps at a time straight up to the office, where, in his telling, he began pawing through order forms and receipts, bank statements and contracts, reviewing for the first time all the deals and numbers he'd left to others.

"And then something terrible dawned on me," said Ambrosio. His voice trailed into silence that first night in the telling room. He pressed his lips together, and Carlos and I sat listening to him breathe for a while. All of this was so unexpected—the turns of the story, the

---

* Later he would tell me a story. "I have a little jar in my cave," he said, "a four-liter jug, the last wine made by a good friend of mine before he died: Joselito. It is now the second anniversary of his death, and I'm always thinking of him. I think of how he might have laughed at this joke, or that moment. Any little thing will remind me of him. And once in a while I want to drink his wine. I want to drink *him,* not his wine. I take a swig of it, of *him,* and I put the cork back on him. Maybe someone who hears this thinks I'm off my rocker, but this is what I believe: When I give anything—wine, a tortilla, my cheese—I am inside that. And of all the people who eat what I offer, only a special few realize that there's a spirit present, that there's my love."

† 1991: *still* bad.

imposing stranger who now sat bereft before us, shoulders rounding in grief, his secrets spilling forth on the table, shimmering like a catch of fish. "The cheese didn't belong to me anymore," he said at last. "It belonged to *him*. It was in *his* name, or the names of those with whom he was collaborating. Because he was very clever."

Who was very clever? I asked.

"Julián," said Ambrosio. "There was no question in my mind that we would have laid our lives down for each other, but he's the one who ruined me. He stole the cheese. He put the contracts before me, knowing that I would sign them without reading."

"Julián duped you into signing your company away?" I asked.

Yes, said Ambrosio, waving a hand. "And, worse, I'd signed it away two years before."

He continued: "At first it was impossible to believe. It all went rushing through my head, all those happy years, right back to my father lying sick in bed. I fell into shock. And denial." Despite the looping evidence of his scrawled signature on paper, he thought he could merely put everything back together again, as if the wind-shorn branches on the ground could be picked up and reattached to the trees in order to create the illusion that there'd never been a storm at all. He would go see Julián and undo everything.

"So I took the contract," he said, emphatically jabbing the knife back into the table again, "and went straight to Julián's office and said, 'Hombre, tell me, what's the meaning of this?'"

Julián, who was seated behind his desk, obviously hadn't been expecting Ambrosio. "He had this habit, when he was nervous," said Ambrosio, reaching to his neck to demonstrate. "He would pinch a little skin below his Adam's apple and make this sound"—Ambrosio cleared his throat, and made a sharp staccato report, like a car engine trying to turn over in cold weather: *huh-huh-huh-huh-huh-huh*. Clear and cough.

And when Ambrosio confronted his best friend with the contract bearing his signature, that's just the sound he remembered gasping from Julián's mouth. *Huh-huh-huh-huh-huh-huh-huh . . .*

"I trusted you."

"Huh-huh-huh-huh-huh-huh . . ."

"Why?"

"Huh-huh-huh-huh-huh-huh . . ."

"How could you?"

"Huh-huh-huh-huh-huh-huh . . ."

When Julián finally spoke, he denied it all. And yet the documents didn't lie. And the nervous tic didn't lie. And Julián's evasiveness—the strange, fearful look in his eye, his inability to hold Ambrosio's gaze—didn't lie. As he looked upon Julián there at his desk, Ambrosio realized that it must be true: Páramo de Guzmán, the family cheese, no longer belonged to his family. He'd been checkmated by greed, by legal mumbo-jumbo, by the backstabbers of this modern world. He wandered out of Julián's office as if having forgotten why he'd come in the first place, the armpits of his shirt soaked with sweat. In his bones he knew, but he was moving into shock, had the sensation of departing his body and watching from above.

"The pain and loss that I felt wasn't for the loss of the money," he said, "but because I was betrayed by my best friend. And I couldn't admit it to myself."

Ambrosio lifted the *porrón,* spun the wine in it, and replaced it without drinking. "If you rob a bank and walk out with a million dollars," he said, "you've accomplished something. If you planned it out, and you have the ability and the intellect to achieve your objective, a monument should be built to you. You're still a robber and it's wrong, but it has some merit. But if you steal from a child—or cheat your wife—what merit is there in that? The betrayal of a friend? These are sins a thousand times worse." Here he sighed, then continued. "I always thought that whoever has the *cojones* to work hard would eventually get ahead. But the thief who is spineless, who undoes all that work, that guy will be buried in his own misery and eat shit for the rest of his life."

Both his resignation and lamentation seemed as complete now, in this moment inside the telling room, as it must have been a decade earlier. "I went back to the cheese factory," he said, "and I gathered the cheesemakers and told them what had happened, that I'd been betrayed and was done. I told them that the cheese factory was no longer mine. When I walked out that day, all but one followed me—one whom I'd trained from the beginning, one from Guzmán. He knew the mechanics, and he could go through the motions of making the cheese in my absence."

When he walked out of that earthly mansion—the warehouse full of packaged cheese, the cellar full of sleeping cheese, the factory full of newborn cheese, there in case his father grew hungry—he entered his own waking nightmare. How would he tell them all, his parents and brothers, his children and theirs someday? For years afterward, he couldn't taste anything he ate.

"He stole my soul," Ambrosio said.

6

THE SUNFLOWERS

"Divinity, not machines."

E IGHT HOURS AFTER ENTERING, WE EXITED THE TELLING ROOM. Day had turned to night, which had turned to very early morning: *1:32 A.M.*, read Carlos's watch. Ambrosio fumbled with an oversized key to lock the door behind us. The sky radiated with such a multitude of stars that everything—the church tower, the stone ruins, an abandoned tractor in a field below—appeared in bright snowdrifts in the silver night air. The beams were so thick you could nearly cup them in your hands. It was bizarre, that cosmic snow.

And that silence. (Some Almighty finger had pressed Mute.)

Ambrosio came up, and we said our goodbyes. For such a solid man, he conveyed a sense of emptiness now, a fleeting inconsequentiality. We were quite far from lodging options, he said. He offered to call ahead to some roadside motel somewhere *out there*. When I assured and then reassured him that we'd be fine, and after he'd lingered a moment longer to demonstrate his concern, he said goodbye the way they said it here, *"Ta' lo,"* which was percussively short for *hasta luego,* and translated as "until later" or "see you later." But in

Guzmán the phrase meant the following, all at once: *hello . . . so long . . . how are you again? . . . until we pass . . . we are passing again . . . oh, hello! . . . goodbye! . . . again? . . . again! . . . and round we go!* At first one might have thought everyone here had short-term memory loss, but it was a rat-a-tat adaptation meant to capture the circularity of life in a small village and a reminder that, though very much alone and seemingly shipwrecked in the world, these sun-scorched orphans of Castile could at least depend upon seeing each other one more time. With our brief admittance into this circle, it was assumed that we'd meet them all again, too.

Now we shook, his rough hand enveloping my computer-soft one, and parted ways outside his *bodega:* us to our car and him to his house. We watched as he slumped past the dark mouths of caves burrowed into the hill—including the one where we'd first met with the *porrón*—then he went twisting down among the cubist jumble of stone houses, finally dematerializing through the narrow, unlit streets that by dawn would hum with tractors on their way to the fields. There he went, Ambrosio Molinos de las Heras. Or: Ambrosio of the Mill and Field. Bearing the halo of his agrarian virtue.

Carlos and I collapsed into the car. I found myself reeling, but oddly exhilarated, too. I turned the ignition, the engine gurgled to life, and then we were drifting toward somewhere that was nowhere, into the nothingness below us, held by the nothingness above.

On the ride I prodded Carlos for first impressions.

"I was really surprised by him," said Carlos. "He's a big man. He has beautiful eyes. Very nice, very warm. He was almost crying at certain points while telling the story of his cheese. As if he'd lost a child."

We swooped down the hill, along the same winding road we'd earlier climbed, descending to the *coterro*'s floor with the windows open, cooler air gushing now. I crouched over the wheel in an alert stupor, trying to register everything that appeared in the headlights—

stones in the road, stray grapevines, pellets of sheep shit—when suddenly came a silent, yellow explosion, like flashbulbs firing. Sunflowers! We were immersed in a sea of them. Perhaps it was the hour, or the giddy sense of freedom I felt after having sat for so long cooped inside a cave, but the car guided itself to the side of the road, and before Carlos had time to question I shot out and waded into them with palms open, as if expecting low fives.

A light wind rustled the flowers, and I zigzagged about ten rows deep, until I was more or less hidden. My feet sank into the loose, granular dirt that filled my sandals, itchy and still warm. The flowers wafted a mild, leafy smell, the sky cathedraled overhead. I could see the car from where I stood, its headlights in a sodium pool on the road, and Carlos blearily struggling to release himself from the seat belt. They were amazing creatures, these sunflowers, unthreatening, listing toward me as if to get a look.

I could hear the hum of stars, and I could locate the sound of myself thinking.* How long had it been since I'd had the clarity, or peace, to hear the gears engage or the rustle of watery thoughts flowing toward some deeper pool? And, standing there,† I had, well—call it what you will—a fibrillation of insight, or a crumb-sized epiphany.

The intervening voice was simple, almost corny, for it felt so good: *Belong to this.* But to what—a sunflower patch? Or the silence of the Old World? And did I *already* belong, or was I *supposed* to belong, aspire to belong, change my life to belong? There was a problem: If I belonged *right here,* then I didn't belong *back there,* with my wife and son, in the noise of the New World.

---

* Says Marcus Aurelius: "Tranquility is nothing else than the good ordering of the mind."

† To get the full impression, one must imagine the singer Peter Gabriel, in earlier guise, with his band of sweater-wearing hippie-nerds, Genesis, during the experimental, prog-rock days of the seventies, taking the stage as Flower Man—floppy petals framing his pale, painted face. Said one of Gabriel's unsuspecting and most laconic bandmates the first time he caught sight of the singer in costume, creeping onstage with his flute: "Oh, bloody hell."

The impulse out in the sunflowers* that early morning was to stay absolutely still for a moment, sucking in fresh air, immersed and drawn under by a deep and powerful silence. Looming before me was the mesa known as Mon Virgo, looking every bit as much a landing pad for extraterrestrials as it was Ambrosio's heaven of bodily evacuation. It called up Ambrosio's earlier phrase, when he'd described the way they gently and soulfully offed their chickens here, but really had been describing their underlying ethos of life.

"Divinity, not machines," he'd said.

It could have been the cheesemaker's slow-food manifesto, silk-screened on a thousand farmers' market T-shirts, his utopian ideal writ large, inked on the sandaled-shaggy-man's placard in Times Square.

Divinity, not machines.

Standing among the sunflowers, I craved divinity. I was thinking about how Ambrosio had said he spoke to animals, as if they were close friends, confiding in them. What so moved me about this notion? Not just that I wanted to talk to animals like that—though I did—but more: I wanted to live in a realm where I *could* talk to animals, where all the generations of my family had once resided, where I might take daily strength in them, and where I'd live a life antlered by meaning and mysticism. Instead, I'd grown up in suburbia, with

---

* A practical word about sunflowers that goes beyond their place in van Gogh paintings: In Castile, among arable hectares for crops ranging from sugar beets to rye and lavender, sunflowers rank third after barley and wheat. As prices for sunflower oil continued to rise in the world markets—tripling in the five-year period between 1999 and 2004 (and from there doubling again by May 2008)—and given Castile's perfectly sunny climate for growing the flower, which requires at least six hours of light a day but thrives with additional rays, more and more land at that time was dedicated to the crop. So—around Guzmán, you'd find sunflowers in the *barcos,* on little diamonds of land scrunched between other crops, in languorous fields. While the bull had once been the great symbol of Castile—and still theoretically was—the sunflower conveyed its own reflection of tempered optimism, a heartiness willing to take its place in the unrelenting natural order of things here and, for its own brief moment, to thrive.

our nearest family relations six hours by car, and a scattered sense of my own heritage. Standing among sunflowers, I suddenly felt an urge to reverse the ships, play history in rewind, spur an inverse diaspora so that I might return to the ur-village, become a cobbler or farmer, working shoulder to shoulder with my brethren.

Those, as far as I could tell, were my brethren: farmers on my mother's English-Irish-Scots side, tradespeople on my father's Italian side. Certainly every family possesses its creation myth, and one of mine revolved around my grandfather, Gaetano of Sicily, who, upon entering the waters of lower Manhattan aboard the *Giuseppi Verdi* in 1920—and passing through Ellis Island—became Thomas of America, an Italian immigrant, an opera-loving barber (and barber's son), a peaceable man who liked nothing more than to make wine.

The story went that during World War I he'd been captured by Central Powers troops and hauled to a prison camp in Romania, where he was left to molder and starve. Until he hatched an escape plan, one that resulted in the killing of a guard, the traversing of icy ravines, the loss of a companion along the way. He traveled this enemy landscape until he came upon railroad tracks, following them to trains. He hid by day and rode the trains by night, holding himself underneath the cars until he snuck back into Italy on foot.

I've often imagined my grandfather beneath those trains, and questions spark to mind: Is this physically possible? And assuming it is, what sustains and gives him the strength to undertake such a harrowing journey? The answer, I imagine, is the village of his origin, Tortorici, where everything that matters most to him resides. Can he taste the ripe peaches of home, the sweet water? Can he picture his own father, in the barbershop, waiting for him now? News from the front has been bleak. There are already four dead Paternitis from the village, but his son Gaetano has not yet been listed among them. The father, Antonino, stands there, his astral face reflecting in the mirrors, and he, the son, who is beneath the train, imagines reaching up to kiss his father good morning—*buona mattina, papa*—then readying the hot towels and combs, sharpening the scissors and straight razors, and finally taking his place beside the old man, waiting for the day's first customer.

That's how I imagine it, at least: the village on the mountain, the narrow streets, the barbershop—all of it giving him more strength than he has. That's how he rides home half alive, and how he feels the first mists of lower Manhattan from the deck of the *Giuseppe Verdi,* borne by that one dream of home. After him, the rest of us are scatterlings.

So perhaps I envied a man like Ambrosio, whose strength seemed to derive from the pulse of the earth in this place, from being an Old Castilian who accepted the violence and vicissitudes of nature. And yet he'd found the key to his universe in the multitudes contained by a piece of cheese, by its absolute grandeur.

In my mild delirium, I eventually found it hard to think, or easier not to; I just allowed myself to register the feeling of existing there among the sunflowers. And the longer I stood, and the deeper I settled into that loose dirt, the more I became part of it, resolved to it.*

With the approach of dawn a few hours off, the air turned a little sweet, carrying with it a trace of chamomile. My limbs, so tired and sore from so much sitting, felt light and loose; my whole body lifted. What I felt then was an all-consuming peace, or perhaps that lack of bodily awareness. It was, I suppose, a feeling of oneness, though I would label it the cessation of an anxiety caused by the speed and decibels of every day. I breathed in one last time to remember it by.

By now Carlos had trudged out into the field, where we exchanged delirious words. "A different planet, huh?" I said.

"Yeah," said Carlos. "Incredible."

And then I took a picture of him, and he took one of me crouched

---

* "You were never no locomotive, Sunflower, you were a sunflower!" screams Allen Ginsberg in "Sunflower Sutra." "We're not our skin of grime, we're not dread bleak dusty imageless locomotives, / we're golden sunflowers inside. . . ."

among the sunflowers, as if they were celebrities we'd met at a barbecue, photos being proof that we'd met them.

When we left that petaled forest to go back to the car, and then
subsequently left the country to go back home, I already had it in
mind to return. I already had it in mind that the cheese was now part
of my legacy, too—and my young family's. After I'd followed it here,
Ambrosio had conveyed me into his telling room and, summoning
ghosts, told me a story of a terrible betrayal, one so cruel and monstrous that it fired not only my own sense of empathy and justice, but
invoked every betrayal visited upon *every other human who ever lived.**

At the same time, Ambrosio had given me a brief glimpse of a
different, compelling sort of life, a life in which there seemed to be
more time for family and conversation, for stories and food, a life I was
desperate to lead now as an antidote to my own. It was okay to squander a day, a week, a year, sitting in that telling room, summoning
ghosts, because no one saw it as squandering.

No, if you squinted a little bit, maybe what seemed like wasted
time was, in fact, true happiness.

---

* And this includes people, or even proto-people, on Earth-like planets in distant,
as-yet undiscovered galaxies. I felt Ambrosio's injury so deeply, in fact, that a review of the transcript of that original conversation finds me uttering to Carlos,
with Barney Fife–like authority, "We're going to find this Julián, and we're going
to ask him some questions."

II

"Now look, your grace," said Sancho, "what you see over there aren't giants, but windmills, and what seem to be arms are just their sails, that go around in the wind and turn the millstone."

"Obviously," replied Don Quixote, "you don't know much about adventures."

MIGUEL DE CERVANTES, *Don Quixote*

7

THE VILLAGE

"...a moment of pure, gustatory pleasure..."

UPON MY RETURN HOME, I PINNED A PHOTOGRAPH TO THE WALL by my desk in the attic and then carried on again, living in clips, in the interstices, on the go, on the run, on the flyover, in rental cars, on takeout, during commercial breaks, between appointments and dirty diapers and ringing phones, adrenaline begetting adrenaline, packing bags and passport, on hold because of bad weather, de-icing, taking off, gathering speed on the cloverleaf, missing connections, missing my wife and son, checking in and out, mentally filibustering until the deadline had passed and it was time to pull an all-nighter to get something done.

Why was one always *behind*? And how did one get *ahead*?

Of course, the photograph was of Ambrosio, though it could have been from a hundred years ago. During our visit, he'd led me down the thirteen steps beneath the telling room, and I recalled Ari's line from that old Zingerman's newsletter, "The cheese is taken and *aged in a cave,*" one that stuck because it seemed most folkloric of all. I'd had visions of a gaping maw surrounded by boulders, wafting forth fragrant cheese—or perhaps cathedrals of cobwebs, bats hanging upside down from stalactites, albino salamanders, the echoing drip-drop of an underground pool. Instead, it was a close, tight space, maybe thirty by fifteen feet, clean, dry, and well ventilated, with PVC pipe running to the surface for air. The floor and walls were stone, and several electric bulbs hung from the ceiling. After that oppressive summer heat it had been surprisingly cool down there, too, "air-conditioned by nature," as Ambrosio had it.

Along one wall was makeshift wooden shelving where the cheese had once been kept. Now the planks sat empty. Back in the left corner was a cubby with more rickety shelves where the family stored its homemade wine in unlabeled green bottles.* Even as Ambrosio talked on and on, he ducked into the corner, rummaged a little, and returned with an old wooden box. He unclasped its hook, reached in, and lifted out something wrapped in chamois—one white tin emblazoned with the black script and gold medal of the original Páramo de Guzmán, all that remained of Ambrosio's grand experiment. *One tin.*

I asked if he'd let me take a picture. He pulled a wooden chair into the middle of the empty cave and sat, holding the tin in one hand and the oversized key to the *bodega* in the other. Framed by the rock walls, he gazed directly into the camera, conveying measures of pride and mournfulness, nonchalance and seriousness. But there was no doubt: Here was a human being concentrated in the moment, with an elemental kind of weight and grace.

---

* Ambrosio's wine was made of Duero grapes harvested in September, fermented for only four months, and was ready to drink by Christmas. His was a young wine, light, almost effervescent. He had no doubt that it was the best made in Guzmán—confidence being his strong suit—but even within his family, his brother Roberto made a heavier, fuller wine that also laid claim to high praise, so the debate never ended. (Roberto's wife, Mika, who never lacked for honesty, summed up Ambrosio's with one word: "Shit.") In fact it was the way of the village to while away the hours criticizing and celebrating one another's handmade wines, much as the common American male might deconstruct with great nuance his favorite, or most hated, sports teams.

In explaining the cave's former function as a storehouse, Ambrosio had conjured the Old Castilian again, the one who had planted and scythed wheat by hand, who had made the casks for carrying wine out of the hardened bodies of gutted goats. The goat-casks were, then, carried up to the caves on the shoulders of field hands, to the song of *jotas,* where a man sat in *el contador,* counting everything brought from the fields. In that day, the field hands had worked for the lord—the man named Guzmán who had lived in the palace and, one imagined, received the tallies of the day.

Meanwhile, there I sat in my attic, tallying—words on the page, hours until deadline, the age I would be made a grandfather if, optimistically, Leo had a child of his own at the age of thirty.* I sat attached to my machines, typing to keep my editors at bay, staring at the photograph of Ambrosio, day after day.

What was it I saw in him? Freedom? Guidance? A simple life? He was a link to the past in a digitized time when the past had become somewhat irrelevant. Ambrosio had defined this phenomenon by a phrase. He called it "the disability of memory," which he felt was the blight of modern man—and which I took to be the blight of *me.*

But what did it mean?

"Everyone is rushing forward," he said, "so I must go back."

That's what the photograph was trying to say to me, too: *I must go back.*

So I DID. I bought tickets, spending money that probably should have been set aside for Baby's college fund. The mere act of purchasing those tickets, though, made me feel good, autonomous. And because

---

* . . . sixty-six! And when that grandchild could drive: eighty-two! And when that grandchild graduated college: ninety! And this telescoping of time sparked its own pang of depression and a primal call from deep within: Stop eating potato chips . . . *now*!

Carlos had classes to teach, I convinced another fluent friend, Jeff, to come along this time.*

Thus began what would become the familiar act of return: the plane from Portland to Newark, the race to the gate (it was always a tight connection), the satisfactory push back—and then the overnight flight, the rental car, the drive up and over the Guadarrama, the buffeting wind, the Meseta stretched out below in its umber robes, the narrowing road beneath the wheel. I could feel my skin tighten in that cold, dry air. I became a drum, alive to the vibration.

I was going back three months after our first meeting, in November, to make sure Ambrosio Molinos had been, in fact, real. I packed my tape recorder and notepad, but why? For an eventual book or magazine story? Even as I first began to make my record of Ambrosio and Guzmán, I didn't know. Or have a plan. Or care to hold myself to the normal journalistic standard, for I wasn't entirely playing a journalist here. I was playing myself for once.

On the Meseta, you can drive for miles without signs of civilization, wondering if you've landed on the most lonesome patch of flash-baked clay in the world, and then from a far hill comes the outline of a church tower, the silhouette of a castle, the clustered homes. Exiting the national highway at Aranda, I scoured the horizon for my phantom village until, with a sigh of relief, we finally came upon the perched lookout of Guzmán again, driving the last of the serpentine road as if climbing to the sky. No longer awash in its summer

* A translator's note here: In all that was to follow, Carlos would handle about 70 percent of the translation; Jeff about 5 percent; and, at the end, my friends in Barcelona, Gerry and Anne, the last 25 percent. On other occasions, those in the village who could speak English—Ambrosio's daughter, Asunita; his brother Angel; Mika—would translate. And sometimes my wife, Sara, did. On rare occasions I muddled through on my own, taping so I could get a proper translation later. While I came to understand more and more of the language, and eventually could grasp the substance of a conversation if not the specifics, my own verbal aptitude was best summed up by Ambrosio's pal the stonemason Cristian, after I asked him a question in Spanish. "How many years have you been coming here?" he said. "And you *still* speak like shit!"

colors—the bright, brushed greens of grapevines against the orangy earth, the sunflowers in yellow bursts, the fiery wand of the sun—the village and its fields appeared in dull, vernal, nearly metallic bronzes, silvers, and grays, like a painting by Braque.

At the summit, as we looked back at the *coterro,* the land rolled away from the village, grapevines twining and tumbling to the foot of Ambrosio's favorite mesa at Quintanamanvirgo. Across the fields to the southeast and rising on its own hill was the aforementioned metropolis of Roa (population 2,500). About twelve miles south, a couple of lonely settlements—Haza (pop. 28) and Fuentecén (pop. 249)—could be faintly seen at the edge of the Duero Valley, named for that same river that runs the length of Castile. Mimicking the lives here, the Duero's waters meander and slice among the vineyards, picking up velocity in frothing gallons through a cut into Portugal, and eventually pour out into the Atlantic Ocean, carrying the silt of Iberia to the world beyond.*

Ambrosio was waiting for me on the steps of his parents' house. If I'd had any misgivings about my perceptions of him, they were instantly erased by the boisterous way he approached our reacquaintance, crushing the space between us, growling hellos, clasping my hand, pulling me in, showing me around the house, reciting family history.

---

* In a helpful visual, I was later told by University of Burgos prehistory professor Marta Navazo Ruiz to imagine the Meseta and its surrounding mountain range—the Cantabrian—as an amphitheater, with the mountains as a hemicycle of seats and the Meseta itself as the stage. But the Meseta's stage had its own striations. Like a cake, said Ruiz. When the European and African tectonic plates had collided millions of years ago, the Meseta, which was perhaps something of a swampland (a wok of trapped water, thought I), had lifted a bit at one end (like a tilt maze, thought I), and the watershed began to drain west in the torrential downpours that characterized that time when the glaciers receded (though glaciers didn't reach as far south as Castile), collecting in the sluggish Duero River and flowing toward Portugal. The water moving across the Meseta had caused various degrees of erosion, sculpting the multilayered plains of Castile: the river gorges, the *coterro* (or what I took to be the middle ground), and the *páramo* at the highest elevation. The flowing water also left high points of sedimentation, called "witness hills." It was on top of one of these witness hills that Guzmán found itself perched.

The house was beautiful inside, rough-hewn handmade beams, wide stairwells of limestone slabs smoothed by the tread of generations. It had been recently renovated by Ambrosio's brother Angel, who was still living in Argentina—and had transformed a house on its way to dereliction into one that might have graced the pages of *This Old Castilian House,* if such a magazine existed. The first floor consisted of a tight galley kitchen, an eating room with a long table, a TV room, and a few stairs leading down to a half-cellar, which had been fashioned into a rathskeller. The second and third floors held bedrooms, including the one in which Ambrosio himself had been born—and the fourth floor was a bright, open space with a sitting area, an enormous, formal dinner table surrounded by perhaps a dozen wooden chairs, and a second, more spacious kitchen. On the walls hung Angel's hunting trophies—an oryx, a hartebeest, wild boar—and there was a picture of him in Africa posing with a lion he'd killed. The top shot, however, was the skybox view out the east-facing windows that opened onto the vast Meseta below.

Ambrosio pointed out a stone pile across the way in Roa. "My factory," he called it. He pointed to Mon Virgo, "the shitting spot." "Beautiful," he said. As alive as he'd been in my memory over the past three months, I'd forgotten how physically encompassing he was, how locked into his orbit one instantly became.

He wore one of those dress shirts again, unwrinkled with his initials on the pocket, his ample girth spilling over his beltline. After a stop in the downstairs kitchen where he searched out a stick of *morcilla* (blood sausage), he said he had something he wanted to show us, so we bundled ourselves up—he in a field jacket and big muddy boots—and trudged the sloping land to his barn, his broad back nearly blotting the sky, us tailing behind him like kids from the city in clean knickers, the ground crunching beneath our shoes.

The village receded, shuttered and nearly silent. Two dogs barked, almost yodeling at each other. Across the fallow fields nothing moved but a flock of birds that startled from their pecking near a glade of trees. Ambrosio didn't walk so much as stalk with such purpose that, when he approached the door to the barn, the padlock seemed to undo itself. "Follow," he said.

The barn was not your red New England variety, but rather a long industrial storehouse made of corrugated metal. Dark, empty, and cold inside, it was three-quarters the size of a football field, with clumped sod on the floor and wooden pens portioned out on either side of an aisle running down the middle of the vast room. A diffused light filtered through dirty windows; the musty smell of dried animal poo wafted thickly. This was where the sheep had been kept. Ambrosio looked on the empty cavern as he might have surveyed the vacated rooms of a house where he'd once lived.

"We loved these sheep," he said. "They were very special sheep, Churra sheep."* From the end of May to September, when the land was in bloom, they ate the dry grass and herbs, the chamomile and sage, which created more protein in their milk as well as the perfect balance of fats and oils, and this, he said, was all fermented into the cheese. "You need to imagine this barn full of living, breathing sheep, and in the morning when I arrived, I said good morning to the sheep and they said good morning to me."

Ambrosio assumed a glum countenance. "Of course, they were sold," he said, then, for the first time that morning, he fell silent. It was Sasha, the hunting dog, who roused him again, appearing at his side, licking his hand, which made him smile. He crouched down, scratch-

---

* Churra is a uniquely hearty Iberian breed of sheep with a shaggy topcoat and soft undercoat (occasionally giving the impression of a spindly-ankled Upper East Side socialite in bulky fur coat and high heels), one that, because of its durability and resistance to disease, became the first breed of sheep introduced in the New World, co-opted by force and trade by tribes like the Navajo for its lean, flavorful meat and fine, lustrous fleece. But it was the milk of the sheep that interested Ambrosio most, being the lead ingredient in Zamorano cheese, a cheese from the Zamora region, ninety miles west of Guzmán, that was nuttier and more piquant than Manchego, aged for six months and cured with olive oil, which darkened its rind, a process similar to that of his own Páramo de Guzmán.

ing her ears. "How are you, dear?" he said. He held her snout in his hand, making eye contact, listening to her whine. "She wants to hunt rabbit," he said. "Come this way."

Ambrosio navigated a patch of detritus—old planks with rusted nails at weird angles and shatters of broken glass—and rounded a corner to a small tack room. In the darkness it was hard to make out much until three metal forms appeared, glowing like spaceships from an old movie. Ambrosio smiled. It was here where he made the family's wine—1,200 bottles to carry them through a year*—and he wanted to check his latest batch, which was nearly ready. "The grapes were very good this year," he said. "We may have our best wine yet." A long-stemmed glass appeared in one of his hands, and with the other he removed the lid from one tank and dipped the goblet in. He held it up to the light, admiring the wine's color, which was actually many colors: There were carmine and amethyst and plum, worlds within worlds. Ambrosio poked his nose into the glass, inhaled, then took a long sip. He licked his lips, pressed them together, contemplating, then nodded . . . *yes*. He swirled the goblet, watching as clear glycerin gripped the sides and slipped down as liquid plane settled upon plane, then repeated the whole thing, ending with a long, loud, gurgly sip.

"*¡Puta madre, está bueno!*" he said. "Here, some lunch." He filled a glass and pushed it toward me. I drank—and then again Ambrosio refilled our glasses.

"When you put something alive in your mouth," he said, "it makes *you* more alive. The people who produce wine are mostly pedantic and stupid," he continued, jabbing the air with his glass, sloshing the dregs. "They don't make wine; wine makes itself, God makes wine.

---

* It averaged out to about 3.2876 bottles a day, shared primarily by Ambrosio, Angel, and their father, and yet this was deceptive because they seemed to drink so much more, at the bar or visiting with compadres, from bottles that were given to them, for the exchange of homemade wine was a custom among friends. It seemed the 1,200 bottles were truly meant as a foundation. Some years, as Ambrosio said, "my father drinks so much, we have to go out and buy much more. He drinks so much he has a groove in his front tooth where the stream from the *porrón* has worn it down."

They may keep things clean and in good order, but the grapes make the wine. Whenever I serve my wine, not only is it cold, but there's an aroma that invades the whole table. You have to listen for what the wine itself says, not the people who make it. And worse are the people who buy the expensive stuff. They don't know shit! They couldn't care less about the aroma and finer nuances of drinking wine. They don't hear a thing the wine is saying."

We lingered in the tack room until we were feeling mighty and powerful. Then Ambrosio led us out of the storehouse, tromping along a footpath that transected a fallow field below the town, circumventing the village itself. He pointed up to the mesa, Mon Virgo, by way of reminder. Again we were off somewhere, boots squishing in the mud. We passed a cluster of trees bowed by the wind and, nearby, a fenced garden with raised beds that were fruitless mounds now, with an open cistern full of dark water. "It's my secret spot," he said. "If we need the perfect ripe tomato or green pepper or head of lettuce, I come here. When the wheat is up and the leaves are on the trees, the garden is invisible. I could write a book just about my relationship to this spot."

We walked on, crossing the road, climbing a short hill to an old granary. The doors were huge slabs of metal, and out front sat a big granite sculpture, a phallic slab chiseled into the face of a woman. Ambrosio went to a stone wall that snaked around the granary, counted off seven rocks, then removed the eighth, grabbing a hidden key. "This place belongs to my friend Cristian," Ambrosio said. "He's an artist, my age."

He fumbled with the padlock until it fell open, then he muscled the doors and we were inside another lightless room with a strong scent of fermenting straw and clay. Ambrosio climbed a short set of stairs and threw open the shutters, illuminating everything. What appeared were a dozen sculptures in various states of completion, each one a naked woman. There were pale shoulder blades and voluptuous breasts, long arms and soft netherworlds. Bundled and cold, we'd intruded on some equatorial expression of desire locked behind metal doors in this opaque village. Ambrosio nodded. "Incredible, isn't it?"

Indeed—especially in a village of old people, a profound tradition of conservative Catholicism, and an abiding prevalence of Franquistas, or Franco supporters, still up on two feet. Incredible it was for its honesty and audacity, its rustic realization, its bald transgression among the devout. Incredible it was for the secret it kept right under their noses, all these naked women cavorting in a warehouse garden.

"This is what your friend does?" I asked.

"No, in the village he's a stonemason," said Ambrosio, surveying the bodies, light gathering to hips and breasts, the long plane of a neck. "There are geezers here who would die of cardiac arrest if they saw this."

"But why women, as opposed to anything else?"

"Because his wife left him," he said. "And there are no women left for him here."

We stood for a while among the unsheathed damsels. Clearly, there was something in each expression of stone that moved Ambrosio—or held him enthralled. Here was a woman with her arms unselfconsciously overhead; here was one gazing down upon her smooth thigh. For him, the half-finished damsels seemed to convey desire, but not of the erotic sort. Rather it was artistic desire, the impulse that drove his friend to hammer rock into objects of beauty. Ambrosio's voice rose, heavy and ragged, evoking the cheese again like an old lover.

"Cristian makes the thing he longs for," he said, "and I long for the thing I made."

BETWEEN 2000 AND THE END OF 2002, I returned a handful of times to Guzmán, in each season of the year, and each brief visit felt like stepping into a gilded text, zooming from the liquid-crystal speed and madness of America—the sudden decimation of two skyscrapers, then two wars abroad—to this moon-dusted Castilian world hovering out of time, a peaceful place that seemed ennobled with integrity. I had a need to believe in this place, and each visit drew me more emphatically into Ambrosio's circle: at the *bodega* with his brother Angel and often his father, the older Ambrosio, and a rolling cast of friends. On excursions to meet more friends. At Ambrosio's house, where an invitation to join his nuclear family for *comida* turned into an open chair for me at the table. At these meals his wife, Asun, appeared from the kitchen with a cornucopia—salads drenched in olive oil, deviled eggs, tasty chorizo, a potato soup, a good piece of meat or fish, a bottle or two (or three) of homemade wine, brandy, some flan—while Ambrosio sat expectantly, rubbing his prodigious belly, joined by whichever of the now almost-adult Molinos children* happened to rotate through that day.

Back home during this time, we'd had another baby, a girl named May, sweet and insistent, a beautiful force to be reckoned with. Now it was double the diapers, double the wake-ups (make it triple, because this kid never slept), double the joy and worry. Equal partners in every way, Sara and I found our roles briefly adjusted. During these, her childbearing years, I also bore more responsibility for supporting our family. After a first book came talk of another, something important for important times, having to do with our country's all-consuming obsession with revenge and war. I went to Manhattan for meetings to write a book about John Walker Lindh, the American Taliban, who'd been captured on Thanksgiving of 2001 at the age of twenty, fighting in northern Afghanistan. He'd been roundly

---

* The entire brood was alarmingly good-looking: Daughter Asunita, the oldest, twenty-two when I first met her, possessed a husky voice, a flashing smile, and a well of creativity. Newly returned to Madrid after a London sojourn during which she'd worked for a cheese and wine importer, she was an artist; her work graced the house, including some of her earliest paintings, which were of the cheese. Next came Josué, three years her junior, standing ramrod straight with hair that flowed to his shoulder blades, who'd just finished a degree at agricultural school and had begun to share more and more duties in the family fields. And finally came Kiké, the baby and an enigma at sixteen, playing in a punk rock band. He wore a green Mohawk and ripped clothes, but if this bothered his parents, they never showed it; instead they loved to tell a story about when he was young, how he had literally climbed the walls. You might walk into a room, they said, and Kiké would be suctioned up in the corner, looking down with a smile on his face.

condemned in the American press: for his conversion to Islam at sixteen, for his unchaperoned wanderings through Yemen and Pakistan,
for the traitorous militancy that led him straight into the middle of a
prison uprising at Qala-i-Jangi, one in which an American CIA officer had been killed. Even the president, George Bush, had weighed
in, calling the bearded and robed young Californian "some mis-
guided Marin County hot-tubber." Lindh became a symbol of treachery and betrayal, but I saw in his story something more complicated:
the mirror reflection of an America I couldn't quite recognize. I conceived the book as an update of Tocqueville's *Democracy in America,*
remembering its prescient lines, written in the mid-nineteenth century: "This uncivilized little nation possesses arms, and it alone
knows how to use them." Or: "If democratic people are naturally
brought toward peace by their interests and instincts, they are constantly drawn to war and revolutions by their armies."

   I left the city with an offer for a book contract, but the truth was
my heart wasn't in it. The project promised to leave me in a war zone
while my children grew up, and I kept thinking about Guzmán and
Ambrosio's cheese. Would it have been absurd, in the middle of all
this war and mayhem, to pitch *that* as a book? In this new world full
of evildoers, could anyone see that a story like Ambrosio's, which at its
heart was about truth and purity, might be more important than
ever? I wasn't willing to test the waters at first, for fear of looking like
a dope, but quietly—I'd say *sheepishly*—I returned to Guzmán to see
what else I might find there, to gather yarn, as the journalist says,
when the journalist doesn't know what the hell he's doing.

   If I wasn't an everyday face in the village with its population of
eighty, it occurred to me that my appearances were like a repeating
cameo in a real-life sitcom in which I, the *americano,* stumbled and
bumbled my way through customs and chitchat, providing comic relief by asking stupid questions about sheep or tractors, or, on one particular evening, why the leading brand of whisky in Spain was called
Whisky DYC, trying to explain what the phrase "whiskey dick"
meant in America, an explanation that was misinterpreted as a heart-

felt admission of my own erectile dysfunction.* Once, while bravely consuming a stew of unknown origin, I reflexively horked up a swine hoof, or something. Another time, outdoors, I drank from the *porrón* in a high wind and ended up looking like a fire hydrant drizzled upon by beet juice. Oh, I was a riot to these farmers, a metrosexual punchline, a tadpole among bullfrogs.

Ambrosio, of course, was my *caballero* gold card. When I was with him, circles opened, drinks arrived, mysteries were solved.[†] Thanks to him, I was fast-tracked past the Naugahyde ropes that hung in the bar's entrance to keep out blackflies and granted immediate entrance to the back room, the inner chamber, the VIP *bodega* where men—some of them toothless, limping, or scarred—related the events of the day, swapped secret recipes,[‡] reviewed age-old leg-

---

* A leading brand of bread, on the other hand, was known as Bimbo—and when I tried to describe what *that* meant, it was taken to mean I was discussing my wife.

† Like, for instance, was there a gremlin artist loose in Castile, one who built cool little rock towers in all the fields? No, there was not. These were *majones,* stone towers built by farmers to mark the boundaries of their fields, a custom perhaps dating back to the Romans. And these had a way of shifting over time, one farmer trying to claim more land, which often resulted in disputes, bad blood, *porrones* dumped over heads, and worse. "It is advisable," said Ambrosio, "to *never ever* touch one of those."

And what of the piles of sticks one saw at the edges of the fields in winter? These were the remnants of pruned grapevines called *sarmientos.* Said Ambrosio: "There's a saying in Castile that goes, 'Don't fall in love with a woman from a town that doesn't have *sarmientos,*' which means there aren't any vineyards, which means there isn't any wine, which means the people aren't very happy."

‡ On his blog, Gerry Dawes, the American connoisseur of all things Spanish, leaves the following record on the occasion of Ambrosio relating a recipe for a dish known as *olla podrida,* or rotten pot stew. Says Ambrosio into Gerry's tape recorder: "First, an *olla podrida* should be made with *alubias de Ibeas,* the little black-red beans that come from around the village of Ibeas east of Burgos and are the best beans in Spain. That is most important. Then, in a clay stovetop casserole, you slowly cook the beans with a special *adobado* (marinated) pig foot, a marinated pig's ear, and pork ribs. The *adobo* marinade is made with salted water, to which oregano is added or, depending on the area, other spices such as black pepper, bay leaves, and paprika, sometimes even piquant paprika. The marinade, which gives

ends. In fact, Ambrosio thought more of these men, or cared more for them, because of their seeming defenselessness against society—and their deterioration—than of those who possessed the ability to push him forward in the world, those able-bodied men in the day's haberdashery with big plans for profit. Whenever it came time to describe one of his posse in conversation, he favored the word *majo,* which for him translated as a great guy, a mensch, a beautiful human, an *hombre muy simpático,* but despite appearances also suggested a being of some higher spiritual evolution, a fellow traditionalist, a hidden angel among the earthbound. Everything these men did, and made, was worthy of hyperbole, of myth. His friend Manuel of the Pérez Pascuas owned the famous local vineyard that had supplied the FIRST SPANISH WINE EVER CONSUMED BY THE POPE FOR NEW YEAR'S EVE MASS. His friend Luis made exquisite ANCIENT KEYS for NO REASON but as a tribute to the EXQUISITE ARCANE BEAUTY OF THE PAST.* His friend Javier of the Cris-

---

the *olla podrida* its strong flavor, also preserves the meat, so it can be left all season in a cool place such as a basement or a cave. Then you put in some fatty chorizo, the one they call *botageo,* because it has a higher percentage of fat to lean, and some *morcilla,* blood sausage.

"But, there is more. Ambrosio continues, 'Once the *olla podrida* is cooked, you make what we call *bolas,* made from toasted hard bread that is then mixed [with] some of the pork fat from the stew to make "balls," which are then fried and served on a platter alongside the *olla.* The meat that was cooked with the beans is served on a separate platter, the beans are also served on a separate dish, and *guindillas,* pickled onions, and other pickled vegetables are served as a garnish. Then all you need is a big appetite.'" Afterward, according to Gerry, "Ambrosio recommended a scandalous precaution, not to be repeated here, for the flatulence he said was sure to ensue."

* One last word about Luis's keys: After the royal decree calling for the expulsion of the Jews, which took effect in 1492, some 200,000 people left Spain, settling around the Mediterranean from Morocco to Turkey, some carrying keys from their old homes, demolished in their wake, that were then passed from generation to generation as heirlooms or keepsakes, symbolic reminders of a lost life. It's unclear whether Luis knew this (in fact, I believe he didn't), but then it explained a silent murmur from the past that perhaps he'd heard, or that guided him invisibly, the fetishizing of those old keys into being, into gifts, into a physical expression of memory, not unlike Ambrosio's cheese.

tóbals owned the BEST RESTAURANT in Roa and grilled the BEST ROAST LAMB IN THE UNIVERSE that EVERYONE AGREED was OF SUCH EXCEPTIONAL TENDERNESS AND TASTE that it FELL FROM THE BONE.*

One February morning when we woke to the village buried in drifts of storybook snow, the roofs all white mushroom fluff, some of Ambrosio's friends gathered at a *peña,* one of many social clubs that I hadn't known existed. They lurked behind Guzmán's corrugated metal sheets, in empty garages, in little apartments with pool tables and kitchens, all of which were thrown open during September's fiesta, when the *peña* members would emerge wearing the bright colors of their club and compete—by singing songs, banging drums, blowing horns, lighting fireworks—at making the loudest commotion around themselves. Though the roads were apparently impassable that day, this *peña* contained maybe a dozen men, some from neighboring towns, all playing hooky in the storm. Ambrosio entered with sausage, someone sleight-of-handed a couple dozen eggs, *porrones* were filled with red wine, and before long Ambrosio had the gas stove going, making a breakfast plate for everyone while regaling the crowd with joke after joke. The laughter came in waves that broke upon themselves, belly laughs, uproarious spasms of joy. It was a roast of sorts—and he went around the room to the great pleasure of the crowd, deconstructing each one of us. In fact, Ambrosio was honoring us with his insults. Who farted the loudest. Whose manhood was permanently compromised by too much wine—or had never worked in the first place. When it came time for me, Ambrosio began by introducing certain unnamed men, famous gauzy figures of legendary ilk, who could take the *porrón* and, rather than aiming the wine into their open mouth, could stream it off their forehead, let it run the bridge of their nose, and shift their mandible in such a way as to catch

---

* Truth was, a quick fact-check often proved Ambrosio right. From the website Chowhound, one foodie who traveled far and wide questing for the finest of this slow-roasted, succulent lamb, called *lechazo,* ended up at Cristóbal's restaurant, El Nazareno, celebrating it as "Castilla y León's 'lamb palace' " and a "lamb temple."

the waterfall driblet as it passed over the septum cliff. Then Ambrosio said, "Hombre, you'd go thirsty waiting for the wine to travel Michael's nose."

Of course, I picked up only bits until the full translation came, but could intuit a little from watching the crowd, which seemed to move in slow motion, eyes lighting, toothless mouths opening, guffawing, then nervous glances cast to assess my reaction. And there I sat with my dim smile of incomprehension, set as usual on time delay. But oh, what pleasure it gave when I did understand! Oh, this was rich! This was really good! If I was receiving correctly, what Ambrosio said was that my nose was so big, so epic, so monumental, that wine flowing from the headwater of the bridge of my nose would take forever to empty into the gulf below it. Mine was a Mississippi, a Zambezi, a Yangtze River nose.

I suspect it took a nose of *some* caliber to recognize a nose of *such* caliber, but what made the moment particularly satisfying was that it went against all notions of Spanish hospitality to insult a guest; thus, with a touch of pride, I realized that I was no longer a guest. I now sat at the *majo* round table, not one of them, but then not an entirely special case either. Gauging my character by Ambrosio's tacit recommendation, these men were willing to allow me to be here, to laugh at me and let me laugh with them—and at them, too. Perhaps it shouldn't have felt momentous, but for me it meant brief admission to a new sort of brotherhood, a brotherhood of forgotten brothers.

I knew that in Ambrosio's presence I was living a fantasy, one in which I'd been freed of all responsibility—no logistics, no late-night wake-ups, no old, incontinent dog to clean up after, no bills or recycling or flat tires. I glommed on to him in the same manner as a barnacle takes to the hull of a boat, as a matter of survival, of one small organism attaching to the force of a larger one. My ardor was portioned in equal parts, for him and then the stories he told: Somehow, of all the millions of villages of the world, from tundra to tropics, from Kirkenes to Ushuaia, I'd found Guzmán and its native son, Am-

brosio Molinos, the great storyteller, who held the real secrets of the
world as well as the key to its happiness.

GUZMÁN'S BAR WAS AS unprepossessing as the village itself, shadowy at
midday and bare-walled but for a calendar and a few *noticias,* a colorful ad for a bullfight, a knitting bee to meet at town hall. There were
a number of plain wooden tables with uncomfortable chairs starred
about, a couple of shelves behind the bar with an unimpressive if potent display of liquor. The top shelf here would have been bottom shelf
elsewhere, and the bottom shelf was swill. The room was a sarcopha-
gus hung with heavy drapes of secondhand smoke. The floor was a
site of archaeological interest: nubbed-out cigarettes and errant nap-
kins, scrips of scribbled notes and receipts, tapas toothpicks and bottle
caps, a potpourri of expended things.

The village had only this one bar at the time, and it was the hub
of social life, of all the feuds and compacts that played out among
Guzmán's diminishing citizens. It wasn't so strange that good friends,
over a period of a lifetime, might never see the insides of each other's
homes, but would meet every day at the table by the window to play a
game of cards. And no matter what the hour, if the bar doors were
open, there was always some sort of commotion inside.

Pinto, the bartender, was both impresario and dictator. In his forties, he lived alone in his family's ancestral *casa.* If you stood on the
bluff behind it, the back of the house appeared as if it had been torn
open by a hungry giant. Apparently Pinto felt no need to address the
destruction, nor the open display of homewares and undergarments
strewn about within. Neglect was his primary coat of arms, his
wrecked modus operandi. It wasn't exactly the trait one expects for
someone in a service industry.

In the normal world, a bartender stands behind the bar and serves
his customers their drinks. But Pinto saw it like this: He was John
Wayne, if John Wayne had been a short, untucked, punchless man

with patchy black hair. And if John Wayne had been wonderful in the kitchen.* Yet Pinto had no problem making the leap. The bar was his stage set. He answered to no man there. And when he wasn't in his own bar, he was either sleeping or trolling other bars as a paying customer in Roa, where there seemed to be an overabundance of watering holes.

Ambrosio said that perhaps Pinto was happiest when walking into a bar in Roa: He'd push through the door slowly, squinting, sit deliberately, light his cigarillo, eye the other hombres, order his poison, and take that first satisfying slurp. After a couple more sucks, emitting plumes of smoke as if on fire, he would get up abruptly, leaving his glass half full, and search out the next stop, his evenings an endless composition of entrances that only he believed held high drama. And while no one understood the fetish exactly, part of its meaning was easier to intuit: Trapped in the Guzmán bar, he was a stationary pourer of libations, while on his off nights he could forever be the shadowy, multifarious man who blew in and out on a dangerous breeze, sipping whisky before pollinating another dark place with his cowboy mysteriousness.

In the Guzmán bar, the rules were simple: If Pinto felt like serving drinks, he would. If not, he might come around the counter and take a seat at one of the tables, cigarillo drooping from his mouth, a washrag slung over his shoulder. He'd prop his feet on the table and watch television turned up to an intolerable volume, drowning out conversation, leaving his irritated regulars to fend for themselves and newcomers to scratch their heads. Was this one of those hidden camera shows?

More than once I heard Ambrosio call him a *culo de gallina,* or "the asshole of a chicken," which only induced Pinto to throw up a

---

* For it was here that his sensitivity and artistry shone through. His catalogue had been rehearsed all those years when his mother was alive, and the townspeople clamored for a *guiso,* an oxtail stew he made, and in particular a snail sauce that Ambrosio said was "technically probably the best sauce in the world, but is more, because it contains all the love of his mother."

hand in rebuke. *Whatever.* Meanwhile, he harbored little love for me, the *americano,* primarily because my Spanish was mostly limited to ordering beer. *"Una caña,"* I might say, and Pinto's reaction was always the same: a smirk that said, "You can't be serious." Half the time, Pinto would ignore me in order to make me ask again. And then when he did fill a smallish glass and delivered the cold beer, he always muttered something, but in a slurry rasp I never understood: Was he reaching out or insulting me?

The answer seemed obvious—and yet even despite Pinto, the bar came alive each evening. The air was hot and close and stale, but that garrulous Castilian conviviality glamorized everything. It was here I met Carlos the farmer. In a town of prodigious talkers, Carlos perhaps ranked as the most voluble. And like Ambrosio—both men's formal education ended at high school—his recall of Spanish history was encyclopedic. Carlos lived in a cluttered house just yards from the front door of the church, and he kept hawks in his attic. He was a sun-stroked ball of energy who kick-started most of his long explications with *"Nahhhh, hombre . . ."* and then was off, flannel-mouthed (in the garbled, not glib, sense of the word . . . never the glib in Guzmán), reciting the precise ecology of the declivity south of town known as the Barco de Siete Palomas (Valley of the Seven Doves). Or how the Romans built fish shelters every thirty miles on their sheep highways, in order to transport seafood inland from the shore. Or how the nineteenth-century monarch Queen Isabella II once took as a lover the son of an Italian pastry chef, which only compounded her obesity.*

Carlos's opposites were the stoic ones: Abel, the most decent metalworker; Manuel, a wall-eyed man lost in the mist of his haunted discombobulation; and Fernando, the man-child with his neatly combed

---

* According to Richard Ford's *Gatherings from Spain,* Isabella, "a pallid, podgy, pampered, and petulant princess" who, when queen, married an impotent man and bore nine children with an assortment of paramours, caused final offense in middle age ("her figure not improved by her penchant for sweets and cakes") by taking up with the civil governor of Madrid, Carlos Marfori, who was, yes, the son of an Italian pastry chef.

hair, polo shirt, and khakis, who never spoke at all, appeared to be entirely mute, and was often seen standing beneath a tree across from the church.

And there were the shepherd brothers—Danielito, Teo, and Victor, all related to Cristian the sculptor. By day they led their flocks up through town and out into the fields, a fan of pelleted sheep shit in their wake. During the broiling afternoons, though nothing moved but a shimmery haze over the *barcos,* the crackling voice of their transistor radio carried all the way back to the village, bouncing through its corridors and alleys. In the bar the three of them sat close together, all with long hair, wearing Che Guevara T-shirts, buying and receiving drinks, talking a blue streak because there's something no one ever tells you about shepherds: They love the social game.

Then, of course, came the old men—including Ambrosio's father, Ambrosio Senior—who after years under the weight of the sun hid for a good part of the hot day, napping, then eventually herded toward the bar. In nice weather they occupied a bench just across from the front door or retired inside to the tables by the windows, shuffling the cards to play *mus* or *julepe.*

One could happily squander the hours in Guzmán's bar, as I did, albeit with much of the action transpiring over my head. While sometimes frustrating, it was pleasant in its way, too, the not-knowing-exactly. I was the slow child, neglected and needing special care, and it suited me. In the throes of giving everything to family and work, of always needing to know, I found it an unexpected pleasure to exist in this alternate reality. And it was a gift whenever I found a Guzmán resident with whom I could speak English, including Ambrosio's brother Roberto and his German wife, Mika.

Roberto and Mika were the village's movie-star couple, installed in a fastidiously maintained wood-timbered house that had once belonged to Ambrosio. They spent the working week in Madrid, where they ran an advertising production company specializing in Roberto's aerial photography, and then they would weekend in the village, where Mika, a former model born in Hamburg, was a dervish, gardening and cooking, boiling and pickling, jarring and canning. She might never be "one of them," but that gave her a certain freedom: She was a Tabasco dash of truth serum in that place, and her opinions were all-inclusive—and sometimes withering. About Pinto's carelessness and his half-wrecked house, she said bluntly, "He's going to die living like that." About Ambrosio, with whom she seemed to share a fractious relationship, she said she'd clawed decades of his cigarette butts from the backyard of the house after they bought it from him. "It was a sty," she said. But they had made it beautiful. It felt like their job here: to improve whatever they touched.

On those occasions when they stopped by the bar, one almost expected the paparazzi to come stumbling behind them. But even they were incapable of putting on airs, mixing easily with everyone. The camaraderie was real and warm, despite any grudges that lay beneath the surface. Considering one of the central paradoxes of the Castilian character—the remarkable acceptance, the stubborn resistance—they still saw themselves as one here. You could travel mile after empty mile seeing nobody, nothing—just the rugged Meseta—and then happen upon an ancient village of a hundred homes, all conjoined and crowded together, enjambed and encircling a church, a castle, each village with its Franco-era *frontón,* linked, for better or worse, in prayer, in drink, in song.

I remember one of my first exhilarating nights in Pinto's bar, which was followed by many exactly like it. Sometime around one in the morning of a summer eve, Ambrosio produced a *charango,* an Andean stringed instrument in the mandolin family, and along with his brother Angel, who was suddenly wielding a guitar, broke out in song: old *jotas,* ballads about heartbreak, and patriotic anthems. Many of the men in the bar joined in; some stood to the side and listened; a few others kept right on with their conversations or card games. Pinto, in a desultory mood, took a seat at a far table beneath the television set, but perhaps the scene of old and young singing at the top of their lungs stirred something within him, for he didn't turn the volume up.

The music went on—and on. Ambrosio relished that spotlight,

singing in a full-timbred baritone. At some point, fatigue guided my feet to the door and then out into the cooling night air. Gazing back through the frame to the warm light within, I saw Ambrosio in profile—his strong, aquiline nose, his mournful eyes—towering over his compadres, reaching for the note, the intonation, the emotion that the moment most called for.

As I slipped out, the stars lit the streets. I found myself moving very slowly indeed, neck craned, drunk. O, wonder of humming stars! O, inscrutable revelation! The strains of music followed me to the edge of some blurry awe. And it had a scent I hadn't anticipated.

By the heavenly light I stood, feet caked in the sheep shit of my enlightenment.

WINTER IN GUZMÁN IS the lonesome season, a gray sky hanging overhead like a slab of ice. The light covers everything in blue gossamer cocoons that turn black with night. The ghosts of the past rise up and howl in the wind, against which the residents bundle themselves. Even some of the place-names—for instance, the vineyard known as Matajudío, or Jew Killer—suggest horrible outcomes one might rather not know.

On this particular evening the bar was closed for some reason having to do with the inscrutable whims of Pinto, Ambrosio was away, and not a soul stirred. I found myself wandering Guzmán with Jeff at about 10 P.M., a burning smell in the frigid air. Cold and hungry, clip-clopping back uphill toward the car, we were surprised by four figures that appeared as hunched shadows lurching down from the palace. Were they Guzmán's own horsemen of the apocalypse?

"Ta' lo," they said as they passed.

"Ta' lo," we said. They carried on down the road until we shouted back at them, "Hey, do you guys happen to know any open restaurants nearby?"

Someone started laughing. "Hombre," said a voice inside a hood, "hasn't anyone told you? This is the moon up here."

Our respective parties started chatting. The two boys, who wore long hair, were Diego and Rodrigo; the two girls with short hair were Beatriz and Lara. They were home for the extended Christmas holiday, on their way to get some lamb for grilling. They knew a guy in a nearby village who might be willing to sell some. Then they were going to the *bodega* to eat and drink. Did we want to come?

Another gesture of Spanish hospitality, but it was no less striking: that openness and trust. We were strangers. We could have been anyone, and that was good enough. Soon we were all piled in a car zooming down the hill from Guzmán. The road wound and unwound. Twenty minutes later we pulled up in front of a house in a nearby village. More Naugahyde roping hung like a curtain before the door. Diego got out, drew back the roping, and knocked, waiting for a while, stamping his feet, exhaling smoky breath. He banged his fist on the door again. After a few minutes, a light turned on, the door opened, and we piled out of the car and followed Diego over the threshold.

The butcher had an acute case of bed head, his hair riding straight up. But he was quite chipper, which was a bit at odds again with the stereotyped image of the wary Castilian.* Now the man put on his apron and disappeared through a door. Aside from a couple of unused

---

* Much has been made of the tribes of Spain—the Basques and their industriousness, the Catalans and their cosmopolitan view of the world, the Castilians and their regal bearing—and the Spanish make much of their own, too: the Basques as contrarian mules, the Catalans as surly grouches obsessed with money, the Castilians as prideful rustics. Unlike an American, it's true, a Castilian won't necessarily greet a stranger with claps on the back and false steakhouse theatricality, but here's an observation that a Swede I know in Madrid once shared with me: We were seated at La Toja one midday for our *comida,* eating a beautiful piece of buttered fish and sipping some very nice wine, and the waitstaff was treating him particularly well. I asked him how exactly he'd become such an insider here, and he said, "The first time you visit a restaurant in Madrid, you come like everyone else—and get treated like everyone else. The second time, the waitstaff may give you a nod, some extra bread, a more generous pour. But the third time, the third time you appear in that restaurant, for better or worse, you're family." So the waiter might whisper tips about what looks good back in the kitchen, smiles all around. If obligations carry you away from that little restaurant for, say, more than a month, the next time you show up, the owner comes out, asking where the hell you've been.

refrigeration units pushed up against the wall, it seemed as if we were standing in a living room.

"He has the best lamb around," Diego assured us.

"Did we wake him?" I asked.

"Oh, he doesn't mind," Diego said.

When he appeared from a back room he came with two separate items wrapped in white butcher's paper, but before sealing them, he opened them up to the teenagers for their approval. The four of them nodded their heads, some coins changed hands. The butcher led us to the door and opened it, exclaiming, "It's colder than a whore's tit out there."

We nodded our agreement, then hustled back to Guzmán. It was one of those rare nights when the hive of *bodegas* on that hillside— maybe thirty in all—sat empty. At Diego's *bodega,* we were greeted by a stuffed deer head hung on the wall and a clock that had long ago stopped ticking at 6:15. It was so cold you could see your breath. The boys went straight to work wrestling snarls of dried grapevines and stuffing them into the fireplace, which they called *la chimenea,* or "the chimney." When they lit the branches, the room instantly filled with the scent of grapes—fruity, sweet, a hint of violets—carried by the clouds of rising smoke. The flames tore through the vines so quickly they gave little warmth, but the point wasn't necessarily to make a lasting fire. Instead, the vines were tamped down, disintegrating into embers, which were grouped together to give off enough fleeting heat to grill the meat.

Meanwhile, Rodrigo rubbed lamb fat on a grate while the girls took pinches of sea salt from a bowl, sprinkling it over each piece of

---

"He feeds you like an angry mother for the first half of the meal," my friend said, "then dotes on you for the rest."

And so it seemed it was like this with Castilians in general. Open and curious, they appreciated any effort you might make to understand them and their land, but when that effort turned to commitment—when you appeared before them with regularity—well, then, you crossed over into intimacy, and they'd do anything for you, even get out of bed late at night to make sure you had some lamb chops.

meat. The chops were placed on the metal grate, and covered with another metal grate that hooked to the first. By this time the embers in the fireplace were glowing jewels of heat, giving off trails of grape smoke. Diego grabbed the grate along with Rodrigo, and they set it about an inch or two above the embers, balancing it on a stone at the back of the fireplace, the room redolent of grilling lamb.

Diego went down into the cave and returned with two bottles of wine, emptying one into the *porrón*. Another *porrón* was brought out and filled with water. Bread was placed on the table, there for the ripping. The chops on the fire were flipped. And though a search was made, no plates or silverware could be found, only a roll of white paper that was used to cover the table for meals. Each person was torn a piece as a plate. "We do everything with our hands here anyway," said Rodrigo.

Waiting on the lamb chops, I'd had a random flash, as I often did on the road, of how much my wife would have loved all of this. In some ways, it often felt as if I was taking mental notes for her, so I could tell her the stories later as she often told me stories about her travels when on assignment. She was an excellent storyteller, whether describing some adventure in a Ghanian refugee camp or riding a mechanical bull in Las Vegas. More than anyone I knew, she, too, would have appreciated the exact steps by which our succulent midnight meal had taken shape, and the utter randomness of our cross-cultural intersection here in Diego's family's *bodega* in the dead of winter. Had she been here she would have jabbered unselfconsciously and laughed her throaty laugh. Even more, she would have reveled in what came next: a moment of pure, gustatory pleasure, the kind associated in our lives with campfire meals or forgotten barbecue stands. The meat, born and raised and sheltered on this land, melted in a grape aftertaste. The salt added a pinch of ocean to it. There may have been thirty or so small-sized chops, and among the six of us we pretty much devoured them instantly. The *porrón* traveled among the assembled. Only crumbs were left on the table.

After we'd eaten everyone sat in contented silence for a moment, and then Rodrigo lit a Fortuna cigarette—these teenagers chain-smoked like the adults they emulated—took a sip of wine, and cleared his throat. Here they were, with these *americano* guests, in his family's *bodega*—in their telling room—with aeons of stories hovering close, and Rodrigo seemed to feel the uncomfortable pressure of having to try to tell one. It was a lot to ask. There was an awkward silence, and then he spoke.

"This is the story of Uncle Eight," he said slowly, with uncertainty, then blew a puff of smoke, which lingered like a scrim before his face. At least he had the gravitas of gestures. "They said Uncle Eight was . . . a little *crazy*," he said. He rested his elbows on the table, stalling, sitting apart from the other three, who were suddenly transfixed, leaning into each other expectantly, without a trace of self-consciousness.

Rodrigo puzzled over what to say next. He started again. "Okay, Uncle Eight . . . who was *crazy* . . . he went to eat in a restaurant . . . and in that restaurant . . . he picked up the menu and studied it." Another pause. "In that restaurant," he said, "Uncle Eight, who was *crazy,* always did the same thing. . . . He ordered *eight* things." He pushed himself back from the table, took a serious drag from his cigarette, and through squinted eyes regarded his audience, the five of us hanging on what might come next.

"No, that's it," he said, waving a hand before his face to clear the smoke. "He always ordered eight things off the menu."

The other three blinked.

"That's all," he said.

Compared to the lush layers of history and hyperbolic spasms of story that came from Ambrosio's mouth, it wasn't much. But then the teenagers did something wonderful. They watched Rodrigo's face when he smiled at them, and they smiled back at him. They were young, they would learn. But this one was pretty funny, too. The story of Crazy Uncle Eight. Like, eight things off the menu . . . yeah, it was a good one!

"I wonder what he ordered," said one of the girls.

"Don't know," said Rodrigo.

The spell broken, Diego reached under the bench and pulled out an old-fashioned boom box. He hoisted it onto the table, punched in a cassette tape, and pressed Play. The room filled with music, a Spanish heavy-metal band named Soziedad Alkoholika. Alcoholic Society. Everyone started jabbering at once, the *porrón* went around again, steam rising from the open mouths as wine poured in. With the music the conversation loosened, more bottles appeared.

"Underneath Mon Virgo," shouted Lara, "there's a cave that was built by the Moors, connecting one village to another. The legend of the cave is that there was once treasure there, and today the two villages meet once a year for the Dance of the Snakes, which represents the mixing of the two cultures, Spanish and Moor."

Diego chimed in. "Guzmán means 'good man,' I think. But that's all I know."

It went on like this for an hour, until we stood to go. They were just warming up, of course, piecing it together, fusing themselves to the past and beginning to channel the ghosts. As the wine flowed and music blared, I had the feeling I was at a birth of sorts, the first time the essential words formed in the storyteller's mouth, and she said, *Once upon a time . . .*

The universe sat rapt waiting for what she would say next.

8

DARK INSIDE

". . . following the arroyo of his deceit."

Huh-huh-huh-huh. TURN IGNITION. *Huh-huh-huh-huh*. CLEAR and cough.

Ambrosio had revisited that day hundreds of times in his mind, went back to it obsessively, and however much he tried to reorder it, the day never changed. It always marked the border between his happiness and madness, his blindness and epiphany. And again: He'd risen that morning, world in perfect order, fluttering in the muslin wings of his oblivious dreams. He buttoned his shirt, buckled his capacious pants, and tied the shoelaces of his worn boots, then passed down the hallway, eclipsing the light, as he floated toward the front door. He drove to his cheese factory in the highlands of Spain—beneath that huge Castilian sky—where his trusted army of cheesemakers was already hard at work. He was their boss, the *jefe,* and they paid a certain deference to his legend. He greeted Pilar and Mari Carmen in the front office: *Who's on the schedule? Let's serve the Duron red today.* And then Fernando and Orencio in the warehouse: *What time is the truck due? Let's repack those dented tins.*

Into the cheesemaking room to inspect the open tanks of coagulating milk, and he grabbed a cheese harp and elbowed his way in between Fidel and José, and combed for a while, harp trawling slowly to and fro, combing to show them, to refine their technique. He was always pointing at something, showing them how to love this cheese, and every moment was a learning moment. His personality was so strong, he seemed to will the forces of nature—the coagulation and ripening—into submission. Everything was symbolic. His task, enormous. Each emerging piece of Páramo de Guzmán had to be coaxed from the earth, from the grass and herbs . . . that were masticated by the sheep . . . who made the milk . . . which came to these heated tanks . . . to form the curds . . . that became another individual planet of cheese . . . that was then set aside, spinning alone in black space for months, aging veinlessly, until it was brought out again into the light, packaged and made ready for the table.

In Ambrosio's mind, no matter how big the operation grew—no matter how many tins Fidel Castro ordered, or Julio Iglesias, no matter that it was served at Buckingham Palace, to Queen Elizabeth or Frank Sinatra or Ronald Reagan—each wedge was still meant for his father. Each wedge was gratitude and humility, its own reflection of God. *This* was religion—and it was as if with each new batch Ambrosio took his pocketknife and sliced that first piece again, then carried it to the *caseta* as if cradling something alive. On that day when he'd opened his hands and his father accepted the offering and slid it into his mouth, when his father began to chew, lost in the powerful, herbaceous onslaught of the cheese, the old man had been overcome by—what was it? Grief-happiness? Joy-pain? And the son watched his father's eyes as the memories flooded behind them.

Ambrosio had seen himself as more than a cheesemaker—or less than one. "I'm a middleman in a natural process," he liked to say to visitors at the factory. "I'm just the person who receives in his hands what nature gives. The cheese makes itself. I just put in that little piece of myself. If I'm going to make a cheese for my son, I'm not going to cheat him. If there's a pail of milk that's no good, I'm going to throw it out. That's the love and care that comes to us from the past, that you carry into the present. That's what you're tasting, and feeling, when you eat this cheese."

The *queso* had been a bold gambit, carrying with it a certain nationalistic fervor, which was also a legacy of the Molinos clan. Until this time, what the world had tasted of Spanish cheeses was limited to Manchego, Roncal, Cabrales, Zamorano, and not much else. Unlike the French cheeses that came with their own reputation, Spanish cheese had no legend.[*] And then, suddenly, along came this aggressive, artisanal *queso Castellano,* made from sheep's milk, exploding with taste. It was a bafflement, a pure delight, a cheese on the leading edge of Europe's burgeoning Slow Food Movement.[†]

---

[*] Wrote Richard Ford of nineteenth-century Spanish bread and cheese: "The Spanish loaf has not that mysterious sympathy with butter and cheese as it has in our verdurous Old England, probably because in these torrid regions pasture is rare, butter bad, and cheese worse, albeit they suited the iron digestion of Sancho, who knew of nothing better: none, however, who have ever tasted Stilton or Parmesan will join in his eulogies of Castilian *queso,* the poorness of which will be estimated by the distinguished consideration in which a round cannonball Dutch cheese is held throughout the Peninsula. The traveler, nevertheless, should take one of them, for bad here is the best . . ."

[†] The Slow Food Movement, led by Italian gourmand and food writer Carlo Petrini, sprang from two incidents: the 1986 deaths of nineteen people from cheap wine cut with methanol in Petrini's home region of Piedmont, coupled with protests against the building of a McDonald's near the Spanish Steps in Rome. In a Parisian theater in 1989, Petrini codified the movement's manifesto, along with "delegates" from fifteen other countries, calling for the protection of the old ways of agriculture and cuisine that, according to Petrini and his compadres, were under attack by the multinational food companies. The tenets of the movement were in part identical to those that Ambrosio and other small producers had been espousing for years: the preservation and promotion of local products and their lore, the creation of an "ark" of heirloom seeds, the celebration and privileging of local cuisine, all to stave off, as Petrini's manifesto put it, "the universal madness of the Fast Life."
In its place, the movement advocated the conviviality of past customs. So read the manifesto: "Against those, and there are many of them, who confuse efficiency with frenzy, we propose the vaccine of a sufficient portion of assured sensual pleasure, to be practiced in slow and prolonged enjoyment." To have joined Ambrosio at the *bodega* for a Sunday meal would have been the living proof of such tenets—and his cheese, then, as much as any editorial that could be written, became *his* manifesto.

Ambrosio saw himself as the needle and thread, stitching backward in time, unifying epochs. The awards had validated the idea
that you could still make old food, the old way, and enthrall. When
The Independent had described Páramo de Guzmán as a wonderfully
"eccentric cheese," he took it to mean a cheese that brought forward a
lost taste from the past, and so created a synaptic connection between
generations.

At lunch he drove to Guzmán, to check on the sheep. The Churra
sheep were famous for the quality of their milk, not the quantity, producing about half of what other breeds did, which was an ongoing
problem. He had words of advice for the shepherds, too, about where
to steer the flock (the Barco de Valcabadillo possessed the most aro-
matic caches of herbs), about an exact method of milking (he swore
the fingers had to be positioned just so on the teat), even about the
wine they brought with them to the fields for refreshment (Hombres,
too acidic! How can you show these sheep your love if you drink this
wine?).

There was no time to rest, of course—and resting wasn't something he did anyway. He ate and jabbered, laughed and sang, but rare
were the moments when his body reclined horizontally for even a
quick siesta after the *comida*. He stayed up late, rose early. He drank
coffee and smoked his Camels; for him, red wine seemed to act as a
stimulant. On this day he skipped the *comida* altogether, riding down
from Guzmán to Roa on the high road—up over the *páramo* itself, in
that thin, ecclesiastical light, then down through the villages of Villa-
escusa and Pedrosa—which brought him past Bodegas Viña Pedrosa,
one of the best-regarded wineries on the Meseta (of course, he stopped
in on his friend Manolo, which meant a little snack of chorizo and a
glass of wine, and he, in turn, supplied the cheese, warming it over a
flame until it perspired, then slicing the wedge in clean rectangular
wafers), and when he returned to the office, feeling a certain amount
of contentment, that's when the secretary came to him, and said, "We
have a problem."

Something about money, was it? Or the lack of it? Even as buyers called in orders from near and far, and even as enthusiastic fans sometimes came to the factory directly, drove right up from Madrid to try it, Páramo de Guzmán was running up unsustainable debts.

On the spot, Ambrosio began his own inquiry, which led him to review the documents, proffered by Julián, that he'd signed without reading. What he found there was nearly impossible to comprehend, a contract bearing his signature, giving controlling ownership of the company not to the Molinos family, whose cheese it was, but rather to two investors, friends of Julián's, who had been conscripted when the company had left Guzmán and moved to the new factory. He checked the contract with his scribbled name there, squeezed his eyes shut, and when he reopened them it was plain to see: The company didn't belong to him anymore—and hadn't for some time.

He went to see Julián in his office, then, needing to hear the truth from his own lips. When Ambrosio burst through the door—waving the papers, booming, "What is the meaning of *this*?"—Julián looked terrified. Cowering, he fumbled his way through an unsatisfactory denial—*huh-huh-huh-huh,* cough and clear, *huh-huh-huh-huh.* . . . "It was the only way to afford it," Julián spluttered. He couldn't, or wouldn't, answer the basic questions, just kept making that drowning sound. When Ambrosio later replayed it in his mind, that sound became, for him, the emptiness at the center of the universe.

So began the humming in his head, a spinning so fast that the blood inside his body centrifuged to the walls, leaving a funnel of hollowness. But what was to be done? There was no script when gravity let go. He immediately went to the warehouse. He thought of the long days he'd worked to happy exhaustion since signing away the cheese, all the times he'd driven the high road from Guzmán to Roa in that holy light, suffering under the delusion that everything was right with the world. He thought about all those days he'd engaged his family— his parents, his wife and brothers—in conversation about the cheese, how it had organized everything. And how meaningless those most meaningful encounters of a life now seemed!

When he returned to the warehouse, he gathered his workers

and addressed them: He, Ambrosio Molinos, the founder of Páramo
de Guzmán, the *giver* of cheese, was here to announce—how to say
this?—he'd been bamboozled by certain dissolute connivers, pur-
veyors of greed, chop-shop entrepreneurs from a Spain he no longer
recognized. There'd been a contract, controlling interests, ownership guarantees. He didn't understand it himself, he told them,
but the company was no longer his. Effective immediately, he was
leaving. When he went to go, nearly all of the cheesemakers went
with him.

Only one—José—stayed behind.

Then Ambrosio was driving away, hands numb on the wheel,
until he came to his home. He passed through the door, unlaced his
boots, slouched back down the gray hallway to his bedroom, let his
body sit, then recline. He lay in bed, unable to move. Telling his wife
and parents was going to be the hardest part, and their pain, which
they wouldn't be able to conceal, would soon exacerbate his own.

At first he did what came naturally. He flailed to build a story, to
order these events as they were happening, based on the facts as they
presented themselves: *I'm a farmer,* he thought, *and Julián's rich and
educated. I've become an authentic person and he's become a superficial
one.* But Julián was his twin, as trusted as his brother Angel. While
there'd been so much left to accomplish with the cheese, there'd been
so many days of friendship left to share, too.

"The human mind is a very complicated thing," Ambrosio would
later say. "Jealousy is born in the small details. Maybe it started when
Julián and I were walking down a street and an old friend came up
and shook my hand first. Maybe I danced with a girl he liked. Each
man is his own world, and maybe this jealousy grew into the idea that
one day he was going to get me. And then he waited for that day."

But what Ambrosio's mind kept revolving back to was his signature on the page. The unwitting scrawl of his own name obliterated
his dreams and intentions. It undermined his legacy and inheritance.
It had robbed him of the most beautiful thing he'd ever made. No,
he'd never read the document, just signed it—like all the rest that

Julián had put into his hands. Because Julián had put it there in front of him. Because if Julián couldn't be trusted, no one could.

GRIEF IS AN IRRATIONAL force. Under its sway, we are given to wild leaps of mind. The cord of life is broken and so goes one's grip on sanity as we begin to revolve. "Round and round," writes C. S. Lewis of his own grief after the death of his wife. "Everything repeats. Am I going in circles, or dare I hope I am on a spiral?

"But if a spiral, am I going up or down it?"

Ambrosio claimed that the loss of his cheese was like "a death in the family"—and afterward, he took the downward spiral. He became listless, drank too much. Where he'd once been a strong 260 pounds, he became bloated and physically weak. He withdrew from his family, filled with shame, then fury. He'd staked not only his name on the cheese, but his entire *patrimonio,* or inheritance, on it. And he now stood to lose that, too, as creditors kept turning up at the door, demanding payment. They came for everything he owned. He entered the years of what he called his "crazy nightmare brain." He couldn't find work, let alone the desire to do work, especially when recent evidence suggested that it all came to naught. When people asked why not make another cheese, he couldn't explain how impossible, how inconceivable, such a thing would be. He'd given everything to *this* cheese—and now he was broken, if not broke and in debt. At night he went to the top of Mon Virgo and, fueled by wine, bellowed and raged on his heath.

Here was a man who once had a story for every day of the week, every person passed on the road, every field and landmark. He loved the toothless misfits and defenseless children. He could sit and listen all day to the stories of old men. Soon he found himself telling only one story, obsessively—how he'd been set up by his best friend, betrayed, stripped of the family cheese. In this tale he was always the chivalric defender of the past's honor. But the story had no ending. He needed an ending. On Mon Virgo, he sat at the edge of the precipice, smoking and drinking.

What was the ending?

The wind lashed, and he could always hear it, that drowning sound. The factory was just over there, down to the south, in the bundle of darkness at the edge of Roa, tucked in against the ramparts of the village. His lost kingdom, there in the dark. He smashed his empty wine bottles on the rocks. *Huh-huh-huh.* Cursed Julián. *Huh-huh-huh.* And as the drowning sound reached its pitch, he had an inspiration: He would hold the head down, push it down, until the drowning noise stopped. Until there was complete silence.*

This thought gave Ambrosio a new sense of purpose, and in its way organized his descent—just as the cheese had organized his ascent. Suddenly, the world held so many inspiring options. He would burn Julián in the fields, hang him from a tree in the vineyard. He would take his powerful hands and wrap them around the man's Adam's apple, crushing ligament and muscle, popping spine bone and windpipe. *Huh-huh . . . arghhh.* He would shoot him. Catch him unaware, put the bullet clean between his eyes, drop him in front of the factory or in the driveway of his house or in a bar before his friends. He knew Julián's every move. It was an unfair advantage, like following the tracks of a paralyzed body pulling its sickly way through the dust, following the arroyo of his deceit.

Now Ambrosio would think, *I want to kill him but I don't want to. I can't do it, but I might have to.* And then: *I will.*

He began to study military manuals at home, by the desk lamp where he'd once studied ways to optimize the taste of his cheese. He feverishly researched the end of his story. It took a long time—hundreds of pages—but then he came upon the perfect resolution. It would in-

---

* To wound an Old Castilian was to invoke a kind of biblical wrath. Even in the recent past, when the reach of the Spanish legal system fell short of the countryside, the formation of makeshift citizen tribunals known as "Seven-Man Justice" was meant to keep matters from turning violent. But when the verdict didn't satisfy the aggrieved party, a primal drama was often quick to unfold. The danger was real: In Castile, the distance between the seed of thought and the deed itself was a very short gunpowder line indeed.

volve telling *cuentos,* and then some prolonged suffering. ("Torture" seemed the wrong word; perhaps "justice" was better.) He would cast himself as Scheherazade in an upside-down version of *Tales from the Thousand and One Nights.* In the trunk of his car he placed a rope, a candle, and a cutting knife. He planned to justice Julián.

And then he waited.

Soon it seemed everyone in the Duero Valley not only knew Ambrosio's tale of woe, but whispered of what he might do to Julián. In fact, there were those who lived by the old code, too, who wondered how they might "assist" in the matter, but Ambrosio waved them off as a point of pride. This was his alone to resolve.

Though it had been a relief to distract his mind with a murder plot, it wasn't lost on Ambrosio that he was contemplating a transgression from which there'd be no recovery. Yet what would have been considered illogical under most circumstances made a crystalline sort of sense now. The faster he spiraled, the more urgent it became. No one could console him, not Asun, not Angel, not his mother or father. He drove by his factory every day—"to take his poison a little at a time," as he put it.* But in certain moments, his delusions led him to believe the factory was still his. He stewed and boiled while living in his parallel mind, the one in which he could be found driving to work at the factory again, now harping the cheese, and now taste-testing another batch before it was tinned and set loose in the world. He called out to Orencio, greeted Fidel. But when he came to the factory entrance, he never slowed or braked. He drove on, powered by his fury.

With debts to pay, he found work driving a truck—or rather, his brother Angel bought a truck for him to drive—and on long hauls through Europe, at border crossings or waiting to deliver a load of melons, or crates of juice, or olive oil, he foraged through the past to

---

* His mother, on the other hand, would never drive by the factory, for if she did, she was stricken with acute stomach pains.

try to find the clues and incongruities that might have led to the betrayal. Search as he might, there was so little to be found. That's what felt most disturbing: either he'd completely missed the signs, or there hadn't been any. Which moment was it that had turned Julián? It was true that in recent years Julián had seemed more distracted and rarely visited the *bodega* anymore. Ambrosio's wife had pointed that out, and Ambrosio had said, No, he has some family issues. It's not personal.

Wasn't that how the closest friendships worked? Three days, three months, three years—you came and went, eclipsed and effaced, taking care of the stuff of your life with the full trust that your *majo amigo* would always come around again, on a Sunday afternoon, for some wine and *chuletas* up at the *bodega*.

In the months after his departure, he heard rumors about the company: They were skimping on quality, buying inferior milk. The company was sold—and sold again. The reputation of the cheese waned. For anyone who asked why, he had an answer, the same one he'd given all those years ago to those enthralled by his cheese: In order to make a magical cheese, you have to pour in your love and goodness. The cheese is an obligation, a referendum on you as a person, your purity and rectitude. What they were doing now was production-line stuff, making soulless cheese from soulless milk. Taste buds never lied: Scallywags and *"putas,"* as Ambrosio put it—businessmen and robots, too—made horrible cheese.

The desecration was complete.

It was one thing to steal the cheese, and another to ruin it, though of course they were one and the same. For Ambrosio the question remained: To kill or not to kill? "If you listen, nature tells you everything," he was fond of saying. So it was only fitting that when Christmas Eve arrived and the whole family had gathered in Guzmán, nature spoke.

Angel was there, Roberto, Ambrosio Senior. They were sitting around the table, and Angel said, "Why don't we go check on the cheese?"

He was not speaking of a midnight run to the factory but to the family *bodega* where Ambrosio had stored a couple tins of the original cheese, from the very beginning, all that was left. The mere mention of it struck fear in Ambrosio, for the tins had taken on great importance—like icons.

"Let's just leave it to God," he said, but then his father rose abruptly and put on his coat. And then everyone put on their coats, and briskly followed the old man out into the cold night, under the stars-upon-stars you see there, the bold Spanish sky that started Columbus to the New World. In silence they walked down through the shuttered town and up to the *bodega,* where they unlocked the door, descended the thirteen steps into the cave, and lit candles. Someone uncorked a magnum—the Gran Reserva 1989 from the Pedrosa vineyard, given as a gift by Ambrosio's friend Manolo.*

There they sat in a circle, passing the *porrón*. Ambrosio unclasped the wooden box that held the tins of cheese and unwrapped one from a purple chamois cloth. His hands trembled as he put the can opener to it. Could it ever live up? And why ask it to? If it was a cheese of memories, then best to remember it alive in its heyday. He dawdled and stalled, cutting the lid as slowly as possible while talking about the price of grain . . . the prospects for spring . . . the drivers he'd met while traversing Europe.

"*¡Puta madre!*" his father burst out. "Let's go, open the damn thing! Before I die."

Ambrosio was thinking, *Shit. Okay. There are no guarantees. It will be what it is.*

When he slid back the serrated metal top and candlelight fell on

---

* The significance of that wine, on this night, wasn't lost on the assembled, for at that very moment the pope, John Paul II, was celebrating Midnight Mass at the Vatican with the same Gran Reserva. It had been a point of pride for Spaniards everywhere that the Holy See had chosen this Castilian wine over Oremos, the Hungarian Tokaj he usually drank on Christmas Eve—the first time a Spanish wine had been picked for the occasion.

the cheese, he spied a white frosting of calcium over its surface. He pushed gently on it with his finger. It gave—and gave back.

With the tip of his pocketknife, he stabbed one of the two wedges and removed it from the olive oil. He cleaned the wedge with a paper napkin and smelled the knife, then cut away the rind and went inside and realized that it was dry and hard and very good, almost flaking. He parceled pieces out to his father and brothers, who couldn't believe it either. For so hard a cheese, it melted so readily, releasing the chamomiles and herbs of the *páramo*. And it complemented the wine perfectly. *That* amazed Ambrosio.

Later, in the months and years to come, they would talk about this night as a kind of miracle. It was yet another story they told, the cheese in all its power and glory, coming back from exile, coming back, despite Julián's betrayal, from the dead.

Ambrosio had been waiting for a sign. Gazing upon his cheese again, he felt flooded with wonder. How could it be? He saw it as young and vibrant, and he said to the cheese, *Damn, what tolerance you have! What stamina!* And the cheese said, *I'm here for you.*

When it came time for the last morsel and Ambrosio took the piece from the plate before him, when he held the cheese up in the flicker of candlelight like a wafer, he listened for its voice again, for the wisdom of ages to speak.

To kill or not to kill?

Get that son of a bitch, said the cheese.

9

THE QUEST

"Whoa!"

THE DIAPER-SWADDLED CHILDREN WERE ASLEEP FOR A BLESSED moment, and Sara was in bed, febrile with fatigue, cuddled around her book, a tome so harrowing it seemed to emanate a radioactive glow. Since the time we'd met at Storytelling School in our tender twenties, we'd come to live overlapping lives. She had written a book, and bounced around the globe chasing stories for magazines, too. Even with our growing family, every assignment presented an opportunity. If the timing was right, if the faraway place seemed benevolent enough, if we had enough frequent flyer miles or we could combine our work, we made a pact to try to travel together as much as possible.* And the pleasures were immense: Sara wandering the streets of Havana with Leo, dawdling before street musicians playing *son* as I tried to arrange a meeting with Fidel Castro, then all of us joining forces for a tasty meal at a *parador;* or Leo and I riding an el-

---

* While I myself never left the country (except to go to Canada) until I was sixteen, Leo's passport bore the stamps of more than a dozen countries by the time he was five, a true twenty-first-century kid.

ephant in a Phnom Penh park while Sara reported a story about baby laundering, to return by day's end for a meal by the Mekong. These blurred divisions had always made perfect sense to us because they'd always led to the greatest serendipities.

On this night Sara was researching an article about toxicity—and what she read was riveting. It turned out that everything in our house was toxic, from water bottles to baby formula, and these items could, would, and *were* poisoning us. The book's title was something like *Total Cancer* or *We're All Toast*. Lying there beneath her cloud of infiltrating phthalates, my wife wore an expression of intense concentration.

"Been thinking about Ambrosio and Guzmán," I said, settling on my side with a bowl of popcorn, munching.

She nestled deeper. *Why is he talking to me?*

"What would you say to moving?" I continued.

She turned a page so slowly it made a creaking sound. "Move to Spain," I said. "Ambrosio says there's a place we could rent in the village. He says no one's living there, so we'd get it cheap."

Sara had long ago learned to ride these hypotheticals out—but she also realized their danger.* And once it dawned on her that I might be gaining momentum, she reluctantly lifted her head, shaped

---

* Once, when we'd been young and broke, I'd devised a plan whereby various tourist boards would sponsor a trip of ours to Scandinavia, believing us to be a semi-connected writer/photographer team thanks to a noncommittal letter of introduction I'd begged from a friend at an outdoors magazine. Though Sara had misgivings, and no background in photography whatsoever, we were soon traipsing over glacier, tundra, and taiga, me wielding my notepad, she carrying the camera case she rarely remembered to open unless I reminded her. Which was not great for the relationship. The last straw came in the forests of northern Norway, when we met up at a rustic lodge with a real eight-person team from a glossy German magazine, including a chatty photographer and his two assistants who wanted to talk shop. She would never live down that moment when, before their boisterous crowd, she unzipped her small case to reveal one sad camera. "That's it?" roared the photographer. "No filters, no lenses?"

"I'm a naturalist," she'd said indignantly. "And I travel light." Then, at bedtime: "I want to go home now."

a quick mountain of pillows, and fell back with her arms crossed. She wore a faded college T-shirt that read "Spring Party Weekend," and her hair was mussed. She emitted a sigh of exasperation. I had the feeling that husbands sometimes have in the presence of wives roused from near sleep: a certain awe at her unself-conscious beauty and a sinking sense that I was yet one more child in her life.

"We need to find a new shower curtain," she said.

"But what about Spain?" I said.

"It might be safer," she said. "The EU bans more than a thousand chemicals that the FDA won't."

"Really?" I said, and then she told me about the essential changes in human DNA caused by the chemicals in everyday items. As she spoke, I was thinking about the glories of snuggling with the kids in the morning, spending time with them that wasn't borrowed or stolen, reading to them for hours at night, living off the grid for a while, just the four of us.

"I haven't written a piece in almost six months," she said. She averted her eyes to her book and its itemizations of our slow, painful dying by chemicals. After childbirth, she was aching to reenter the same journalistic fray that I was now eager to exit. Then she turned back to me and said, "The kids are so small."

What remained unspoken was a laundry list of reasons that we both knew made a move impractical: We had—and needed—jobs, for one. It would be expensive, for two. We didn't speak the language, and out on the Meseta we'd be miles from medical help, let alone supermarkets or a Starbucks. In truth, we'd most likely be living in a dark hovel, in a village of mostly elderly people and a bunch of half-feral dogs.

"It would only be for a while," I said.

"Like how long?" she said.

"A year maybe?"

And so began the negotiation, me painting a picture for Sara of a young, vibrant family that drops out of the American rat race and finds more time for each other in a small Spanish village. Children become instantly bilingual, wear black berets and Continental shoes. Husband and wife dance in the village square. When Sara retreated to her book that night, I knew the adventurer in her had been stirred.

"We'd have a lot to work out," she said, "but I'm not opposed."

A MONTH LATER, I flew down to Manhattan to meet with my book editor. We sat in a nice restaurant with white tablecloths and rectangles of flavorful fish topped with capers and "confettis of herbs." The clientele wore suits and ties, and the murmur of gravitas, of business being done, was unmistakable. Meanwhile, I was an interloper in jeans, trying to fake seriousness. There was some talk again about doing a war book. Ideas were batted around—and nixed. Finally, my editor asked if there was a story I was dying to tell.

I hesitated for a moment. "Well," I said, and it came pouring out: the small Spanish village, the cheesemaker and his family recipe, his best friend, a revenge plot . . .

As I spoke, my editor's face bloomed with the most quizzical expression, and she said, "Wait—what you're saying is that you want to write a book about *a piece of cheese?*" To which I replied, "No— *Ambrosio's* cheese!" To which she replied in genuine mystification: "Ambrosio *who?*"

That lunch precipitated a number of calls between my editor and agent. In the suddenly fraught and dangerous world of 2002, there were so many important things to write about—why this? But now that I'd said it out loud, I knew there was nothing *but* "this," because "this" was all I ever thought about. Every time I'd been to Guzmán I'd run my tape recorder—*mi grabadora*—for hours and scribbled notes. A random dive into my backpack at any given moment would have revealed a cache of arcane Iberian-themed books—*The Bible in Spain* (1843), *Spanish Raggle-Taggle* (1934), *Tales of the Alhambra* (1831). Ambrosio had told me that he longed for the cheese he'd once made; I longed for something to make, too. Out of words, on a page.

And I kept wondering: Would it be possible to tell a tale so powerful, so fantastic and true, so ridiculous and redemptive, that it would in one fell swoop resurrect the cheese, stop a murder, lionize this cheesemaker Ambrosio Molinos, exact revenge on the *puta* Julián, and memorialize a waning way of life, all the while giving someone like me an excuse for sinking deeper into the soil of Guzmán—i.e., drinking copious amounts of fresh red wine in the telling room while listening to stories, or breaking free of my current life, which left me feeling trapped, distracted, and a little depressed?

I wrote up a thirty-page book proposal in which I described the story of the cheese, as well as my attempts to convince my wife that "we should move to Guzmán for a while, in order to find more time. Time for family. Time for conversation. Time to eat." The conclusion read, "Whether it's all a foolish romantic dream or the only true path to happiness on earth, I hope to be able to tell you."

And then I waited, like an expectant father. When I heard the book idea had been accepted, I couldn't quite process the news. Did this mean someone else believed in Ambrosio, too? The advance gave us money to make the move to Guzmán a reality. To top it off, a British publisher had bought the book, too, providing a little more cushion. Now, late at night as I tried to fall asleep, Sara sat with a legal notepad, scribbling the master plan:

"I think we should take language courses in a city before going to Guzmán," she said.

"Time away: less than a year, more than six months," she said.

"We need to nail down lodging," she said.

Then she started moving mountains. The to-do list never quit. There was mail to be forwarded, an old dog to be cared for in our absence, a house to be readied for renters. We packed ourselves into four oversized bags loaded with, among other items, diapers in two sizes (6's and 2's), a Spanish-English dictionary, a corkscrew (for all the Duero wine in our future!), winter jackets and summer shorts, a dozen Binky/pacifiers of similar brand, an army of Playmobil figurines, baseball mitts, swimsuits. We were a ridiculous circus of car seats and strollers, luggage and diaper bags, missing only the bearded lady and her husband, the sword swallower. "Wow" was the last word out of my father-in-law's mouth when he dropped us curbside at Logan Airport, watching our wagon train lumber under gray, still-wintry skies into the warm, amber twilight of the terminal. It wasn't "Wow, good luck on your wild adventure, you intrepid kids!" It was "Wow, do you *really* need to be doing this?"

Flying overnight through London and Munich (thanks to frequent-flyer-mile routing), we landed in Madrid midmorning and were forced by the sheer scale of our impedimenta to take two taxis to a hotel on Campomanes Street, a few blocks from the palace and its lawns and gardens. We changed diapers, ate ravenously, drew heavy curtains over the floor-to-ceiling windows, and fell asleep. When I awoke some hours later to the pleasing music of slumbering kids, under the low-cost grandeur of fifteen-foot rococo ceilings, it occurred to me that we'd done it, the four of us. Exactly as I'd dreamed it, back among the sunflowers, up in my office with all the pinging and ringing—we'd reached mach speed and broken free of our American life. But then again—why? So that I could be closer to a man I half knew, with the hope that I still might come face-to-face with a world-famous piece of cheese I'd seen in a deli cooler nearly fifteen years earlier? Or so I might restore that man to power, and in so doing reunite him with his destiny?

Oddly, the answer to both questions seemed to be yes.

MADRID* WAS LEO CHASING pigeons in the Plaza Mayor—and an orchestra playing Mahler there at midnight as May screamed and cooed. It was getting mealtimes all wrong, searching at noon for lunch only to find that the restaurants opened at two for *comida*. It was going to see the paintings of Goya at the Prado—"that small container over-

---

* The origins of this name are murky but may be partially rooted in the Latin for "land of bears," to signify the abundance of bears when the Romans arrived. That and/or the equally abundant strawberry trees, *madroño* in Spanish.

flowing with good things," as Mavis Gallant once had it—and Leo
nearly smudging a Velázquez with fingers of melted chocolate.

Enthralled, we could have made ourselves quite comfortable in the
big city, down the alleys of Chueca, out in its squares—my favorite the
touristy Plaza de Santa Ana, with its old bullfighting hotel, *chuleta*
restaurants, and cafés—but soon enough we found ourselves riding a
bus to Salamanca, one of the great Renaissance cities of Europe, where
we settled in for a six-week intensive course in Spanish at a small private language school teeming with foreigners like ourselves.[*]

On the western edge of Castile, near the Portuguese border, Salamanca[†] happened to be only a few hours from Guzmán, and one Fri-
day after class we rented a car and drove up through Valladolid,[‡] and
then east toward Guzmán, through a green landscape soon to be desiccated by heat. When night fell, we laid up in the picturesque town
of Peñafiel, in a hotel housed in a former flour mill. Out our window
hovered a lit medieval castle.

The next morning we drove to Guzmán, running the low road to

---

[*] In the melting pot of that school, known as Sampere, we befriended a Swiss sta-
tionmaster and a shy Swedish postman. We became fast friends with a couple of
frat boys from Virginia, and clung to them as if drowning. We found a cozy (read:
shoebox) apartment next to a wonderful park, and so began more adventures: One
day in the park my wife met an old man and learned from him the precise Spanish
for "Do you mind if I fondle your cantaloupes?" Meanwhile, on the soccer pitch
with Leo, I approached a group of young boys, none of whom came to my waist,
and, hoping they might include him, fumbled an opportunity at international di-
plomacy by blurting the first words that sprang to mind, "*¡Está bien, por favor!*" or
"It's good, please!" Also, we spent an inordinate amount of time trying to find diapers. Another fine evening, after going on a two-hour manhunt for a can opener
(*un abrelatas,* I found out after much pantomime), I returned to our apartment,
holding the device triumphantly aloft, to find the kitchen on fire (small blaze,
eventually contained, set off by wife's misreading of Spanish burner instructions).

[†] Salamanca is famous for the ham of its acorn-fattened pigs, as well as for having
the oldest university in Spain, founded circa 1218 by King Alfonso IX of León just
over a hundred years after the death of El Cid.

[‡] Valladolid: Once the capital of Spain, pronounced *Vay-ah-do-leeth.* Among its
pleasures are the house in which Columbus died, and another in which Miguel de
Cervantes wrote part of *Don Quixote.*

Roa, which was socked in by mist, over the Duero River, which flowed a sluggish gray-green, then skirting Roa itself, passing by in the shadow of the cheese factory, and eventually rising through the vineyards to Guzmán. The children were bandoliered in their booster seats, chirping obliviously. I could see Sara's expression soften, eyes following the script of the landscape—the grapevines and sunflowers—and the absent finger-twirling of hair that signaled growing curiosity. I felt oddly anxious. We were about to enter my dream world. What if it really was just a bunch of crumbling buildings on a hill?

"Africa," Alexandre Dumas was alleged to have said, "begins at the Pyrenees." What he seemed to be saying was that Spain, located to the south of that granite range and tagged like an alien remora to the underbelly of Europe, was not European at all. It was a rough, bastard land full of warriors, misfits, and half-breeds; slackers, dreamers, and bandits. (And rabbits as well: The word "Spain" derives from the Latin *Hispania,* which in turn probably derives from the Phoenician *i-shephan-im,* meaning "island or coast of rabbits.")* Next to the cultural refinements of London and Paris, the voluptuous living of Rome and Venice, the supposed homogeneity of the Viking north, Spain was the Other, a chaos of violent, fiery people in a place down under that the Greeks, after coming upon Gibraltar sometime around the tenth century B.C., mistook for the gates of Hell.†

---

* Rabbits were endemic to the Iberian Peninsula but they weren't commonly found elsewhere until the Phoenicians began exporting them from Spain on their travels around the Mediterranean. The proof of Spain as Europe's first rabbit hutch was solidified when a 2.5-million-year-old fossil of a rabbit was found near Granada. (However, a 55-million-year-old proto-rabbit has been found in Mongolia.)

† Geologists guess that approximately 5.5 million years ago Africa rammed into Spain, sealing shut the Straits of Gibraltar. Then, over the next 2,000 years, the Mediterranean evaporated, until the Atlantic Ocean breached the elevated isthmus between today's Spain and Morocco, creating a "mega-fall," a waterfall thought to be twenty times higher than Niagara and up to six miles long, that replenished the Mediterranean over the next hundred years.

Observing the Spanish in the first century, the Greek geographer Strabo felt that certain commonalities existed between tribes: unstinting hospitality, chivalrous manners, brimming arrogance, an acute indifference to hardship, and a particular aversion to outsiders telling them what to do.* The character of the land—from the African south to the alpine north, from the rainy, almost English west to the balmy, Alabaman east—shapes the character of the people here. The Basques are thought to be a moody, unconquerable race of inscrutable tongue clinging to their cloudy mountain valleys; the Catalans are considered industrious if a bit cold behind sunny smiles, after aeons of protecting and exacting their interests against foreign powers who have washed up on their gentle coast; the Andalusians are notoriously breezy and fun loving, some say too lazy in the heat to finish even their half-swallowed sentences; and, by contrast, in the rough-hewn interior, the Castilians are somber, intense, and wary until they suddenly burst with laughter, generosity, road directions. Castilians love to give road directions.

For all the tensions between regions, the modern Spanish state still maintains an instinctual if at times blustery consensus against the world. Which is ironic, given how much of the world has passed through the peninsula. From Neanderthal to Cro-Magnon to the cave dwellers of 15,000 B.C. who drew on rock walls at Altamira, in Cantabria, from the Phoenicians who established their first colonies at Málaga in 775 B.C. to the Carthaginians who occupied southeast Spain and exploited its material wealth, from the vanquishing Romans who

---

* History is rife with stories about Spanish intransigence. In roughly 134 B.C., as the Romans continued their drive to subdue Iberia, the Roman general Scipio Africanus the Younger laid siege to a town called Numantia (near present-day Soria) by establishing a blockade in hopes of starving the Iberians inside. After nine months, realizing the hopelessness of their predicament, the Numantians got drunk, lit the town on fire, and died in their self-made pyre rather than surrender to the Romans, a version of events later immortalized by Cervantes in his play *The Siege of Numantia*. In Cantabria, people shouted and sang victory slogans while being crucified; mothers would kill their children rather than let them be taken prisoner by the enemy.

brought roads and a legal system between the years 218 B.C. and A.D. 476 to the Visigoths who gave way to the Moors in A.D. 711, Spain has been a crossroads for the three major religions of the world (Christianity, Islam, and Judaism), a hotly contested land bridge between Europe and Africa, and a living museum to all the cultures who have come and been vanquished on its barren field.

This, too, is a source of pride for the tribes of Spain: their ability to withstand, everlast, and overcome. *Si Dios no fuese Dios, seria rey de España, y el de Francia su cocinero* goes the old Castilian saying, which means: If God were not God, he would make himself the king of Spain, with the king of France as his cook. As the Duke of Wellington once put it, boasting of Spain's strength is the national weakness.

My first vision of Spain, however, suggested postapocalyptic desolation rather than any show of strength. It came on the overnight train from Paris while I was backpacking Europe in the mid-1980s during my junior year abroad. Sometime after dawn, I remember waking high in the Pyrenees when the train jerked to an abrupt halt. There was a long wait at the break of gauge on a lonely mountain pass, then the train lumbered forth again, entrance to the kingdom granted. Somewhere on the scree-draped slopes a single shepherd appeared with his flock. He bore a crook in one hand and a goatskin bag in another. This was ten years after the death of Franco but it could have been a hundred years ago.

The train had descended from the Pyrenees in a rush, as if we were a procession of maurading Celts or Gauls, Vandals or Visigoths. The mountains gave way to the Meseta, what was thought to have once been a single, Paleozoic volcano until it blew up and left this tableland of limestone covering about 40 percent of the country's interior. At one time it had been thicketed with oaks, junipers, and evergreens, but deforestation beginning with the Romans left behind this desolation.

Atop these high plains we rode, sighting faraway villages and their silhouetted castles (hence the name Castile), then climbed over the Guadarrama and slid down into Madrid, a city that left a hard, jittery first impression: the thin, pale light washing the buildings of their dimensions, the bellicose expressions of the heavily armed *guardia civil* provoking fear. After the cafés of Paris with their exquisite wines and creamy fromages, crepes and steak tartare—screaming *Adore me!*— Madrid was these store-bought hunks of unyielding cheese and brick-hard baguettes, consumed in leafless Buen Retiro Park.

Yet there was still something about the city, though I couldn't say what at the time, something that grew on me later as I came and went, sometimes as a tourist, sometimes on assignment. It was Madrid's authenticity, its unwillingness to bend, a naked trueness of self perched high on the central plains of Spain that, say, the whole Moulin Rouge show of Paris couldn't claim. Madrid, dressed as it was, tasting as it did, prideful as hell, didn't care what you thought about it on your junior-year backpacking trip. That was your problem.*

Perhaps some of that indifference epitomized the Castilian character. While Americans are quick to cast themselves as rugged individualists, the Castilians have a much longer history of going it alone against the world and, when need be, against each other. Before its rise as the lone global superpower in the fifteenth century, Castile was born a weakling, bereft of natural riches and defenses. For centuries the region between the Tagus and Duero rivers remained mostly un-

---

* By contrast, enter Barcelona: On the overnight train to the City of Counts during that same trip, a family with whom I shared a sleeping car invited me to stay in their apartment for *as long as I pleased*. They were as innocent as the turtles of Galápagos, warm and open and willing. And soon there I was, crashed in their guest room, playing with their kids, Sunday walking at Gaudi's Park Güell and out on the Ramblas, the famous boulevard leading to the Mediterranean, the night Barcelona exploded for some soccer victory or something I could never quite determine. Bottles of wine were passed in the squares, the people spontaneously broke into song and then suddenly dance—dancing dances so beautiful in those golden-lit city squares, all of these Catalans wearing their buoyancy so colorfully that one couldn't help but feel momentarily blinded. Soon pure joy turned to something deeper and more considered. Everyone stood for a moment in silence, the eighty-year-old couple hand-in-hand with long-haired teenagers, waiting for the music again. As the evening wore on, they seemed to be dancing less for Spain than for themselves, their own history, their tribe.

inhabitable due to the pillagings of other kingdoms. For those who staked their lives there, the water was so fetid they were forced to brush their teeth with urine. It's said that Sancho III of Navarre (d. 1035), whose son became the first king of Castile, slept with a horse in the royal bedchamber, always at the ready to ride against invaders. The mind-set persists.[*]

This life of danger and action, this prerogative to defend one's precarious hold at all costs, is perhaps what gives such weight to the communal rituals of Castilian life, in particular the planting and harvesting of food, the fiestas, and even *los toros,* the bullfights, which belong to all of Spain. The bullfight is said to have had its origins in the mysterious Mithra religion, which took as its divine figure a young man killing a bull. One rite called for soldiers to be drenched in the blood of slaughtered bulls so they would be invincible in battle. And Castile especially prides itself on the invincibility of its legendary warriors, from the eleventh-century knight El Cid to the footballers of Real Madrid today.

Of course, as a junior in college, I knew none of this. It wasn't until later that I found myself enthralled by Madrid—and more so by what I found beyond its frontier, in the Castilian *campo.* Here, the sun-stroked faces of the old men met the arrival of a stranger with mild curiosity, but they wanted nothing from you. They only wanted to make sure you weren't invading, and once that was settled, you were tolerated, allowed, and over time, perhaps even accepted.

To MY GREAT RELIEF, when our day-tripping family came upon Guzmán that first time in the spring of 2003, my wife leaned forward

---

[*] Writes Américo Castro in *The Spaniards: An Introduction to Their History,* the Castilians "did not bother to foment culture; they cultivated the art of being 'lords' rather than exercise the faculties of the intellect or imagination. They did not develop a philosophy or science of their own, but they did create personal ways of being that would, in the future, make possible imperial enterprises and literary forms of expression still admired and studied throughout the world."

on the dash, gazed up at the village, and said one word: "Whoa!"
When she met Ambrosio and he bear-hugged her, singing her name
in his rumbling baritone, she was smitten. When we walked the
streets with our kids, the women approaching with candies, she'd felt
so welcome she kept repeating, "Oh, they're so nice." And when she
responded in not-so-bad Spanish, there were gales of giddy delight.

We ate *comida* with Ambrosio and Asun in the warmth of midaf-
ternoon at their telling room, and Sara seemed to fall more deeply in
love with the cheesemaker and his wife. Meanwhile, Leo clambered
up the hill above the *bodegas*. He had a stick that he wielded as a
sword, and Ambrosio kept talking to him. *"Mira,"* said the giant,
picking some thyme from the ground, crushing it in his hand, and
holding it out for Leo to smell.

"Our son is mesmerized," Sara said.

After six weeks in our cramped apartment in Salamanca, what a
relief it was to find ourselves in open fields, orchards, and vineyards!
And our kids—everyone kept doting over the kids. It was like inher-
iting eighty grandparents, this one holding hands with our son, this
one pinching the cheek of our daughter. "Everything you said about
this place is true," said Sara, in near disbelief.

So at the end of May we left Salamanca and moved to a house on
Calle Francisco Franco, living with the ghost of El Caudillo himself.
Our neighbor was an eighty-year-old gentleman known as Don Honorato, who lived in a humble manse with an anomalous patch of
green lawn that he watered constantly. From our perch on a cusp of
land planted with olive trees, we felt like the giant cranes we'd seen
nesting on the high church tower in Salamanca, surveying all of creation below.

Almost better, there was no TV, no house projects, fickle cell-
phone coverage, and it took forty-five minutes to reach an Internet
café. Without all the distractions, we quickly became reacquainted
with each other, taking long walks, lingering over meals, sharing ob-
servations or delighting in some little thing our kids did (May's first
step, Leo's first loose tooth, May's first birthday, Leo's first ride on the

toilet). So it was that, if only briefly, we'd broken the cycle. We'd stuffed away our old life, jumped an ocean, and unpacked our bags, laying our clothes into dresser drawers belonging to others. We slept on their beds and piled our books on shelves of preexisting books written in Spanish. If it was a fool's errand to chase Ambrosio and his cheese, so be it. I was here to suffer the consequences.

10

REVENGE AND OTHER TRIVIALITIES

"Here is the Lord of Vizcaya you acclaimed."

THE FIRST-EVER AMPUTATION WAS RECALLED BY THE ROMAN Aulus Cornelius Celsus in A.D. 1, a case of trying to stanch gangrene. His advice was simple: Never cut through a joint. Minimize blood loss. Leave enough skin to cover the nub. The early amputations—the ones before anesthesia in the nineteenth century—relied on speed. You made your incision quickly, in a circular motion, slicing muscle, tendon, nerve, and vessel, then hacked the bone. The burst of blood was controlled and coaxed to hemostasis by hot pitch or oil. The great amputator in the field, Scottish surgeon Robert Liston, who plied his trade in the 1800s, was world famous for being able to dispatch a leg in twenty-five seconds.*

It gave Ambrosio an idea, in a beam of clotted light at his desk, as

---

* Key to his success was Liston's enormous left hand, which he used as a tourniquet while his right hand did the cutting and sewing. Before anesthesia, when time was of the essence, Liston was described by one writer: "He was six-foot-two, and . . . sprung across the blood-stained boards upon his swooning, sweating, strapped-down patient like a duelist, calling, 'Time me, gentlemen, time me!' to

he studied an old military manual. The page looked something like this:

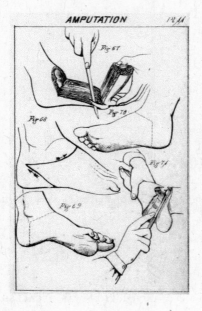

He obsessed and mulled, paged deeper, and slowly a thought dawned on him: He could kill Julián while keeping him alive. After all, there were things he felt he needed to share with him. The scenario he imagined was simple. A rope, knife, and candle in the car; a distant cave. He craved revenge that could last, in terms that were final: blood, snot, ligament, bone.

He took to the roads in the winter after he'd lost the cheese, skim-

---

students craning with pocket watches from the iron-railinged galleries. Everyone swore that the first flash of his knife was followed so swiftly by the rasp of saw on bone that sight and sound seemed simultaneous. To free both hands, he would clasp the bloody knife between his teeth." However, Liston's reputation may have gotten the better of him when, during "a bravura performance," dressed in his familiar bottle-green coat and Wellington boots, he allegedly amputated one patient's left testicle, as well as two fingers of an assistant, both of whom died of gangrene soon thereafter.

ming through the vineyards like a vapor. There were nights when he turned off the headlights and drove by the moon's luster. How many times had he found comfort in the undulating land here, in every bend of rural highway? But in his stricken state, the scene brought him unbearable sadness: a tree with a fallen limb, a gutted car in a field, the old factory with dark windows. The force of projection was too great, and gravity too weak. He would fry himself by flying head-long into his own black sun.

Of course, he knew Julián's every move, exactly where he was at each hour of the day. They'd had telepathy, hombre; for instance, if they were in a crowded room of people they might look for each other at the same exact moment—they were the same height, which was a head taller than the rest—and meet eyes, and start laughing, laughing at the telepathic joke they told each other over the heads of all the people standing between them who would never know their joke, be-cause they didn't possess anything like the telepathy Ambrosio and Julián had, that secret channel.

He'd picked an abandoned *bodega,* of which there were hundreds in this part of the country. He would turn the engine off, and in the plot he'd concocted, the one he'd fantasized about,* he would drag Julián, bound and gagged, from the trunk of his car into the cave. Killing him with a gunshot or garrote to the throat would have been an act of cowardice. If you really meant to kill your best friend, to change him in death, it should have to be long and slow, thereby pro-viding repeated edification.

The moment of truth: Julián bound tightly in a chair, the knife and

---

* By the way, this murder plot was no secret. Ambrosio told his story far and wide, in the bars of Roa, Aranda, and Burgos, to his vast circle of friends, and in the *bo-degas* of trusted allies throughout the land. It was a tale of two men who had loved each other like brothers, the one who trusted and the other who cheated. It pitted purity against greed, creation against destruction, heart against spleen, the Old Castilian against the new. And when a listener asked what kind of justice might be done, Ambrosio would say, "I could kill him." Part of the joy he derived from con-cocting Julián's slow, delicious death, one might surmise, was the relief (or surge of power) he got by telling people the details of what he planned to do.

candle on the table. Ambrosio would start by leaving him in the dark for a few days to think about things. Then he'd appear with cheese and wine. Expansive, jovial. Light the candle, drip a bit of wax on the coarse tabletop, and prop it there. He wouldn't yell; he wouldn't hit. He'd sit down and eat and drink in front of his good friend—sucking, slurping, masticating, wine dribbling from his lips, as Julián sat swollen and parched. And night after night, he would tell him stories, "the thousand and one stories of our friendship," as Ambrosio had put it.

Do you remember our first merienda *at the* bodega? *We stole the wine, just the four musketeers, right? Can you picture Enrique's face, when he was still alive? And do you remember the story we told that night about the Witches of Peñafiel . . .*

The stories would unfold in slow motion. He would tease out this intricate detail, that funny strain. He would make beautiful origami out of memory, out of innocent tales of childhood, and then hang it there from the cave ceiling. Afterward, he would dispense with the niceties and let his mood swing to the affliction of his mind. He would approach Julián, picking the knife from the table, and in one motion he'd slice an earlobe. To stanch the blood, he'd cauterize the wound with the lit candle. It was so easy, the way you could begin to edit and delete a body. They were so far from civilization the screaming merely sounded like the wind. But even that didn't feel like enough. He wanted to give more by taking more. He would tell a story for each amputation. He had so much to give.

Do you remember the fiesta? Do you remember the girls at the Burgos dance?

He needed Julián to live, in order that he might understand what Ambrosio meant by "the disability of memory." He wanted Julián to live forever, in order to remember how it had once been when they were young and innocent and most alive. He would bring Julián to a place where there was no such thing as time.

Night after night, Julián heard the stories and songs. Even in his diminishment, he still clung to life, to the sound of Ambrosio's voice. But Ambrosio couldn't help him live forever. He knew there'd come a night when Julián would remain motionless. Perhaps Ambrosio, who could be moved to tears by an old dog with a limp or young child with his hair parted just so, would feel nothing except a final flash of anger. *¡Puta madre!* It seemed this brother of his, Julián, was, for the moment, dead.

Back when I went to Storytelling School, we encountered a parade of visitors from beyond (usually New York City), all the real and amazing writers, agents, and editors of our day, who came bearing grim news: What we were doing was madness. A suicide mission. No one had time for stories anymore. No one cared. Look, this is 1991, they said, unleashing an elephant hose of icy water on our fantasies. You can't compete with *Murphy Brown, Designing Women,* or *Murder, She Wrote.* There are thirty channels of something called cable. There are *one million* Americans using something called the Internet. Statistically speaking, we were told, there was barely a chance for any of us. Maybe one day if Johnny Carson retired . . . or if Charles and Diana separated . . . or, if in some space-age future, they invented a handheld device that acted as phone, camera, and portable multimedia player (and because of that, people started buying Macintosh products again, ha, ha, ha) . . . well, if all of *that* somehow came to pass, then one of us just might* make it as a writer.

Leaving those roundtable sessions with our heroes, my colleagues and I bore the countenance of the damned, eyeing each other as if weighing the possible toll on our psyches if we started cannibalizing the weakest. But our biggest, saddest thought balloon was transparent to all: Why hadn't we been told all of this *before* we opted out of law school?

At the time, I was reading the great Jewish-German essayist Walter Benjamin,† which, for once, should have lent me an air of intel-

* . . . *might* . . .

† The genius-esoteric but ever impractical Benjamin died of a morphine overdose as he fled Vichy France in 1940. Detained at the Spanish border town of Port Bou,

lectual rigor and credibility at the coffee shop, had it not been combined with my habit of drinking hot chocolate topped by frilly mountains of whipped cream. In his 1936 essay "The Storyteller," Benjamin posits that the storyteller, as well as the story itself, has lost primacy in a world that craves information, progress, and speed. The teller of tales is therefore left "remote," an endangered species. The storyteller, in the oldest sense of the word—i.e., the one who imparts counsel or wisdom, who carries forth the oral tradition of tales—has been eclipsed in Benjamin's mind by the stultifying demands of modern life. "Every morning brings us the news of the globe," he writes, "and yet we are poor in noteworthy stories. This is because no event any longer comes to us without already being shot through with explanation. In other words, by now almost nothing that happens benefits storytelling; almost everything benefits information."

---

he was essentially quarantined at a local hotel and, believing he was at risk of being captured by the Nazis, ended his life. Though his traveling companions soon resolved their bureaucratic snafu and found themselves on a ship to America, Benjamin's left-behind body became the subject of another controversy. He was misnamed in death and mistaken for a Catholic, and evidence of his grave was lost in the cemetery above the Mediterranean. In Michael Taussig's *Walter Benjamin's Grave,* the author writes of the confusing transpositions: "You see this name in the receipt made out to the dead man, the *difunto* Benjamin Walter, by the Hotel de Francia, for the four-day stay that includes five sodas with lemon, four telephone calls, dressing of the corpse, plus disinfection of his room and the washing and whitening of the mattress. You see it in the receipt made out by the physician for seventy-five pesetas for his injections and taking the blood pressure of the traveler, *el viajero,* Benjamin Walter. You see it in the death certificate—number 25—made out on September 27, 1940, for Benjamin Walter, forty-eight years old, of Berlin (Germany—as noted). You see it in the receipt tendered by the carpenter to the judge in Port Bou for making a cloth-lined coffin for the dead man, *el difunto,* Señor Benjamin Walter, a receipt that includes eight pesetas for the work of a bricklayer closing a niche in the cemetery for Benjamin Walter. And you can see it in the receipt made out by the priest dated October 1, 1940, for ninety-six pesetas, six of which were for a mass for the dead man and seventy-five for 'five years' rent of a niche in the Catholic cemetery of this town in which the cadaver of B. Walter lies buried.' "

The irony, of course, is that in death he's confused with someone he isn't, the confected, ever-mysterious Señor B. Walter. And though his body can't be found, his voice still rings in our ears.

I could feel the pain of this, even wearing my whipped-cream mustache. I craved to write a story, however impossible, hewing to Benjamin's penchant for fable and "a chaste compactness which precludes psychological analysis." But here was something else I was beginning to recognize: Even if I did, or could, nobody would *ever* read that story. No—like a nomadic tribe, the mass story consumers of our day had unstaked their tent poles and moved on, craving news and sound bites, reprogrammed by predictability and sentimentality, by television and the big screen of the Story Industrial Complex.

Perhaps Benjamin had identified the most precious sorts of stories in order to protect them. They were, in fact, like Ambrosio's artisanal cheese, needing to be recovered, revalued, remembered. Unlike the Industrial Story—written by committee and writing team, flattened and familiar, with Hollywood product placement or commercial breaks—they connected us to the larger floe of history and dream. They seemed to be tales that were local, personal, and oral. They might have been the stories we swapped over bottles of beer at Old Town Tavern or at our student mailboxes or on the steps of the graduate library, where Sara and I had first met, hauling out certain mythologies about ourselves.[*]

It didn't seem to matter if these stories corresponded to exact truth, as the fictions we wrote for class weren't expected to either. And by the time I was done with my own fictions, the truth was unrecog-

---

[*] On this note, I'm reminded of the Eskimo storytellers whose tales tend to be divided into two groups: 1) ancient communal ones, and 2) newer local ones. The ancient tales are the well-practiced ones that hew to a pleasing, memorized script, though they make allowances for the peculiarities of the narrator (tone, gesture, and so forth), as well as for the occasional mapped digression. Meanwhile, the newer local stories require the Eskimo storyteller to weave brand-new tales, often concerning recent events. These are infused with asides and mysticism breathed to life by the teller, as surely as the original storytellers filled the original stories with spirits and phantasms, forming, as one ethnographer has phrased it, "myths of observation." That phrase now seems so beautifully apt—*myths of observation*—as if describing what we call history or the genre of writing known as nonfiction and memoir, as if describing the truth of all storytelling really by the fallacy of its scientific/factual investigation.

nizable, not out of deviousness but because, under pressures barely accounted for, I was building the stories I needed to hear. Or making the truths I needed to believe.

A BRIEF SURVEY OF Spanish history shows Pedro the Cruel, ruler of the kingdom of Castile from 1350 to 1369, to be the most vicious, repugnant slug ever to darken a medieval throne room, the most bloodthirsty snake to lay fangs on the royal apple, the most demonical scepter-wielding conniver ever to cry paranoid foul. Famous for having insurrectionists boiled, burned, and hanged, Pedro seemed to have had a flair for eliminating his imagined enemies. On one occasion, he had a powerful cousin killed (suckered in by the king's false favor and trust, the cousin was left to defend himself with a small knife against the king's knights as His Excellency looked on), then ordered the body thrown down onto the plaza. "Behold!" he shouted to the throngs below. "Here is the Lord of Vizcaya you acclaimed." It's also believed he had a hand in the death of his own wife, Blanche, whom he hated, and of his two younger half brothers, Juan and Pedro, both just teenagers, who were held in custody for most of the king's reign.

One might ask: What made Pedro so cruel? And how do we know all of this nearly seven hundred years later?

The answer is the storyteller—in this case, Pedro López de Ayala, author of the medieval text *Crónica de Pedro,* which either exaggerates Pedro's distemper or tells it like it is. But as one of Pedro's trusted courtiers, López de Ayala lays claim to a tantalizing kind of authority, that of eyewitness. As the scholar Clara Estow points out in her wonderful book on the medieval king, López de Ayala, "the consummate dramatizer," weaves a masterful tale, incorporating bits of dialogue— some borrowed from speeches and letters—to voice opinions he avoids as the "objective" storyteller, while manipulating "certain key episodes to exploit their dramatic potential and emotional impact." And nowhere does the monarch seem to show his true colors more than in the story about his poor brother Fadrique.*

May 1358—and Seville appears beyond the alcazar window, a city of orange blossoms and incense wafting on benevolent breezes, an oasis of abundance in comparison to the harsh Meseta. Here in the alcazar surrounded by waxy palms and fecund gardens, Pedro is far from the wife he despises, living with his lover, María. Like his father before him, Pedro adores this place over all other Spanish cities, most especially the seat of royal power in Valladolid.†

But he can't escape his own embered mind, obsessed now with what to do about Fadrique. Recently his brother has been caught with seven hundred troops on the Portuguese border, trying to foment revolution against Pedro. He repents and swears his loyalty. As a test of fealty, the king has asked Fadrique to reclaim a fortress at Jumilla, in Murcia, belonging to another of Fadrique's former rebel allies. When the king receives word of Fadrique's victory, he calls him home to Seville for what Fadrique assumes to be a hero's welcome.

Fadrique arrives at the castle and, separating from his men, pays his first respects to the king's lover, María, but there's something amiss in her expression, some uneasy signal she's trying to convey. (Is it that she herself can't stomach the king's ruse?) Fadrique senses this, and looks to escape. But he's apprehended in the courtyard by two reluctant guards, and brought to an antechamber of the king's quarters, where from a nearby room the king orders his men to attack him, not

---

* Fadrique is really Pedro's half brother, born of Pedro's father's twenty-year liaison with his longtime mistress, Leonor de Guzmán, an affair that produced eight more illegitimate offspring, of which Fadrique had been the fifth-born, with a twin, Enrique. To Pedro, the whole lot of bastards wasn't to be trusted.

† The Castile of 1350 was a land divided, with Seville acting as a southern colony of sorts. In the wake of victory over the Moors, which drove them back across the Straits of Gibraltar to Africa, 24,000 Castilians had been repatriated to Seville, and the king was soon to embark upon an ambitious renovation of his castle there.

even dignifying Fadrique with a face-to-face death sentence. The guards do their business and leave him for dead.

Meanwhile, the king scours the castle for the remainder of Fadrique's now scattered men, finding one in María's quarters holding his daughter hostage, whereupon Pedro sticks and drops him with his poniard. Soon after, he stumbles upon Fadrique's body, apparently not yet dead. Drawing a knife, he hands it to a lowly page, commanding him to finish off his half brother. After the deed is done, the king orders a feast to be eaten in plain sight of Fadrique's body (*blood, snot, ligament, bone*), but whether there's cheese on the table, and whether the food tastes better in that rush of revenge, with the thick scent of death-treacle in the air, the storyteller doesn't say.

NOT EVERYONE BELIEVED THAT Ambrosio intended to *kill* Julián, and of those who did, few were in favor of the idea. Relatives from the north called one evening for a hushed conversation with Ambrosio Senior: *Does something need taking care of?* It would be nice to settle this the old way, said Ambrosio's father, but no, that's a sure course to insanity. He reiterated to his son that a life in jail was hardly an even trade for having something, even the family cheese, stolen from you. It would be a double captivity. Others in the extended family urged Ambrosio to take refuge for a while at a nearby monastery, to cleanse himself of his anger, which was an idea he gave serious thought to. But the deeper Ambrosio fell into the meaninglessness of his life without Páramo de Guzmán, the more he lost a grip on his equanimity, the more vehement he became. If other people doubted his intentions, he felt all the more resolved.

This kind of sudden disorder, this upending of happiness, this complex of futility, loss, and violent fantasy, gives rise to many strange bedfellows—drink, depression, self-loathing. Having seen Julián so completely as a doppelganger, Ambrosio lost his bearings. Yes, revenge was paramount, but was there something more to this wish to kill Julián? Was it a wish to kill some part of himself, too—to silence his mind? And was it possibly more useful to keep an enemy, thereby keeping yourself intact, than to eliminate him?*

On the Meseta, you might drive thirty, forty, fifty miles to nowhere, a bunch of ramshackle buildings, and bump into the very person you're hoping to avoid. There was a story about the time Ambrosio had taken his place at an out-of-the-way bar in Haza, a virtual ghost town. Ambrosio sat with his back to the door, and Julián had allegedly entered in the shadows, seen Ambrosio from behind, and instantly retreated, while Ambrosio's poker-faced friends betrayed nothing, until much later, when they were sure Julián was long gone.

Two years passed in this way, and who knows how many near misses there might have been, Julián entering a bar five minutes after Ambrosio exited, Ambrosio stopping for gas where Julián had just bought cigarettes. Ambrosio went on living his life, stalking Julián in his mind, ready for him when the moment arose.

LET US RETURN NOW to the king, once more at his table, before the lifeless body of his half brother. How are we to read this man who is stuffing his gullet? As bloodthirsty murderer and irretrievably disturbed individual? Or justified somehow in his actions?

In the *Crónica,* López de Ayala is quick to itemize Pedro's revenge killings (sixty or so in all), as well as the granular bits of his grumpiness. It's a wholly damning bit of storytelling. What shines through

---

* In this way perhaps, Julián ceased to be a real person, or never fully was. He became a foil, an adversary, a bugaboo. Perhaps he was the ghostly embodiment of one Count Julián, a Spaniard from history blamed for the collapse of King Roderic's Visigothic Spain in the eighth century. Rumor had it that Roderic had seduced Julián's daughter. To exact his revenge Count Julián aided and abetted a Muslim leader named Tariq in battle against the king, whose army fell in surprising fashion, thus relinquishing the entirety of Spain to the Muslims, who would remain on the peninsula for the next millennium. While the story was completely untrue, Count Julián had served as a convenient scapegoat. In order for Spain to believe in her own greatness, her downfall could only be caused by another's horrible underhandedness.

the centuries and leaves its afterimage isn't the king himself. It's not
Pedro's own version of his life, or that of his lover María, or the sweet
reminiscences of his children, if they were sweet at all. What endures
is not kindness or empathy or intelligence, though Pedro's supporters
argue that he was cruel only in avenging the wrongs perpetrated
against his citizens.* They point to his tolerance of Jews and Muslims,
a trait not shared by his Trastámaran half brothers,† as proof that the
king had dimensions, perhaps even a greater compassion and sense of
egalitarianism than those of his day.‡ But in general, for as much pain
as Pedro may have inflicted, he has become a victim of the storyteller.
And so he's died twice.

The first death is simpler: Fadrique's twin, Enrique, stages a night
march that catches Pedro and his troops by surprise, and in an attempt to wriggle free, the king strikes what he believes is a deal with
one of Enrique's lead commanders, Bertrand du Guesclin: the king's
freedom in exchange for six towns and 200,000 gold *doblas*. When the
king arrives at the commander's tent, dismounts his horse, and enters,
urging the commander to hurry, he finds the entrance blocked—and
in strides Enrique, fully armed. Though at first Enrique fails to recognize his half brother (it has been years since they last met), he draws
his dagger and stabs Pedro to death, which begins nearly 150 years of
Trastámaran rule in Castile. In symmetry with Fadrique's murder,
the king's body is left lying on the ground for three days, while Spaniards come to mock him.

---

* "Proud, high-spirited and confiding, his confidence was met with treachery by
one after another of those he trusted," reads a 1911 *New York Times* review of a
book sympathetic to Pedro. "Rebelled against by his brothers, he sought reconciliation with them to be again deceived. He trusted his mother; she conspired against
him." The headline of the article, however, says it all: "Pedro the Cruel of Castile:
A King Who Has Had the Ill-Luck to Be Portrayed Only by His Foes."

† After Pedro's demise and the ensuing fall of Toledo, Enrique auctioned off the
Jewish citizens, ostensibly as slaves, in order to pay his army.

‡ "Oh noble, oh worthy Pedro," says Chaucer in the Monk's Tale, "glorye of
Spaine."

But the second death of the king is more ignominious in some ways, for it is repeated over and over, as many times as readers pass through the gates and into the *Crónica de Pedro*. What is really happening here, behind the words? One answer comes from the scholar Estow, who argues that López de Ayala, an aristocrat, lieutenant, and chronicler par excellence, who became one of the first "caballero historians," needed to justify his own betrayal of Pedro,* whom he supported until quite late in his reign, at which time he jumped to the Trastámaran cause. His account, she says, is a "literary gem" that mimics the truth even as it may veer radically from it. But then, these are the plots and subplots of the storyteller, too: the grab for power or meaning, the self-glorifications and justifications, the critique of a subject other than oneself to divert attention from one's own failings (or unconsciously reflect them).

It leaves one to wonder: If Pedro seems unusually cruel, and is a projection of the storyteller, then what great cruelty is cloaked within the breast of the storyteller, López de Ayala, himself?

---

* After all, one need only have glanced one kingdom over, toward Pedro's contemporary Pere III, the king of Aragón and Catalonia, who may have been much more paranoid and creatively zealous than Pedro when it came to persecuting his enemies. In one case, after quelling an uprising of the Unionists of Valencia, Pere ordered his men to melt down the bell used to call meetings by the rebels so they could "taste of its liqueur." The molten lead was then poured down their throats.

11

AMBROSIO OF THE MILL AND FIELD

"Give praise."

THE WINDOWS OF OUR BEDROOM WERE COVERED BY METAL SHUT-ters meant to block the Meseta's relentless glare, and yet at dawn first light came oozing like lava through the crannies, setting the bedroom ablaze. Sara and I would groan and bury our heads beneath the pillows. The patter of feet flurried down the hall, and our kids did their morning ambush, if they weren't already sprawled between us from the night before.

How did the Spaniards do it? They drank each night with cele-bratory élan, started their *cena* somewhere between 10:30 and 11:00, popped up early in the morning, and started all over again, cleaning, talking, walking, cooking, farming. I'd read somewhere that in all of Europe, the Spaniards ranked themselves highest in sleep satisfaction. Meanwhile, we'd never slept less.

The village rooster didn't help, of course, nor did the dogs living next door, whose call-and-response with Chanticleer created a rush-ing pandemonium of first wakefulness that sounded an alarm. The sun was pulled a little higher on its string, and some days, not more than fifteen minutes after sunrise, we could feel the heat pulsing through the walls, as if we lived in some fairy tale about the strangers who came to town and chose, to the confusion of the natives around them, to live in a Dutch oven.

At first, time seemed limitless. We threw open the shutters and ogled the view. Having partly eschewed the world of commerce and commodification, I felt the book could wait a couple of weeks while we settled and explored, which was part of the book, too. And while I waited for my buddy Carlos, whom I'd hired to help for a month. As it was, my Spanish had progressed from *inexistente á rudimentario* during *seis* weeks in Salamanca, but I was a long way from understanding anything obvious, let alone nuanced.

Our arrival coincided with Ambrosio having work—a stretch of truck trips—that took him out of town. In his absence, I soon found that our version of village life organized itself around the ascendancy and final daily importance of doing nothing. Sitting on benches, ambling aimlessly, going to the bar or the *pantano,* the swimming hole, pretty soon *that* became everything. I was the busiest hombre in town, cramming in tons of back-to-back nothing. In that newly made space an alternative reality rose, a nest knitted by ambitionless being, the sound of breathing and laughter, and behind it, an all-engulfing silence. Would it be possible to submit blank pages, ask my editor for an earnest edit of those blank pages to include no marks at all—and hours on the phone saying nothing to each other—and then publish it at three hundred pages of white space, regarded as the ultimate bit of performance art in our harried times, *The Book of Silence and Nothing: A Meditation in White*? I feared ruining the best, wordless part of this world by trying to capture it in words.

The morning hours were luxurious, if touched by the faint boredom of another planless day sprawling before us. What would we do? Who knew? There was no phone ringing, no e-mail to answer, no immediate deadlines pressing. There was only this feathery weightlessness, the exhilarating and claustrophobic prospect of permanent together time. Wasn't this exactly what I'd been after?

At first the magic moments were plentiful. Unhurried breakfast seemed a surreal phenomenon, languorous conversation a gift. A lot of time was spent trying to decipher the news on Radio Cinco. If the heat was reasonable, Sara and I might trade off runs out to the *fuente,* a spring directed by pipe into a rectangular stone catch tucked into a ravine on that vast plain above the village.* Nearby, sunflowers burst their yellow petals; a small hill rose with an ancient stand of majestic *nogales* trees. Something about the place, stranded out in all of that openness, moonlike but with the grace of shade and the music of burbling water—the stone cistern always full, but somehow never overflowing, the sunflowers nodding yes and hello—always inspired a deep sense of well-being and peace.

If the heat was instantly too much, we'd go to Plan B, run a hose from the garage to a little plastic pool we'd bought, and let the kids splash around. We followed exercise with a slow breakfast of stewed fruits and vegetables along with cereal or eggs, and coffee for the adults, dressed ourselves, and took our first tentative steps out into the morning, where as the hours ticked by, certain less idyllic truths about our family reared their ugly heads: May and I were known to turn surly when not properly fed and hydrated; Leo became slightly irascible when separated from his baseball or when people tried to redirect him away from his extended knight fantasies. And Sara was known to hit a point on the hottest days where, with all energy sucked from her body, she might refuse one further step.

About baseball: We'd arrived in Spain at the height of Leo's fixation on the game,† thus he demanded to play daily. After breakfast he

---

* Eventually I would sort out some of the names for the land, and I offer one last refresher here: The land above—what was identified as *arriba* by those in the village—was also the *páramo,* the high flatland. The undulating land below the village was called the *coterro,* but also where it dipped was called the *ribera,* which also described the previously mentioned *barcos.*

† He was a doomed Yankees fan living in Red Sox territory back home, and I could never get over how often people, old and young, went out of their way at the doughnut shop to disparage the Yankees cap of a three-year-old, as if the kid were the conglomerated reincarnation of Babe Ruth/Joe DiMaggio/Mickey Mantle/

and I would mosey from the house—me with the mitts and a ball, him dragging a small bat—and trundle through the village, stopping here and there on our zigzag to the *frontón*.*

Ten feet or so from our front door came our first stop, a quick hello to Don Honorato as he stood each morning watering his lawn. Don Honorato was a beautiful old man, with neatly parted white hair. Short, with the bearing of an eagle, he stood stock-straight with rubber hose in hand, water glubbing forth, wearing two pairs of chinos for some reason I never quite gleaned. (You could see the one beneath hiked higher at the belt.)

"This is a lawn of courage," he announced the first time we met. "A lawn of miracles. How can it survive heat as hot as this?" He gestured at the patch of green beneath his feet. "My wife loved this little lawn."

She was gone now, and he was still in mourning. They'd been famous in Guzmán for their dancing. They'd won local competitions. There were trophies to prove it. In a village this small, they'd been Fred and Ginger, dancing not only the *jotas* but the fandango, the bolero, the *zambra*. Now he stood alone, examining the clumps beneath his feet. On this dusty plateau, his was one of the rare lawns of

---

Bucky Dent and every other reminted Yankee who'd at one time or another eviscerated the dreams of Red Sox Nation. Here in Spain, he refused to remove the plastic Yankees batting helmet that had become his signature. He ate in it, played in it, tried to sleep in it—and no one cared, or knew what team it was. They just treated him like a three-year-old.

* The *frontón* was a relic from the times of Franco. It was said that El Caudillo had provided these handball courts for all the northern towns—and most especially in Basque country—in hopes that people would forget some of the atrocities that had been done unto them during the Civil War. One can almost imagine the Caudillo's line of thinking: *Remember the bombing of civilians by the Luftwaffe at Guernica, the rubbled town, the hundreds of innocent dead? Well, it's time for amends, folks . . .*

The *frontón* in Guzmán stood at the base of the village, to the south, about halfway between Abel's soldering shed and Ambrosio's long metal *caseta*. It was L-shaped, with high green walls. No one really played handball here anymore, but the shepherds kept their sheep in its penned-off area, which meant the ground was covered at all times with little pellets of sheep shit.

green grass, perhaps only ten by ten feet but as thick as the hair on his head. We left him there, murmuring to the grass.

Along we went—fifty yards to the end of Calle Francisco Franco, then a right-hand turn skirting the side of the *palacio* to its front stairwell. This was the spot where, more often than not, we might encounter Clemente, another old man who always seemed to step out of the same shed, a bit more spry than Don Honorato, taller, lankier, same head of thick hair, clad in checked, collared shirts, with loads of advice and dire warnings. "You must remember to lock your doors!" he scolded, in exasperation. "And put down your shutters in the heat of day!" Of course, I never asked how he knew our doors were never locked, as I never asked anything, finding it impossible to get a word in edgewise. At the end of his diatribe, he'd look down on Leo in his batting helmet, perhaps convinced the poor boy had a head injury of some sort, and speak kindly, almost softly to him, taking pity. *"Precioso,"* he said, and fished a sucker from his pocket, then knelt to look him in the eye. "Hombre, I have a little secret for you. In this place, you will burn up under that shiny hat of yours. Take water as often as you can."

We continued our strolling, for that is exactly what it was: *strolling.* This was not something I did in real life, either. It was always more like "rushing," or "hustling," or "guy-walking-like-weird-Olympic-walker." Sometimes, for no reason, I'd break out running, just to get between two points more quickly, because I was always behind, or so it seemed. But strolling—this was really something *astonishing*!* The sky overhead kaleidoscoped with clouds and colors, flecks of orange, blue, green; the road below our feet was etched with fault lines and signs of life. I took my son's lead in this happy distraction. Look at the ants, in the middle of their own rush hours, streaming over the rocks!

---

* Writes Henry David Thoreau in his famous essay "Walking": "I think I cannot preserve my health and spirits, unless I spend four hours a day at least—and it is commonly more than that—sauntering through the woods and over the hills and fields, absolutely free from all worldly engagements." He also advises one to "walk like a camel, which is said to be the only beast which ruminates when walking."

And over here—a piece of aquamarine glass! Now we are collecting glass, except we can't find any more, so we're collecting rocks. How many rocks can I carry? As many as Leo hands me . . . *seventeen, eighteen, nineteen* . . . I will leave them in a pile now. He doesn't want them left in a pile. Now I'm strolling with my arms full of rocks, with my son who wears a helmet to protect his head injury, down to the *frontón* covered with sheep shit, to play baseball.

Just like any other day.

We passed the women sweeping their front stoops. This was a competition, really, to see who could appear most fervent and fastidious in the daily ablution of the home. Points seemed to be awarded for the generation of the biggest dust cloud, furiousness in the act of sweeping, and general effort as determined by most times blowing loose strands of hair from face. Caught in the act, the women, in their worn dresses and aprons, would pause, only slightly embarrassed, and once they sighted Leo, come forward into the street to pinch his cheek. "Oh, *cariño*," they chirped. *"Tan serio con su cachiporra para cazar!"* Yes, he *was* so serious dragging that cudgel for hunting! Though I knew next to nothing about these women and their lives, about the frustrations of living in a rigidly patriarchal society, about the loneliness of their days, the scratchy radio inside echoing to the street, knew nothing about the loss that striated their lives—the Civil War, the hardships under Franco, the societal shifts that set the last lance in a village such as this—I think I loved them best, for their sheer exuberance when confronted with a fair-haired beacon of youth. They couldn't contain themselves, and, fluttering like pigeons in their own dust, they shared a kindliness that seemed unwarranted.

On we went, the road gathering a current, Leo's hand in mine, then drawn away, running fingertips over every fleck of mica in the crude stone walls that hid courtyards full of chickens and hung laundry. Bowlegged, he veered to and fro, chased cats, pocketed treasures, and froze in awe, eyes wide, mouth in an O when white clouds—the sheep herd—came up through town, led by the three Basque brothers in their Che Guevara T-shirts. There were forty or fifty fluffy animals, smelling of lanolin, tufted with coarse fiber, flowing past him, while he stood lost up to his shoulders in fleece. That road from our temporary home to the *frontón* may have measured half a mile, but it seemed forever. We were a father and son, bathed in that eternal Castilian light. His hand slipped back into mine, and we carried on.

When the stone walls fell away, the vineyards lay before us, the grapes hidden deep in the vines, trying to keep cool. Everything tucked itself away from the heat. Leaves curled like withered hands; the green fields seemed to wilt toward brown, the grain going critical, until somewhere out there, at allotted intervals, huge sprinklers sputtered on, and everything momentarily revived in a false rainfall. Then the wheel of fire caught again, and heat came pounding back from heaven, flattening the life out of every breathing thing.

We played not on the *frontón* surface but in the shade behind the high wall, in the dirt and rubble. We replayed the same game over and over again, ad infinitum, way up there on the Meseta, a game from thousands of miles away. The Yankees facing the Red Sox, a close contest to the ninth inning, though Leo did most of the batting, and, coming to understand the game and its language, a lot of the talking, too. "Jeter to the plate . . . and *strike two*! . . . Jeter at the bat . . . and *strike three*! . . . Jeter puts on his batting glove . . . and *strike four*! . . ." I threw thousands of pitches behind that wall blocking the sun, and Leo, not quite grasping the concept of a "ball," swung at every one of them. These games always had to end on a climactic moment, a clutch homer, an against-the-odds single to bring in the winning run. And afterward, Leo insisted on celebrations, something at which he excelled. So we threw hats in the air, ran into each other's arms, ruffled each other's hair. Farmers passed on tractors; the shepherds returned; someone schlepped off to his vineyard or out to hunt rabbit.

Then my son replaced his batting helmet and we dragged ourselves back up through town. Leo could scarcely walk. It was blindingly hot, and wet tendrils of hair stuck to his forehead. His cheeks flamed red. This was usually when the whining began—and the parental bribery, too, incentivizing his progress with a highly prized Spanish lollipop. "If you make it to the palace," I told him, "you can have a Chupa Chup." And so we ended up together, sitting on the shaded church steps, the pocked limestone cool against our backs as we sucked the last drops from our bottle of water, and the lollipop appeared. Nearing the midday hour, nothing moved in the streets, not even the cats. The sun was its own kind of death. Two hundred yards from home, it was Everest, and we couldn't find the energy to make it.

Eventually came a hint of the *comida,* the scent of eggs frying, a piece of meat. Somewhere, the *thup* of a cork signaled a cold wine being poured into a *porrón.* We got up and trudged the last inclines, came through the door, climbed the stairs, entered the kitchen to find Sara and May, both flush from their own adventures, May tottering here and there, squawking her first words: *hola, agua.* Her brother called her name, rolling a rubber ball down the long hallway, and she came waddling by as if blown by a huge wind. We began cooking the *comida* while the children played, loath to increase the temperature in the house, and yet that's what people did here, didn't they?* We nibbled on cheese and thin slices of chorizo, nuts and olives, then served plates of

---

* Well, no, in fact, they didn't. We would come to find out that in most of the homes there existed an abbreviated kitchen downstairs, just a galley space for the making of food. This was to keep the cooking—and especially the heat, for nothing was air-conditioned—well away from the living area. Eventually, Clemente shared this insight with us, too, though again, we did not take his advice, cooking in the kitchen on the second floor, which led to the eventual violation of another sacred rule: Because of the heat, we switched our *comida* (the Spaniard's big lunch-dinner) with our *cena* (the Spaniard's smaller dinner-lunch), usually eating the less labor-intensive meal at midday, while our neighbors stuck to their big meal at lunch. Our secret shift represented classified information that we promised not to share with anyone, though I suspect Clemente knew from the first, just by sniffing the air around our abode. One day, when he could stand it no longer, he came to our door, knocked while walking in, and summoned me to behold the cavelike room on the bottom floor that was meant for cooking. "This is where you move your stove, hombre," he said, exasperated, but he knew we were hopeless, and I think something broke in him, then, in regard to us. He summoned his usual goodwill when he saw us and still offered advice—because he was genetically programmed to do so—but he never again let himself believe that we might actually take it.

chuletas and salad, or fish and rice, abbreviating and amending for the kids. Satiated, we led the children to their room, lowered the metal blinds, and let them nap.

They slept in old beds in an unadorned white concrete-walled room. They could have been mistaken for wee Castilians until that moment when the lava light pried their eyelids open again. Then their voices filled the house with *hola,* baseball, *agua.* Leo in his batting helmet, May goosing around in a chubby diaper. New plans were made, and soon we were out in the streets, down to the bar, up to Ambrosio's *bodega,* to the *pantano.* Doing nothing in that dream. Everything.

I'D TOLD AMBROSIO ABOUT this proposed book of mine, or book of his. (So what was it: mine or his?) He understood, of course, what had delivered me here in the first place: his cheese, Páramo de Guzmán. And then what had brought me back: his telling of a slow-food fable gone so awry that murder hung in the balance. I suspect he was flattered by my interest, which he gauged by the questions I asked. And I asked about everything—the fields, his philosophy, Castilian customs, history, and stories—but not as a journalist, it seemed. As an interested party, as a would-be participant.

During our first weeks in Guzmán, then, Ambrosio did a most extraordinary thing: He appeared at the house one morning and asked me to hold out my hand. "*Para tí,* Michael,"* he said, laying a heavy object in my palm. It was dark metal, a couple pounds and ruler length, with a clef at the end. The key to his telling room. "There's a full *porrón* on the table," he said. "You'll write our book there."

It wasn't the first time he'd told me how it was going to be—and it would hardly be the last—but, regardless, the gesture was laden

---

* He pronounced my name *My-kull,* dragging out the *L* sound, giving it ululation and lullaby. *My,* for I was his, and *kull,* conjuring "skull," or "my empty one," which he filled with words and axioms.

with meaning. I looked at the key in my hand and back at Ambrosio. "Really?" I said.

"Hombre," he said, as if he didn't want to hear another word about it.

Ambrosio became our guardian angel. When he wasn't driving his truck on a long haul or out in the fields, he might pull up before the house and issue all sorts of exhortations and invitations: to his house for lunch, to this or that village fiesta, to the bullfights, to a famous monastery or village. He wove us into the fabric of his every day. And the kids adored him, if they couldn't quite figure him out: the giant, ceaselessly talking in that smoky baritone. He mesmerized them. He'd lift them from the ground, fling them around, and loft them to his shoulders, and they would appear wide-eyed, uncertain, looking to their parents, who smiled reassuringly. He spoke to them in encouraging tones, but never pandered. If they fussed, he would drop a pearl of folklore on them—one they didn't understand but for the mock-seriousness of his voice—and their eyes would go wide again. *"Chicos,"* he said, "don't let the wolves hear you."

When Carlos arrived with his family,* he and I spent more of the day with Ambrosio while the mothers and children found adventures of their own. Sometimes Ambrosio led us to the bar at 11:00 A.M. for fortification; sometimes we were in the fields until after sundown. There was no guessing what the day would bring. A run to the grain-sorting machine, an ancient mechanical contraption that sepa-

---

* As luck had it, I'd first met Carlos because my wife was best college friends with Carlos's wife, Melissa. In fact, the two were part of a five-woman posse known as the "Dzawns" (short for "Dzawns") and each bore a tattoo on her ankle of a tiny fish blowing bubbles, as part of some secret Skull-and-Bones pact their husbands would never find out—as if their husbands cared to find out, because they didn't. Might the number of bubbles signify the number of people they'd killed? Probably, but who cared, really. There was so little care about this that I'm ending the footnote *now*. And *now*. Unless the bubbles stood for something stranger than murder. Like the digging up of graves. Or the interstate transfer of spleens. How many bodies did they leave in hotel rooms, in tubs packed in ice? We'll never know, but for the tattoos that no one cares about. At all. *Now*.

rated seeds. To Abel's workshop, where Ambrosio stood among blow-torch sparks discussing an invention he'd sketched on a napkin, an attachment to a tractor that, to Ambrosio's mind, would improve the efficacy of planting seeds. To lunch in Roa, to meet a *majo* with whom Ambrosio was talking about purchasing grapes. The only constant was the *bodega*. It was nearly guaranteed that at some point along the way we'd end up in the telling room with Ambrosio holding forth, in great word gusts of appreciation for the joys of Castile. He slurped wine and let out wondrous sighs, saying, "Its taste reminds me of the old people who once sat here. It's a privilege to drink this wine." It was a privilege to eat the almonds and the chorizo and *jamón,* too. It was a privilege to sit on one's derriere in the telling room and get pleasantly soused while hearing stories. It was a privilege to walk this land, to live in this place, to watch the grain grow.

Each day Ambrosio added more to his *"grandísima filosofía de vida,"* the stylings of which glorified anything representing an antidote to the shrink-wrapped, digital mess of the modern world: an old farm implement, for instance; a certain funny *cuento* about an ancestor;* a meal from the field graced with a bursting tomato or sweet

---

* Ambrosio's great-uncle was known for his good wine, which he sold out of his *bodega* (Ambrosio's *bodega* now) in this strategic way: Some shepherds or field hands might come knocking at the door, and great-uncle would happily greet them. His clientele was often strapped for cash, so he had to devise a way to make them pay more for the wine than they might otherwise. He started by having them taste an admittedly weak wine, while disparaging it. "It's a pity you don't have a little more for the good wine, it's *very* good," he would say, then: "Would you like a taste? It costs nothing to taste." Great-uncle would disappear to a cask deeper in the cave, then materialize with a *porrón,* and the shepherds would drink, agreeing that yes, it was a very excellent wine. But when great-uncle named the price, it was four times the amount of the first. The shepherds would appear crestfallen, and Ambrosio's great-uncle would let a beat pass, then light up with an idea, snapping his fingers. "I have just the thing," he would say. "Come with me." Then he would lead them outside, following a trail that circled the hill. He would walk slowly, saying, "I think you will be very pleased. A nice wine, in between the two others." Partway around he would stop, and if the day was hot, mutter the words *"¡Puta madre!,"* wipe his brow, then pull from his pocket a piece of cheese—the family cheese—and offer his clients a piece, and then another. The cheese was buttery

green pepper. These were the simple, exquisite testaments that he looked for at every turn. And found. If only in Guzmán.

His philosophy might have been reduced to two words: Give praise.

Even the town of Aranda, a mere half hour away, posed a threat to his *grandísima filosofía*. Once, when we stopped at a supermarket there together, Ambrosio seemed lost in the aisles, in the pale-purply klieg light glow of commerce. I couldn't tell if it wasn't just an act—after all, how many forty-something men have never broken the plane of a supermarket's electric doors?—but the moment did have the feel of someone touching down in dusty, cosmic boots, then traipsing lost through a plentiful wilderness of dish soaps and multicolored cereal boxes. In the wine aisle he asked, "Why would anyone spend ten euros on a bottle of wine when the stuff you make at home has feeling?"

He made a point of stopping at the cheese counter and asking after what they had. He listened, shaking his head gravely. He said something I missed, which made the two women behind the counter laugh, and turned back and mumbled something about their cheese being crap. Come to think of it, that's actually what he must have said to them: *Don't you have anything better than this crap?* But he always did it in such a disarming way, with a wink that invited everyone in. It wasn't a threat; it was irreverence meant as humor. Before retreating from the store, he stopped to survey some ham sealed in plastic. He touched the smooth packaging with his finger. He lifted it to his nose and could smell nothing.

---

and tangy, setting off a flood of taste. Then great-uncle quickly led the shepherds into another telling room, one actually connected through the hill to the antechamber of the first telling room, where the wine casks were kept. He disappeared, poured the cheap wine all over again, and this time the shepherds, or field hands, would shake their heads, yes, yes, more than we wanted to spend but for this wine, very nice, very fine. Great-uncle would charge half of what he'd asked for the expensive wine and double the cheap wine, which now posed as the sensible, tasty median. And in this way, thanks to the cheese, great-uncle sold cask after cask of dreggish wine for double the cost.

"*¡Puta madre!*" he said, dropping the packet back in the refrigerator case.

Scenes like this triggered my indignation, too, even though as a boy of suburbia I grew up on plastic-wrapped singles of Kraft American cheese and Steak-umms. Nonetheless: What was up with this lame ham? What was up with these less-than-magical, half-assed cheeses? Didn't anybody respect tradition, making food by hand, the slow way? Hadn't anyone frittered away a Sunday afternoon at the *bodega* gorging themselves on the bounty of the land—the fizzy wine, the beautifully constructed chorizo? What was it with humanity, what secrets had we lost by disrespecting the Old Castilian and embracing Slurpees of otherworldly fluorescent colors? "When you put something alive in your mouth, it makes you more alive," Ambrosio declared. And I had repeated it to my wife, to friends, to whoever would listen. For a while there, I became Ambrosio's mini-me, espousing the simple sayings and irreverent gospel of the big man, repeating his nuggets of wisdom. And somewhere along the way, he must have sensed more than my interest, he must have intuited my malleability. He was going to make me the eighty-first citizen of an eighty-person village, and I would tell his story to the world.

And for a moment I wanted it more than he did.

12

THE LAWSUIT

". . . 42 percent potato . . ."

IT WAS SPRING IN THE DARK TIME AFTER THE DEATH OF HIS CHEESE— and another night atop Mon Virgo, drinking and cursing, psyching himself to kill. Ambrosio Molinos was like the jilted lover, the bereft, boozy father gazing upon his taken child through the fence of the state orphanage. The story couldn't be rewritten, for it was always the same: the same betrayal, the same loss, the same grudge.[*]

What they were doing to his cheese was unconscionable. The in-

---

[*] From the Middle English *gruggen* or *grucchen,* and the Old High German *grunnizon,* "to grumble or complain"—an examination of the word's sedimentation suggests an emotional deadlock also, two deer stuck in antlered impasse, in thick mud that congeals as winter arrives and freezes them there. I once heard a story when visiting my father's ancestral village in Sicily about a very old lady I saw caning down the road, then up a steep incline to the cemetery there. It was said that at her tortoise pace, the walk from home to cemetery and back took up to six hours. What grief inspired such travail: the visit to a departed child or husband? No, no, that wasn't it at all, I was corrected in rather stentorian tones. *Astio,* bitter hatred. It was her archenemy up in that cemetery. Rain or shine, the old woman walked every day to her grave site, just to spit on it one more time.

troduction of inferior milk meant an essential molecular change in the milk that made the cheese, but more, it gave the name Páramo de Guzmán an empty lyricism. Soon there was nothing of the *páramo,* or Guzmán, in the cheese, which meant to Ambrosio that the cheese was officially deceased. "The dead cheese," he called it, or "the soulless cheese." The whole operation, to his mind, was an empty front, a *desastre ateo,* a godless disaster.

He also knew, or assumed, that the workers—he would never dignify them with the sobriquet "cheesemakers," those who had replaced his happy brood at the factory—were clock punchers, like everyone these days, there to do their time and collect a paycheck. How could such automatons make something remarkable, let alone create a delirious, sublime cheese of memory and strength? They, too, were thieves, if unconscious ones, afflicted with the disease of mediocrity. After all, why were you put on this earth, to serve humanity or the *jefe*'s bottom line?

All of this lamenting could bring nothing back now. Ambrosio spit in the wind and resolved himself to it. He fell into his Pathfinder, torqued the ignition, dropped a heavy foot on the accelerator, and the car jumped, shooting loose gravel from underneath the back tires. The *puta,* the unworthy sot—it would feel so good to crush him. It was the hour just before dawn, and the road to Julián led past his own house. Though he had misgivings, he entered one last time, to say goodbye. So here was the dividing line between everything that he could have been and everything he was about to become, between a virtuous life and one of calumny. Or maybe they weren't that far apart, really, and there was no dividing line.

When he came through the front door, he could hear the deep breathing of his sleeping children chorusing through the house. In the dim light, he could see the certificates and medals hung over the desk, all won by his faithful cheese. He walked the long hallway to the back bedrooms, pushed open the door on his twelve-year-old daughter's room, and saw her eyes tracking beneath the lids in some dream that had nothing to do with cheese—or his rage. Her art covered the walls, but it was one earlier drawing that caught his eye that morning, one of her first. This daughter of his, Asunita, had dutifully painted a tin of the cheese, then written in her best hand: "Páramo Guzmán." Yes, the iconic sheep looked a little like a turtle with table legs, but it was so true and heartfelt, rendered in her eight-year-old hand, full of such promise, and the word at the bottom scrawled in script said "Artesano."

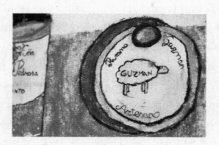

Ambrosio regarded this daughter, drooling slightly in sleep, then gazed at the painting again. Here in this house, nothing stood between him and his daughter, or his sons, or wife. Here no cage or fence or signed contract separated him from what he loved most. It was important to differentiate: The cheese embodied an ideal of love, and he'd loved the ideal. He'd poured himself into that ideal, and animated the cheese with it. But it was his family that loved *him*.

The realization was both profound and inconsequential, for in that moment he wasn't suddenly freed of grief or sadness. Nor his mourning, or pain. He still wanted to kill—yes, he very much did—but what seeped in was this notion of belonging to a collective, his family, and the fear of losing them. After all, this was the same family who'd given everything to the cheese, too.[*] Minutes earlier he'd been resolved to kill a man, and now he unresolved himself.

He made no promises for tomorrow, that he might not try again, but for this morning, at least, Julián would live.

---

[*] Ambrosio would later say: "Maybe I realized I wasn't alone. My best memories of the cheese included my children, when they were very young, putting labels on the tins, decorating them. My wife had named it. This didn't happen to me; it happened to *us*. And we needed to get through it together."

SOMEWHERE IN THEIR ILLUSTRIOUS past, the Molinos family had been milliners in Aragón, and with the rise of Spain their business had prospered and grown. Eventually the family had migrated to Castile, to be closer to the sheep that grazed on the Meseta—and over time, through marriage and wealth, had acquired vast holdings of land, including tracts in Madrid that later became the Chamartín neighborhood. Ambrosio's *patrimonio* had included the fields around Guzmán, and when the bank claimed those to repay his debts, he lost one more part of his family's legacy.

Now he drove in a borrowed car from the slopes of the Guadarrama, teeming with boar and weasel, into exurbia, and then the city itself. He entered Madrid on Paseo de la Castellana and drifted through the bustling capital, past Bernabéu stadium, where Real Madrid played soccer, and on to the Plaza de Colón, sluicing past fountains, foreign embassies, and government ministries. It wasn't a trip Ambrosio relished. The baroque buildings evoked that hollowed-out feeling: Among this many people he always felt alone.[*]

Here was an irony: He didn't have enough money to buy a coffee, and the lawyer's office was situated near the Ritz hotel, the Prado, and the capital's grand park known as El Retiro ("The Lungs of Madrid"). In the hub of Castilian commerce, among luxury apartments, boutiques, and high-powered corporate suites, came the rough-and-tumble, bare-knuckle reality of a modern life Ambrosio eschewed, the business lunches and drinks in fine places after work, the fast talk and

---

[*] Ambrosio later described to me the arc of thought and emotion that had brought him to the city: "For years I planned Julián's death, killing him every single night. Every single night I would create a different movie in my mind, trying to settle on one. I would picture what I was going to do—grab him, put a bag over his head, etc. On a full moon, I would go to Mon Virgo, smoke a couple of cigarettes, and start thinking, 'I want to kill him, but I don't want to. I can't do it, I shouldn't do it.' At the end of the two years that I wanted to kill him, I discarded my personal vengeance and replaced it with a lawsuit. But then it became more difficult to resist the temptation to kick the guy's ass."

instant gratification. Time moved in spasms, businessmen gilled for their bloodthirsty profit, with no fidelity to any idea, furthering their own names and wealth. At least that's how Ambrosio, the Old Castilian, saw it.

Ambrosio found the lawyer in his office, decorated with oriental rugs and pastoral paintings. The man projected an air of equanimity and well-worn wealth. In this cocoon of reassurance, in the calm created by the lawyer's inviting, rather efficient manner, Ambrosio told his story, then listened intently for the possibility of justice. The law of the land, with its precise volumes and impartial scales, would weigh the matter of Julián's deception, said the attorney, but hearing events as Ambrosio unfolded them, he believed there'd been malfeasance, that Ambrosio had a winnable case. As he warned his client, though, justice was a slow-moving process. And there were several issues here to parse out, including alleged fraud and the recovery of back wages. Due to the intricacies of the law, these would have to be broken into separate proceedings. But he was willing to try.

When Ambrosio left that day, he found himself inflating with the slightest hope again. He'd been offered an alternative plot—legal revenge—and grabbed hold, as if to keep himself from falling into that cistern of roiling must.

Still, the lawyer was going to cost money. In order to pay his fee, Ambrosio was soon hauling grain north out of Spain, through parts of Italy, on to Germany. His travels took him to the Black Sea. He waited at border crossings with other truck drivers from the Ukraine, Romania, and Poland. Ambrosio, like most enlightened Castilians, saw himself as a citizen of the world, for every Spaniard knows that Spanish blood is mixed liberally with Arabic and Jewish blood—and that of any invading tribe from the Phoenicians to the Visigoths.

Sunflowers and cocoa to Holland, juices to Austria, wine to Koblenz, chocolate back to Spain: Driving a truck suited Ambrosio just fine. "It's like a research grant to study other cultures," he would tell friends.

He traveled with a store of victuals—including bottles of his homemade wine—to avoid a culinary predicament in which he might be forced to consume fast food. He packed morning eggs from the chickens, and some excellent sausage made by a good friend, and a special jar of fish conserve. Instead of eating a hamburger or "some kind of shit meal," he would pull out a camping stove he kept in the cab and scramble some eggs. In gas station parking lots, he could be found at twilight, gobbling a plate with chorizo. It was part of his mission, to be that man at the stove in the shadows of the neon flow of modernity, to practice what he called *enlazar,* or enlacing, the bringing together, the intertwining of nature and nutrition, the old and the new. At the closest bar, where he always went to take his coffee, he met people easily, traveling bard that he was, and he collected some of their stories, too.

He told one of his own about arriving at a place—a castle-factory, he recalled—somewhere in Germany, and a small man—a dwarf?— magically appearing before him, allowing him through the gates for his pickup of Pringles potato chips. In that odd wonderland, Ambrosio was taken to a bar where he spoke nothing but Spanish while being met with nothing but some dialect of German, and yet never, he said, had he felt such a connection as that day, with that dwarf and his brethren, as they spoke their own languages and understood everything about each other.[*]

[*] Later, when I did some investigation into the origin of Pringles, I couldn't find a German castle-factory that belonged to the Pringle family—but traced the chip to its Ohio inventor, Alexander Liepa, a last name of Latvian and Lithuanian extraction that belonged to a food scientist who worked for Procter & Gamble, the company that began selling the potato chips[†] nationally in the mid-1970s. The name for the product had been picked from a Cincinnati phone book street address, Cincinnati having been settled by Germans.[‡] Of most interest was the fact that the inventor of the distinctive red tube,[§] Frederic J. Baur, asked to have a portion of his ashes buried in one of his cans. Had Ambrosio lied?[||] No—I certainly don't believe so. Or maybe I had something to do with it. It's just that wherever he'd actually been, even if it was half in his imagination, it didn't seem to be a Pringles castle-factory.

[†] In England, where potato chips are called "potato crisps," the saddle-shaped[#] snack food was deemed by the High Court of London to hold too little potato content to qualify as a "crisp," but was rather a British "chip," which would have made it susceptible to a 17.5 percent sales tax.[**] Pringles lawyers claimed that the product

The downside to roaming all that open road was all that time Ambrosio had to contend with memories of his deceased cheese—and also the memories of his oldest, closest friend, Julián—memories that recurred when he was most trying to forget. On the horizon, in a bright sunset, he might glimpse that one scribbled signature on a piece of paper, loops of ink hanging him from the clouds, again and again.

The road does this to a person, impels him backward into memory as he hurtles forward, the episodes of a life flickering in the passing fauna of the land: Here now is the *caseta,* the little stable across from his parents' villa, light outlining the cracks in the door as a man labors late into the night for that first taste of ancient cheese; here are

---

doesn't look, feel, or taste like a chip, arguing that potato chips "give a sharply crunchy sensation under the tooth and have to be broken down into jagged pieces when chewed." "It is totally different with a Pringle," they argued, "indeed a Pringle is designed to melt down on the tongue."

\# The shape is a hyperbolic paraboloid, reportedly designed by supercomputer. Meanwhile the saddle-shaped food product is only 42 percent potato, the rest composed of a paste of wheat starch and flour, vegetable oils and emulsifiers.

** Judge Nicholas Warren ruled that Pringles did not qualify as a "crisp," but the tax office exempted Procter & Gamble from paying the tax. Pringles are sold in one hundred countries and gross over a billion dollars a year. Some of the flavors include zesty lime and chili, screamin' dill pickle, chili cheese dog, ketchup, pizzalicious, soft-shell crab, grilled shrimp (the chips are pink), and seaweed (green).

‡ The word "pringle" actually seems to possess Welsh roots, meaning *prencyll,* a hazel-wood, from the words *pren,* a wood, and *cyll* or *coll,* hazel. Pringle is also an obsolete Scottish coin and the name of a luxury knitwear company named after its founder, Robert Pringle, in 1815.††

†† Now owned by the Hong Kong–based S. C. Fang and Sons, the clothes company released a cheeky cartoon video, describing in a nutshell the forces of mass production. "We take the wool from the belly of the goats because the rest of the wool gets really manky," it begins. "Manky wool is no good to us because we have really high standards." Then, it describes the process by which its products are made: "And then the yarn gets put on to bobbins. And the bobbins get put on to bobbin trees. And all the bobbins start spinning. . . . In the olden days, before we had the machine, we had old ladies sitting there knitting all the jumpers and cardigans by hand but nowadays we make about seven hundred billion jumpers and cardigans a day, and if an old lady tried to knit that many her hands would catch fire and she'd die. Any-

the sheep shuffling on hooves, awaiting an early-morning milking in the filmy light of the barn; here are the strange cars drifting up the narrow lane and into town, windows descending, asking after the rumor of a certain cheese said to be made in the village.

---

way," the video concludes, "... probably everybody else should be banned from making jumpers, and just make socks, because they're crap."

§ The iconic cartoon figure on the red tube with parted bangs and a big brush-stache is known as Julius Pringles, who looks like a German butcher with a red bow tie.

‖ "Lie" is such an incendiary word for a storyteller. His product is packaged and designed to melt on the tongue, to be pleasing. To that end, he offers what appears to be a potato chip or crisp, perhaps idiosyncratically saddle shaped, an *amuse-bouche* to entertain and delight.‡‡

‡‡ One last note here: When I went back to my transcripts to find this story, it varied from what I'd written in my notes. There, I found the phrase "story of Pringles factory," but also evidence that suggested that it might have been "a juice factory." Ambrosio claimed it was in "southern Germany" and at another point "near Vienna." (A Google search reveals a Pringles factory in Belgium.) The word "dwarf" was used by me, apparently confirmed by Ambrosio, but then he never used the word when he told the story. "All the people here were very small and really round and very colorful," said Ambrosio, "like, very red with suspenders and hats. And everybody with their thumbs in their suspenders, and smiles."

What was the explanation for these differences? First, there was the ever-digressive, often-fractured, footnote-within-footnote nature of Ambrosio's stories, which meant that those stories were often revisited with subtle shifts. At the same time he might answer a direct question from me as a "yes" or a "no," perhaps without having heard the question at all, but just trying to rush the story free of my pesky interruptions, of which there were many. Once, in fact, when I interrupted him yet again with another detail-oriented question, he finally lost his patience. "What is it with you, My-kull?" he boomed. "You *always* ask the color of the shirt I was wearing when this or that happened. Sometimes, when you tell stories, you need to use your imagination, hombre!"

As to whether he visited a Pringles potato chip factory in a town of dwarves, my journalistic inclination is to say it was a juice factory with "small people," that this entire footnote is built on the shape-shifting nature of truth and language, the gaps in communication, as well as the journalist's frenzy to nail down a patina of facts and the storyteller's gift for imbuing events with supernatural qualities and "mythological observation." And yet, if put to it, I have no doubt that Ambrosio could lead us all to a village of small people somewhere in southern Germany/Belgium, and much of it might be exactly as he said. The question remains, however: What percent?

Sometimes another vivid flashback played like a film in the windowed screens of the truck, from a time during Páramo de Guzmán's heyday, when the cheese was still being made in the stable across from his parents' house. Ambrosio's idea for expansion had been, he thought, inspired: If the cheese could be made in Guzmán, by the *people* of Guzmán, perhaps an opportunity existed to rehabilitate the *palacio* and turn it into a factory.

With its two towers and an imposing limestone facade, the *palacio* was a no-frills castle. Yet it anchored the village, serving as a secular nexus to the church's religious one. At some point the *palacio* had been left to disintegrate, becoming the public property of Guzmán itself. But it seemed such a tragedy: Gazing up through the gutted, four-story carcass, one could spy patches of sky, birds funneling through torn rafters into the blue. It had become an irretrievable mess, a monument to the disintegration of the village.

Enter Ambrosio's dream: The palace would be revived and transformed into a state-of-the-art facility, with the finest cheesemaking plant, a *bodega* for storage, a tasting room where visitors could try Páramo de Guzmán paired with local wines, and meeting halls to be used by the citizens of Guzmán for town business. Since the village had no money, Ambrosio cast himself in the role of altruistic lord, like the original Guzmán.

Some villagers brought their own interpretation to Ambrosio's designs, however, and as they did, his intentions took on a different quality and texture. By the time his enemies* had their turn with it, the dream was a most pernicious plot indeed. According to them, Ambrosio wanted to turn back time, all right—to the Middle Ages, in-

---

* A group of these formed around his former friend Emilia, the eventual mayor of Guzmán. Perhaps their disagreement had started over religion, Ambrosio disparaging the priest, Emilia as one of the most devout in town rushing to his defense. Perhaps the two were too similar, hard nosed and hard driving, convinced of their rightness, which exacerbated everything. What is true is that over time they entered into an intractable feud, Ambrosio launching his broadsides at her from the bar, while she parried from the streets and town offices.

stalling himself in the *palacio* and ruling Guzmán. Pockets of resistance swiftly formed. A vote was called: yea or nay to the cheese-maker getting the *palacio*. What emerged was a debate not about saving the palace, but about what *los Ambrosios* had up their sleeve.

True, the Molinos clan had long been regarded as Guzmán's de facto royal family—monied, handsome, successful—and had been perceived, rightly or wrongly, as looking down upon their neighbors. Though here in the new Spain the ancient practices of patronage and entitlement existed only in vestigial form, it was an attitude, a bearing, an aristocratic manner that survived. As happens in a small village, the fault line existed. It was just waiting for a seismic event.

Ambrosio was the seismic event. Suddenly the issue became a referendum on *him,* too. Flamboyant, prideful, obstinate—the epitome of Spanish temper and duende*—he wouldn't budge on his plan to restore the *palacio*. Why should he? It would benefit everyone. As much as he was becoming his own cult of personality with Páramo de Guzmán, he was creating a bit of an industry, putting Guzmán on the map as a destination. Travelers might arrive for cheese, but then also stop at the bar for a drink, take note of the village's beauty. Perhaps because the villagers felt Ambrosio thought too much of himself—after all, it was very un-Spanish to elevate yourself over your village†—or because they'd felt inferior to the Molinos family for so long, an unsettling thing began to happen. A campaign was waged against Ambrosio that turned aggressive, and he responded with aggressivity.‡ His

---

* Writes Federico García Lorca: "The duende is a momentary burst of inspiration, the blush of all that is truly alive, all that the performer is creating at a certain moment. The duende resembles what Goethe called 'the demoniacal.' It manifests itself principally among musicians and poets of the spoken word . . . for it needs the trembling of the moment and then a long silence."

† There was a saying that every Spaniard was first from the village, second from the region, and lastly from the country of Spain.

‡ A friend told him: "It's not what you're saying, it's the way you're saying it that's turned people against you. People feel bullied." And perhaps this is where Ambrosio fell short. His proposition was jackbooted: Give me the palace and we'll talk. Instead of: You seem kind of old and tired, Guzmán, let me help you to the

motives—to his mind, absolutely altruistic—were questioned as ulterior and craven. Well, *puta madre,* went the line of argument against Ambrosio, Spain already *had* a king! The communal and sacred monuments of Guzmán were not there to be cherry-picked, for after all, the palace was an emblem that connected Guzmán to Spain, and Spain to its past.

At this time, Ambrosio's family lived in a pretty, three-bedroom home with red-tile roof, the first as you entered the village, set down in a little hollow with neglected tangles of greenery, and, of all luxuries, a swimming pool carved out in the back. On the morning of the vote, Ambrosio left from the front gate of his house as usual—and, to his shock, walked into a blaze of white: fluttering wings of paper like some modern-art installation. He reached down and picked a flyer from the ground.

In the night, something crazy had occurred. Hundreds of leaflets had been spread anonymously, left on walls and doors, littering the streets. The flyer bore a picture of him, Ambrosio Molinos de las Heras, the cheesemaker of Guzmán, and read: DON'T LET HIM STEAL THE PALACE.

He could think of only one word: *Why?* How could one not feel let down and betrayed, surrounded by Lilliputians, all enemies now who would never grasp what could have been? Enough was enough. In the months that followed, with the help of Julián and his new investors, he moved Páramo de Guzmán to the factory in Roa, then moved his family to a house nearby, bitterly washing his hands of the village, while the village washed its hands of him, too.

THE OPEN ROAD FLOWED with memories such as these, as painful as they could be. But then there were loads to haul, pickups and drop-offs to make, schedules to keep. Up in the cab, in the throne room of his

---

bar, buy you a drink, and let's talk about the decrepit *palacio* and ideas for saving our heritage together.

new life, the Meseta gave way to the Pyrenees, rocky mountains gave way to alluvial lowlands and limestone basins, the vineyards and rivers and forests that ran into more mountains—the Alps, Apennines, Carpathians, and Caucasus. Here were the plains of Hungary in gray light, the Crystalline High of Germany in icy blue, the North Sea in green storm. The world was much bigger than Guzmán. Let the village die its own silly death, then. He'd done what he could, offered what he had. And now he had nothing.

He rode, keeping himself company, talking to himself as if split in two, as if he were both driving and riding in the passenger seat. No one could soothe him, he knew, but someday he might soothe himself with a tale that explained it all, a unified theory. Drawn out over Europe, he rehearsed. The body in the passenger seat (himself), listening so intently, believing so fully in himself (the driver self). He built himself back up on the road, and came home, and listened for what the wind said, the vines, the river. He wondered if happiness might ever be possible again, for he hoped it might be. He no longer expected it, of course. He came back to his homeland and drew his head down, waiting for some sort of retributive justice, though. As powerful as he was, he now felt like the victim of everything he'd loved more fiercely than himself.

13

EL CAMPEADOR

". . . he still rides on nights like this."

THE KEY TO THE TELLING ROOM WAS A CONICAL PIECE OF METAL, an artifact, it seemed, from Middle Earth. Because of its weight, I had to steer it with two hands into the lock and then crank it counterclockwise, whereupon the crosshatched wooden door floated open. Up five steps was the telling room itself, with its white stucco walls, benches and table, and the musty smell of hay and wet clay. When I threw open the shutters, the sun and warmth surged, bringing it to life.

Ambrosio had urged me to write here, on the plank table beneath the blue china plate of saints and a poster of Spanish cheeses, with the last precious tin of Páramo de Guzmán thirty feet below in the cave. As often as I could, I came here and spread out my notes, set up my laptop, and then sat staring at the *porrón* full of Ambrosio's homemade wine, so fresh it had a little fizz to it. It glittered scarlet, working its hypnotic effect. Here I was in Castile, trying to live by the old code, and the computer and the *porrón* were at war with each other. My modern gizmo versus the time-honored decanter of the Old Castilian.

A thousand words and then a sip, I told myself. It'd be my reward. Make it five hundred and then it . . . okay, call it two-fifty. Eventually I gave in, wooing the *porrón* as if were my Juliet—*"It seems she hangs upon the cheek of night / Like a rich jewel in an Ethiop's ear . . ."* I tipped it high in the air and drank in big, satisfying gulps.* So many gulps that I soon found myself giddy, singing, mawkish. I banged on the keyboard, amazing myself with verbiage, sometimes writing out the lyrics to old Who songs as if they were just occurring to me. This is how I quickly became disabused of the notion that the writer—your Hemingways and Faulkners, your Dylan Thomases and Tennessee Williamses, in-dulging in smoky spirits, writing legless and bladdered—could some-how, under the influence, muster grandiloquent prose, let alone *any* prose. I often found myself curled up at midday on a hard wooden bench, snoring lightly, drooling on the back of my hand, trying to sleep off my exuberance—and then waking to a headache and a bushel of horrible paragraphs.

Admittedly, it was slow going. I had ten, then twenty pages . . . then twenty-five. Another few weeks, and I had thirty-five. I threw it all out and started again. It wasn't just the wine. I found myself strug-gling with how to capture Ambrosio, who somehow remained just out of reach when I went to render him on the page. His mild recalci-trance to revisiting his loss made it more difficult. *"Hombre,"* he said in response to any question about the cheese, "why would you want to ruin a perfectly good day talking about all *that* again?"

His reluctance extended to the court cases, too, which were still in progress. He allowed that they were proceeding in a variety of courts, in Burgos and Madrid, that there'd been victories and setbacks, but I never was privy to details—and never asked to speak with Ambrosio's lawyer because . . . well, something stopped me short. It was the same

---

* The best descriptions of wine by sommelier, seller, or critic deserve their own literary award. I've heard reds described as "chicory and licorice," "chewy and charcoal," and in one particularly fine restaurant, "hay and sweaty saddle." As for Ambrosio's wine, let's just say it was grape Pellegrino, purple SweeTart, liquid Pixy Stix.

thing that stopped me from going to see Julián, something I knew I'd eventually have to do, and filled me with growing dread. Why? I was a journalist used to getting in and out, asking tough questions, checking off my sources with ruthless efficiency. Here, Ambrosio Molinos was my only source, and for some reason, I kept it that way. Maybe I thought if I started asking around about the cheese it would violate an important trust we'd established, that it might suggest that I didn't take him at his word. And that's all an Old Castilian had in this world: his word.

ANOTHER HINDRANCE TO widening my circle of sources was that I spent almost all of my time with Ambrosio. He became the dominating force, operating under the assumption that I wanted to do whatever he had on the agenda. He showed up early in the morning, and ended each day with "What's our plan for tomorrow?" And although I'd encouraged and invited such intimacy, it took the occasional day off for me to realize how completely I'd fused myself to his world.

One Sunday when Ambrosio was on the road, Carlos and I arranged to visit the cheese factory. We drove from Guzmán to Roa, parked before a chain-link gate topped by spools of barbed wire, and waited. I felt exposed on that roadside, preparing to visit the "dead cheese." As if committing my own betrayal of Ambrosio.

Eventually a man drove up in a clattery car and disembarked, squinting, hand outstretched. He wore a T-shirt under an off-white sport coat that bagged over his thin, wiry frame. He had a scar that ran from the middle of his neck to a spot below the lobe of one ear, and he rubbed his index finger against his thumb as if working a grain of sand. This was José, the alleged turncoat and the last one remaining from the old days, who agreed to see us despite the fact that Páramo de Guzmán was shut down for the weekend.

He unlocked the barbed-wire gate, and we entered.

The cheese factory had recently been robbed. That was José's first declaration after the niceties. Thieves had jimmied the lock on the gate, then backed a large truck up to a corrugated metal building under cover of darkness. After disabling the alarm system, they had broken two bolted locks on the door and then loaded the truck with crates of cheese. José estimated that the heist had cost the operation somewhere between $35,000 and $50,000. "This stuff is gold," he said. When I asked if there were any suspects, he shook his head. When I asked if anyone might have it in for him, he cocked his head, looked suspiciously at me for a moment, and then said, "No one that I can think of."

José led us through the first outbuilding, explaining things as we went in a most accommodating manner. A recent storm had flooded the workroom: every day a new challenge, it seemed. The cheese, he said, took at least fourteen months from the first boiling vat of milk to the dense wedges that went out into the world. Sometimes it was aged for up to eighteen months before being sealed in tins of olive oil. That's what it took, he said, to make an award-winning cheese like this.

Did he see in Carlos and myself prospective cheese buyers or big-time businessmen? I can't imagine we gave off the scent of success, but nonetheless, he meant to put his company's best foot forward, and I felt both an irrational dislike for him born of a protectiveness for Ambrosio and a tinge of pity, as if we were in the act of ambushing him somehow.

"Who founded this business?" I asked him, playing the calculating naïf.

"Ambrosio Molinos," he said, with no hint of malice. "He's originally from Guzmán, but he left town to earn a living in transportation. He still has farms in Guzmán, though. In May and June he's practically living there, planting and harvesting cereal and grains." José continued without encouragement, rubbing his fingers, blinking sleepily. "He was in his thirties when he started, and I was very young, nineteen, when I began here."

"And you're still very young," I offered, though not without a liminal note of sarcasm, for in my mind's eye I could see Ambrosio, a vibrant man full of warmth and good humor who had suddenly aged before my eyes when describing what had happened to his beloved cheese.

"It's my birthday," he said.

His birthday . . . *today?* What was he doing showing a high-school Spanish teacher and a journalist around a cheese factory? He was, it appeared, guileless, incapable of diabolical plot, another cog in the machine. He was someone with parents, secret wishes, a cake with candles, name smeared in frosting. He was someone proud to have a job, who took pride in the product he made. José filled the vacuum created by my sudden silence with a description of how the milk was heated from 4 to 32 degrees Celsius, until it became cottage-cheesy. "We grind it down into little curds," he said. "If you want a liter of cheese, you need to start with five liters of milk. And the leftover liquid becomes a waste management issue: You can't just throw it in the river, because it has high acidity."

He showed us long tanks of coagulating milk, heated until the surface thickened, when cheese harps were employed to separate the curds and whey. He showed us presses where the curds were molded and forced into blocks. There were drum strainers and cookers and hoops. And the overwhelming impression inside that warehouse was that this was no mom-and-pop outfit but one of gleaming technology and an antiseptic cleanliness, of hairnets and silver tanks. There was no straw on the ground. No stable across the street from the house in which the cheesemaker had been born. No "Eurekas" and the joy of discovering a new world. There weren't even sheep to milk here; instead, tank trucks drove up to the gates bearing thousands of gallons of milk from whoever offered the best price.

It became clear that José had no filter, would say almost anything. He told us that Harrods, the famous London department store, had carried, then recently dropped, the cheese. "Our problem is that we have short supply because it takes so long to produce this cheese. They got angry with us and canceled their order." When I asked if he remembered the first time he'd tried the cheese, he said, "When I tasted it, the only thing I wanted to do was cry. I didn't like it at all. It has a very strong taste. It's a very radical cheese. It tastes like the land here. Select clients prefer this type of cheese because it's made the traditional way, the way it's always been made in Castile."

One of those clients, as I already knew, was the king of Spain, Juan Carlos. "Not only does the king love it, but there's an official distributor to the royal family who distributes our cheese," he said. He turned to continue our tour, pointing to a saltwater bath. "After the cheese is pressed, you have to drop it in here so it gets some salt." He showed us to a room full of metallic coffinlike cylinders in which the cheese was aged in order to prevent mold and bacteria from growing. And finally we entered a huge, temperature-controlled space where the cheese, stacked in wheels thirty high, was further aged in temperatures between 7 and 9 degrees Celsius, at 77 percent humidity. In all, José claimed, there was more than 120,000 pounds of cheese currently in storage, waiting to fully ripen and then be shipped out.

Eventually he led us to the back of the warehouse, where we found wooden pallets piled high with those distinctive white-and-gold tins. For a moment I wanted to give that cheese a chance, wanted to believe that it wasn't a satanic cheese at all, or a lame one that hadn't won an award in more than a decade. I wanted to believe that this cheese still embodied the values that Ambrosio had conferred upon it, the ones that had first brought it such attention and acclaim. The abundance seemed nearly perverse, like a garage full of shiny vintage cars or shelves lined with Fabergé eggs. We flitted before those tins, then José conducted us outside, across an expanse of loose dirt, to show off the girders of a new structure, a winery that would soon house an impressive operation to rival, he promised, some of the best wineries in the area.

Of course, Ambrosio felt ever present here. I could almost see him counting canisters of sheep milk or checking on the inventory of rennet. I could see him hulking across the parking lot, falling into his vehicle, heading out to check up on the local shepherds. I could imagine those former halcyon days, the burst of hivelike activity after Ambrosio had first purchased the factory, when everything must have seemed possible, and when the operation had been limited to the old stone building, well before the warehouses had been built. I imagined Ambrosio arriving early and leaving late, perhaps alone in the factory at the end of the day—gazing on the tins waiting to go out into the world to transmit his love, to bring back memory—and for one moment confessing that here he'd left some sort of mark, every day making the king's cheese. But then an Old Castilian knew better than to count his good fortune.

At the end of the tour José took us into the stone building, said to be five hundred years old, the original cheese factory with its underground cellar. He led us down a long stone ramp to the basement, empty now, with cobwebs garlanding the rafters, where Ambrosio had risked his life when that beam broke, had held it in place with his bare hands until they were able to stabilize the structure. That's how far he was willing to go: life and limb, everything for his dear cheese. In the name of Páramo de Guzmán, he was capable of superhuman effort.

Upstairs, in a tasting room, José poured a red wine for us, then reached below an oak counter, retrieving a tin of Páramo de Guzmán. He worked a can opener, *un abrelatas,* until the lid came free. Inside, bathed in olive oil, were two wedges of rich, amber color. It didn't look like dead cheese at all. José offered a piece and I took it, stealing a glance at Carlos, who took another, attaching little ceremony to what otherwise might have been momentous had Ambrosio been our guide.

I took a halfhearted bite.

I'll admit it: It was good cheese. It was really good cheese. But it was all wrong. José watched me closely, gauging my reaction as if a substantial sale depended on it. Under the full force of his attention—his fingers rubbing that grain of sand—I slurped wine and masticated without thought, nodding politely. It was sharp, that much I can say, but had I tasted centuries of love and care, of generosity and perfection, as defined by the Molinos family? Had some mystical transference occurred between this substance and my tongue—and then spread through my body and out the top of my head?

Nah.

I faked it pretty well, though, as did Carlos, and we bought a couple of tins by way of thanking José, the birthday boy, for his time. With that ersatz, soulless cheese stashed in our trunk (hidden there because I didn't want Ambrosio to know I'd met the enemy and paid cash for his contraband), we made our way back to Guzmán, wondering what a tin of the original Molinos cheese might taste like—and if one could really taste a difference at all.

JUST WHEN IT COULDN'T get any hotter, it did—until we felt as if we were living life on a griddle, oil spitting and stinging, our bodies crisping like duck skin. The grapes curled deeper into their vines, and now came that pall of midsummer death moving in wisps and bony fingers, turning the land brown, and the pavement to goo. It drove us toward shade and cool water. In the absence of any discussion about his cheese—any late-breaking murder bulletins or court case updates—we retired again and again to the shadows of the telling room, where, between long pours from the *porrón,* Ambrosio spoke.

"I've seen a big deterioration in humanity," he said, warming to one of his favorite themes. "People don't know how to raise a chicken from its egg. Or how to hold an animal. How to go to nature for answers. Today, we're dependent on medicines and hospitals. We're victims of illnesses that never existed before. And do you know why?"

I pretended to consider. "Um—people don't know how to shit anymore?"

"Exactly!" boomed Ambrosio. "You *are* listening, aren't you! And this isn't a rumor, hombre. There are three highest things in life: to eat, to make love to a woman, and to shit. You can say one is more important than the others, but they are all pretty much the same. What happens when you shit is that your body has taken the most important parts from the food—the nutrients—and the rest is waste. *Claro?*"

Yeah, this sounded right. "So it's the opposite of eating," I said. "It's the end."

"It's not the other side of eating," said Ambrosio, "it's not the contrary. Otherwise it would be called 'de-eating,' or 'not eating.' The opposite of eating is to vomit."

"Then would it be part of the evolution of eating?"

"Yes, in a way," he said. "It's part of your own life, a biological act that belongs to your own life. And yet it's the most spiritual moment. It's the moment when people can't lie. When the death of food makes you most alive."

He again conjured the beauty of collective *cagando* on Mon Virgo. Of having the whole world laid out below you and your friends as you shat. But I was wondering how one was supposed to eat—let alone evacuate one's bowels—with such a fastidious fixation on purity and with such inspiring vistas, when society had become so frantic that we were human versions of Marx's time-saving machines. Yes, of course, with a little burble in the belly, it would have been nice to take an hour or three up on Mon Virgo, shitting it out with friends . . . but seriously. We didn't all abide in slow-moving, single-minded Guzmán. Sometimes, Ambrosio sounded as if he lived in a plastic bubble.

When I told him so, he wagged a finger. "Shit how you must," he said. "I can't do that for you, but it's not hard to eat well." He pointed to the almonds on the table before us, sloshed the wine in the *porrón,* took a drag. "These are almonds that are from the field here," he said. "My father took the time with a hammer to deshell them, and later my mother preserved them by submerging them in salt water. Then, in an old pot, she heated a few drops of olive oil, added the almonds, and stirred with a spoon for a couple of hours—and this is the result."

He handed me one. I slid it between my teeth, salt sprinkling my lip, the hard hull poised, then cracked by molars. Its flesh—the nut itself—was soft and gave, and the wood and mineral was instantly transformed into something very sweet, spreading to the far reaches of my mouth. "Mmmm," I mumbled.

In Ambrosio's presence, under the spell of his words, food had this way of ascending to sublime heights. Chorizo, *lomo,* stews, olives, fish, wine, nuts, *aguardiente*-soaked cherries, lamb, fresh lettuce, bread, cheeses, flan, paella, tomatoes, peaches—in the context of the telling room, around that ancient wooden table, on those hard seated benches, it all set a mouth watering, a body thrumming, and it left an afterglow on those gathered, one illuminated by the same food, the same nutrients, the same molecular transformation that now occurred inside our bodies, while the words washed over us.

"But for me, it's not special or unusual," said Ambrosio. "The biggest satisfaction is to offer a wine from these fields or a little piece of cheese or some of these almonds from my mother. It's another concept of life. It's another way to plant your existence on this earth." He pointed to the jar of almonds. "That's about six hours of work right there."

"Six hours in that jar," I said.

"Six hours by our hands," said Ambrosio. "It sounds like a lot if you're rushing, but in the context of life here, it's nothing."

AMBROSIO HAD BEEN ITCHING to take Carlos and me to the town of Haza, another field trip to have a drink. "The place is essentially abandoned," he said as we drove late one afternoon beneath a chiaroscuro sky. The wind had picked up, some sort of front approaching from Galicia, pushing hot gusts past the window with an occasional burst of cold air that sliced sheets of silt from the *coterro* and set them loose in tornadic rotations. When the weather came on the Meseta, it never meandered in milquetoast indecision but barged forth in ominous combinations: huge orange clouds, winds from competing directions, lightning in the distance forking the earth until the land opened to the faraway rain.

The approach to Haza was a steep climb, a road grooved into a hillside. At the top we passed stone facades of old derelict homes (they were literally only facades, like a stage set), sunlight filtering through the walls in heraldic bolts. A castle stood in disrepair, its turret like a bitten-off Pirouline, its bell tower only a vestige, a half gesture of that word "tower." Gravity seemed to be the village's most active citizen, grabbing down rock and roof, grinding it slowly to rubble. We drove through a cluster of half buildings and parked as cats skittered into a nearby alley.

Leave it to our Ambrosio to have close friends in a ghost town. The bar in Haza was nothing but a small room, cozy in that emptiness. Something about being so high up, with all that weather roiling forth, with all those resident spirits—another town, another legacy: Who had once lived in this castle, and what had befallen *them*?— everything felt more alive, interlinked, interdependent. Carlos and I sat in the warm suburb of Ambrosio, who introduced us to the bartender, and ordered us cold cervezas. "My son comes here sometimes," said Ambrosio. "When you see this tall guy with a back the width of that doorframe, with really long hair that falls to his shoulder blades, you'll say, 'I shit on God, aren't you Ambrosio's kid?' He's so big he needs to bend down to walk through the door." I relished Ambrosio's Bunyanesque descriptions. When Josué took to the fields, his long hair flowing like an Adonis,* the grapes grew larger, more succulent. The sun shone brighter. Ambrosio made no bones about how proud he was, never by saying so, but just in these descriptions of his eldest son as an organic, elemental force of Castile animated by the propulsion of native blood. And this was one form of *enlace,* too, the attachment of the child to the father, and with the passing of time the father

---

* This last happened not to be an exaggeration at all. At twenty-one, Josué (remember: *ho-sway*) was a spectacular human specimen. Just ask my wife, whose Josué crush was famous among those who visited us in Guzmán and others who've seen videotape evidence of her chasing his tractor, chirping "Hola, Josué!" Even Carlos, a happily married man, may have had a crush. "He's a statue," said Carlos one day. "He almost looks like a Viking on a boat. That's how strong he is to me." Indeed, he possessed a bold Iberian nose, soft brown eyes, and despite his stoicism—unlike his father, he went days speaking only the occasional five-word sentence—laughed like a little boy. During the summer he worked long hours, shuttling between the vineyards and the alfalfa fields, his limbs covered in dust and chaff, disappearing into that conversation with the earth, the one bequeathed him by his father. Which merely added to yet another legend, the one of the prodigal son who might pick up the pieces of his broken father and make the dry, rain-starved land turn green and grow.

to the child, so that even in death one lived on, carrying the ghost of the other like a baby inside.

There was some talk about crops, and what the year might bring. So far the heat had caused many to hold out hope about the grapes, as the best yields came from that perfect combination of hot, dry days and cold nights, from the punishing extremes that might push the vines to their own extremes, releasing more sugars into the grapes, making for bigger-tasting wines.

After leaving the bar, we strolled a little, ending up on the bluff, looking back across the *coterro* toward Guzmán, under darkening skies. Haza was a village, Ambrosio said, that now had no reason to exist; for all intents and purposes, it was dead. We were walking on a grave, another example of "the remains of Castile." The only thing left was the nostalgia of a few hangers-on, and the stories about it that had been carried by its scatterlings out into greater Spain. "My fear is that this will be Guzmán in fifty or a hundred years," he said. "I don't believe it's possible, but then probably no one here thought it was, either."

We piled back into the car at twilight, swooping down through the twilight as if it were a substance. I rode shotgun, and there beyond the windshield was that sky again, purple clouds layered over black ones, and now Ambrosio was really talking, shot through with adrenaline, evoking the crumbled history of Castile between drags on his cigarette. Oh, how they'd grown rich and fat on wool here in the fifteenth century, the best sheep in the world, and how, for that one fleeting moment when everything revolved around Castile, Fernando and Isabella* had sent Columbus to discover the New World. The

---

* Los Reyes Católicos were second cousins, and in the consolidation of the lands of modern Spain, they were able to reduce debt, lower crime, and further a Catholic agenda that included the Reconquest, their army marching south to drive the Muslims (and Jews) out of Iberia. They also produced a daughter, Juana La Loca, who later, after the death of Isabella in 1504, became an unlikely queen. Fluent in at least six languages and ruling not only Spain but the kingdoms of Sardinia, Sicily, and Naples—as well as vast holdings in America—she was an unstable monarch, afflicted with severe depression and possibly schizophrenia. In that familiar tale of

shadows flew outside the metal steed that bore us, and now only the thinnest skin held back the past. Ambrosio accelerated, zooming round dark corners, and orange dirt came up in the headlights, a hare at the side of the road, another imploded outbuilding. Rock and shadow gathered and formed the first words of the story Ambrosio gathered himself to tell now, the ur-story of Castile, really, about the great knight El Cid.

In the romantic rendering of El Cid's life (one that flourished through ballads and, most famously, *The Poem of El Cid*),* the plotline was familiar: Rodrigo Díaz, a knight of great courage and strength, pledges his eternal loyalty to Sancho, the Castilian king with whom he lived as a boy, and thus becomes the king's most trusted and fearless defender until that day when the king is killed in a plot by his brother. That brother, Alfonso, then becomes king, and ever distrustful of El Cid, who has nonetheless pledged his loyalty to the new king, banishes the knight from Castile. Distraught, El Cid leaves his homeland, marching down roads lined with grieving well-wishers until he enters the Muslim-occupied hinterlands with a terrible vengeance,

---

royal families, internecine squabbles and power plays were her undoing: With designs of his own, her father, the former king Fernando, outmaneuvered his daughter at court, leaving her isolated and forced into imprisonment, which allowed Fernando to rule again. Such was the template for modern Spain's First Family.

* Of contested authorship, the poem was probably written by 1207, within a hundred years after El Cid's death. Some claim a local abbot as the poet; others claim the story was recited by traveling minstrels. From the first lines—"Tears streamed from his eyes as he turned his head and stood looking at them. Men and women came out to see him pass, while the burghers and their wives stood at their windows, sorrowfully weeping."—the drama crystallizes: El Cid carries the virtue and promise of Castile in his every heroic move, and his leave-taking is so heartrending it convulses the kingdom in paroxysms of grief. When he says goodbye to his wife, Jimena, and two young daughers, he "wept and sighed heavily . . . with such pain as when the finger-nail is torn from the flesh." But once he rides away, he goes from bawling to beheading, transformed into a killing machine of such ferocity that anyone in his path quakes, becoming "anxious and distressed." And this speaks to the bipartite Castilian character, too: great, sentimental love and a bloodless kind of rage, sometimes posing as "courage," bordering on the kamikaze.

sacking whatever foreign armies and villages stand in his way—the Cross prevailing over the Crescent—in the name of Castile. "Who could say how many lances rose and fell," reads a typical description of battle, "how many shields were pierced, coats of mail torn asunder and white pennons stained red with blood, how many riderless horses ranged the field? The Moors called on Muhammad and the Christians on St. James. In a short time one thousand three hundred Moors fell dead upon the field." In episode after episode, he sends heaping tributes back to the king who has banished him, in hopes of one day returning to see his home again.

Of course, in these idealizations, the Campeador reigns as a man for all seasons, chivalric to a fault, ever obedient to the crown, brutal when need be, empathetic and humble in turn, and unparalleled as a provider to his wife and two daughters, even in wretched exile. The poem is exactly what it sets out to be, blatant hagiography, mixing fact with a great deal of fictive flourish, invented events, and ersatz characters to further gild El Cid's every utterance and action.*

Ambrosio was an unquestioning booster, but for me, it was the *way* he told the legend: its immediacy (as if it had taken place yesterday); the emphasis he put on El Cid's devotion to an ageless code (which was Ambrosio's code); his admiration for El Cid's allegiance to first Sancho, and then Alfonso, which was his allegiance to Castile

---

* So important is El Cid's place in the mythology of Castile and the tale of Spanish nationhood that scholars and historians have for years tried to determine the truth of his life, or, as important, struggled for control of the El Cid narrative. In Richard Fletcher's book *The Quest for El Cid,* the author contends that the extant version of the Cid that mixes fiction and fact—and was the basis for Charlton Heston's portrayal of El Cid in a movie seen by millions—is the invention of El Cid's most influential modern biographer, Ramón Menéndez Pidal. As Fletcher argues, Menéndez Pidal's 1929 bestselling book, *La España del Cid,* "is a tract for his own times disguised as history," one that presents "his countrymen with a national hero in whom they could rejoice and to whose virtues they should aspire." Most important, Fletcher writes that, for Menéndez Pidal, "there was no disjunction between history and legend. The Cid of history is as flawless in his character and deed as the Cid of legend." And his Castilianness becomes one of his greatest virtues, or rather, he becomes Castile itself, the two interchangeable. Fletcher quotes Menéndez Pidal to this effect: "Thoughout the history of Spain, Castile has played a unifying and

above all things (for no land in the world was more worthy of such allegiance). Then there was the heartache felt by El Cid at having lost his friend, the former king Sancho—and finally the terrible betrayal by Alfonso that turned him out. To be turned forever out of Castile, out of this land right here before us, the pine forests and plateaus falling away in the dusk as we drove, what an impossible thing to imagine. In that low rumbling baritone of his, Ambrosio described El Cid riding into battle on his giant horse, Babieca, an enormous man towering over mere mortals, bearing a sword that, he said, would take five others to lift.[*] For a moment, through Ambrosio, El Cid was alive again on these plains, trying to stand up to his betrayal and losses, as Ambrosio imagined himself fighting for that same Castile, the one vanishing out here before our eyes.

"Even after he'd died," said Ambrosio, "they roped him into his

---

anchoring role. Castile is not the whole of Spain, but her spirit *is* the unity of Spain."

But what of the real Cid? Evidence suggests his virtues might have been more self-serving. As a renegade professional soldier he was profligate in his partnerships, hardly discriminating between Muslim and Christian employers, with an eye toward creating a kingdom of his own, which eventually he did, in Valencia. And for whatever chivalry he possessed, he may also have been another violent, hotheaded, ambitious artist who found himself on the outs with King Alfonso's court. In a letter from one battlefield rival, the Count of Barcelona, he is accused of placing more trust in auguries (in particular, attempting to read the future in the flight path of birds) than any good Christian should, and as Fletcher says, "The general sense of the count's letter was that Rodrigo was a boor and a thug." But it's the eighteenth-century work of Dutch orientalist Reinhardt Dozy that first debunked the legend and led to later charges of "Cidophobia" by Menéndez Pidal. Fletcher sums up Dozy's final assessment as follows: "The Cid of reality was a *condottiere*. He was neither humane nor loyal nor patriotic. On the contrary, he was a harsh man, a breaker of promises, a pillager of churches, only interested in pay and plunder. Cruelest cut of all, Dozy described the Cid in the last paragraph of his essay as 'more Muslim than Catholic.' "

[*] The name of the sword was Tizona, which means "burning stick." Made of Damascus steel, it bears the inscription "I am Tizona, made in the year 1040," though it weighs only about two and a half pounds. "By one swing, he was able to cut off six heads with that sword," said Ambrosio.

saddle and sent him to battle at the front of his brigade. The enemy were so petrified, they fled from the field."* By this time night had fallen, and Ambrosio had moved himself to great emotion. "Look at the hair on my arm," he said, holding it out in the dark. "This is what happens when an Old Castilian talks about the Cid."

I'm not ashamed to admit it wasn't just Ambrosio. In that car I was a boy again, imagining the primeval world in which El Cid brandished a sword that five men together couldn't lift. I felt the presence of warring hordes, the cloud of rising dust out of which galloped the Campeador, teeth clenched with animal ferocity in defense of his homeland, of everything right. Intuiting my thoughts, Ambrosio said, "I believe he still rides on nights like this." And I could have sworn that somewhere out there the shadows took shape around the Cid, and he came into view out the passenger-side window, riding astride Babieca at full gallop, his face set in strong Iberian profile, his body in a purple tumult of fury.

ARRIVING HOME THAT NIGHT intoxicated by more than a day of intermittent wine consumption and barroom spirits, I found Sara on the

---

* This flourish seems to have come later in the evolution of the El Cid myth. In the *Estoria de España,* a thirteenth-century chronicle Fletcher terms "bizarre," El Cid is visited by Saint Peter, who predicts his impending death, while calling for one last V: "God so loves you that He will grant you victory in battle even after your death." The Cid ceases eating or drinking soon after, except for a daily regimen of myrrh and balsam, thus embalming himself. After he dies, his eyes are pried open, then he is clothed and perched upon Babieca, spurs and all, and conveyed back to Castile, where the king at first takes the Cid's appearance as a miracle. Meanwhile his compatriot Álvar Fáñez defeats the king of Tunis on the battlefield. Only at some later point, when the two events are conflated by some unknown storyteller, does El Cid lead the charge. In fact, according to the *Estoria,* the deceased El Cid is seated on an ivory stool covered in silk near the high altar of a church in Cardeña, where he sits for seven years until visited by a Jewish mischief maker, who sneaks in to tweak El Cid's beard. Just before the deed is accomplished, however, the dead Campeador's right hand reaches to unsheath Tizona, and the horrified prankster converts to Christianity.

roof patio, bleary after having put the kids to bed. She sat beneath the same sky, too, enjoying the cool air, but when I began to gush about the night I'd just spent, she let me carry on for a while—the ghost town! the sighting of El Cid! the glory of Castile!—and then she cleared her throat as if to announce something important. I stopped short at her expression, which was querulous, squinting at the figure of this man, her husband, standing on a roof patio above the Meseta, in a delusional babble.

She put her hand on mine. "I'm worried," she said.

"Worried?"

"About your book."

"*My* book?" I said. She squeezed.

"Well—are you getting anywhere with it?"

"Of course," I said, "I'm getting *all over the place* with it."

"But aren't you writing a book about Ambrosio's cheese?"

"Yes?" I said, palms up, in messianic pose.

"Yet you aren't asking any questions about the cheese because you seem afraid to—as you keep saying—*hurt his feelings.*" Obviously, she'd been waiting a long time to spring this, giving me the full benefit of the doubt, observing my comings and goings for weeks now, quietly gauging the material I'd accumulated with the final determination that we had only six weeks left before returning to our American life, and while I could have told the whole history of the farm plow as I'd gleaned it from Ambrosio, I couldn't have said much more about the cheese than when we'd first arrived over five months ago.

"He won't answer any questions about the cheese," I said.

"Have you asked?"

Had I *asked*? Oh—ha, ha, ha. That was rich. "Not recently," I said. "I've tried, though—it's not easy."

"I mean this in the kindest way," she said, "but you seem confused. Or even a little—I don't know—*emasculated* by Ambrosio."

Had she really just used the word "emasculated," in the kindest way? (Debatable.)

"What do you mean, exactly?" I said. True, I was a journalist, accustomed to asking intimate questions, but in my mind this wasn't a job at all, and intimacy was something to be earned by long periods spent *not* asking intimate questions, especially when trying to gain the trust of someone who didn't want to be reminded of the greatest failure of his life by the asking of intimate questions by his awesome new friend, one who was now in training to become an Old Castilian.

"You're afraid of him."

"Oh—okay, I'm afraid."

"Not *afraid* afraid. More like Gilligan and the Skipper."

"Wow."

Sara was smiling now. She'd made herself laugh. "I just think you need to level with him."

"This book is much bigger than a piece of cheese," I said, with a last, truculent exhalation.

"No," she said. "It's the same exact size."

14

THE MURDER

". . . arms outstretched in surrender."

AUGUST WAS THE MONTH WHEN SPAIN TOOK ITS SUMMER vacation: The cities emptied and people fled to the seashore or their home villages, luxuriating in four weeks of freedom. Guzmán briefly resembled a thriving, if still tiny, dot on the map, its population ballooning to two hundred or so. New faces that were old faces kept appearing. A rush of fleeting conviviality reigned.

Up in the telling room, I'd managed by limiting my wine intake to rack up forty more pages, for a grand total of sixty-four. But none of them belonged to me, they belonged to Ambrosio. His voice was all I heard in that room, and I'd simply become his willing parrot. The more I wrote, the more I kept wondering if all of this was a dream or a joke of some sort. (It would start: *So a guy tells this other guy a story about some cheese, and a murder plot, and he believes it. Then he goes to New York and sells it as a book. . . .*) Even when I tried to fit the story to my own life—conjuring those who'd "done me wrong," whatever that meant—I realized I wasn't plotting anyone's murder, let alone

wasting energy on hating anyone. Could this kind of grudge be justified, or even real?

That was the question bouncing around in my head one evening
at the *frontón* with Leo. During our time in Spain, my son had discovered this little soccer team known as Real Madrid, and players like
Zidane, Figo, and Casillas had become his new *galaticos*. Gone were
the bat and batting helmet; instead he proudly wore Real Madrid's
white jersey—of his favorite, #7, Raúl*—and sported a sprout of a
ponytail, trying to emulate that of the team's newest acquisition, David
Beckham, who wore his hair like a gladiator's.

We were booting the ball, playing an imaginary game against FC
Barcelona, when a voluble man approached on his *vuelta,* or evening
walk. His name was Pelayo. Born in Guzmán and back on a visit
from Aranda, he taught English, he said. While he was quick to apologize for his "bad speaking," he wasn't about to pass up an opportunity to converse with an American, especially one with more than a
passing interest in his birthplace.

Pelayo had a wonderful way with words. He called the church
"the Master's house." He described a man from his youth, Pepe Ortero,
as "a cunning success at cutting hair." "I passed him many times cutting the hair of animals," he said. And I could envision the barbershop, all the animals sitting in chairs. So had that been a lucrative
trade at one time, animal barbering? According to Pelayo, there were

---

* Raúl González Blanco, the all-time leading goal scorer for Real Madrid: Handsome, speedy, prolific, he represented a fluency that Leo now found his three-
year-old self aspiring to. The game's geometry and constant teamwork, its action
and its postgoal celebrations, all coalesced in his mind as something greater than
the New York Yankees. When we procured tickets to see a game at Bernabeu, Real
Madrid's 85,000-capacity home stadium, his conversion was complete. Before his
eyes on that emerald pitch came the new knights of Spain, and Raúl had a true,
alert, generous playing style, scoring two goals that night. I only wished that Leo
would follow Raúl's muted postgoal ritual of kissing his wedding ring, but soon at
the *frontón,* there was Leo after scoring, shucking his shirt, waving it like the more
flamboyant megalomaniacs of European soccer as the tractors passed.

the *barberos,* cutters of human hair—named Martinino and Glada—and then the *esquiladores,* cutters of animal hair, led by the noteworthy Pepe Ortero. Later, after consulting a dictionary, I deduced that Pepe actually had been a sheep shearer, but in that moment, as in so many other moments when I only half understood, I let my mind float away with the myth, as silly as it was, of the animal barber shop, the dogs and goats and pigs all gathered to improve themselves at the hand of a kindly hairdresser spiffing them up with Vidal Sassoon product.

Pelayo wanted in the worst way to convey the importance of this lost world, if only he could make the sentences work. He told about a lightning bolt that once struck the bell tower of the church, leaving a twenty-foot gash. He remembered when the village had possessed two grocery stores, a pharmacy, five bars, a doctor, and a dance hall. He quoted a proverb—"It's better to be a mouse's head than a lion's tail"—which, he said, described the central predicament of village life. One could be in charge of one's small enterprise, or contribute to the bigger whole. In Guzmán, he said, everyone wanted to be the mouse's head, and because of that "some people are friends and some are enemies."

"Is that what caused the fight over the *palacio?*" I said.

Pelayo did a double take. The controversy was almost fifteen years old at that point, and he must have wondered how I knew, let alone why I might care, which is when I added an addendum about my friendship with Ambrosio.

"Ambrosio is very clever," Pelayo said. "And is nice. A friend for many years. And strong. He told everyone, 'I got sheeps, and I got their milk, and I make cheese. The *palacio* is in ruins. Let me fix it and move the cheese in there.'" Ambrosio first offered his house in the lower part of town, with its pool and gardens, in exchange for the building. "But the people became very, very angry," Pelayo said, "and fought him."

This was how it had always gone, said Pelayo. This is exactly what he was talking about, this small-mindedness on one side and this

self-righteousness on the other, all of it wrapped in fierce indepen-
dence.* "You can't be free in a small village," he said. But at least no
one had been hurt. Not like that other time, when someone had been
"felled and killed by the people."

He dropped the phrase in such a way that I almost missed it.
Wait—*who* had been felled and killed by the people? Leo was dribbling the soccer ball, which topped out at his knees. As the ball rolled,
sheep pellets attached themselves to it and pinwheeled off. He kept
shouting out my name—my soccer name, *Zidane*. And when I didn't
respond he hollered, "Daaaaaaaaddddd!"

"Who was felled and killed?" I asked, the ball ricocheting off my
shin.

"A brother," he said. "But no one can talk about this." Pelayo was
inadvertently telling me anyway, and, realizing this, he seemed uncomfortable, shifting his weight from one foot to the other. We were
passing through some choppy strait to the concealed truth, and unlike
my recent encounters with Ambrosio, I was steady on the throttle.

"What happened?" I asked, knowing that it would pain him to
turn back.

The story, or what remained of it, went like this: In the years before the Civil War, there'd been a marriage, a woman from Guzmán
betrothing a man from away. On such occasions the groom was expected to throw a tip to the hometown boys, as a gesture of respect, to

---

* This mule-headedness had otherwise served Castile well at its inception. According to a Library of Congress study of Spain, Castile was born as a loose collection
of strongholds in the tenth century, when the kingdom of León looked to create a
buffer between the Christian north and the rest of Spain, which was Muslim. Castile not only had the blessings of the kings of León but was granted *fueros,* which
were special dispensations that left it virtually autonomous. "Castile developed a
distinct society with its own dialect, values, and customs shaped by the hard conditions of the frontier," reads the study. "Castile also created a caste of hereditary
warriors whom the frontier 'democratized': all warriors were equal, and all men
were warriors."

When it came to the *palacio,* the sense among the townspeople was the opposite:
that all men weren't created equal, that *"los Ambrosios"* were trying to take what
they saw as theirs, and this gave rise to an atavistic fury.

say in effect, "Okay, I'm taking one of yours, but here's some money in exchange: Go have some wine and lamb, and we'll call it even."

For some reason, on the day of the marriage the groom didn't pay the tip. One of the local men was a Republican named Martín—or Martínazo, because he was very tall—and he started heckling the groom. Things escalated. There was shouting and shoving. Martínazo was pushed to the ground, and as he lay there, the father of the bride lifted his cane—some people said it was a knife—and before he could strike Martínazo, Martínazo drew a revolver and shot him.

Martínazo was subsequently tried and sent to prison. When the Republicans came to power in Madrid, however, he was freed and returned to Guzmán, where he became mayor. If once he'd been abrasive, went the legend, he came home a more moderate man, addressing people politely.

Yet, after the Civil War began in July of 1936, Martínazo was forced out as mayor, and a man named Alfonso—of the opposite political persuasion—took over. With the first spasm of war came some of the worst atrocities: "Savage acts on both sides," said Pelayo.* Martínazo believed, rightly it seems, that Alfonso wanted him dead, so he fled, exiling himself to a forested area a couple miles across the *páramo*

---

* Depending on the source, fatalities would total more than 350,000, including tens of thousands of "enemies of the state" who were murdered after the cessation of hostilities, and tens of thousands who withered of starvation. In addition, some number of children (sources claim anywhere from "hundreds" to 30,000) were forcibly separated from their leftist parents. Atrocities by the Nationalists, known as the White Terror, outnumbered those by the Republicans. The bombing of the Basque town of Guernica by the Condor Legion of the Luftwaffe on April 26, 1937—an incident that claimed up to 1,000 lives and was immortalized by Pablo Picasso—became perhaps the most famous, but a brutal incident at Badajoz on August 14, 1936, was more typical: a massacre in which civilian "prisoners" were gathered in the town's bullring and then systematically slaughtered by firing squad, leaving between 2,000 and 4,000 dead, some tortured and mutilated by *bandillero* lances. Meanwhile, the Republicans' response—known as the Red Terror—featured attacks on the Spanish clergy, including a parish priest in central Spain who was forced to reenact a parody of Christ's crucifixion and was finally shot, and the Bishop of Jaén and his sister, who were allegedly paraded before thousands of ecstatic spectators and put to death by a female executioner nicknamed *La Pecosa,* the freckled one.

from Guzmán. From here Martínazo could keep watch over the high fields, but it had to have been a rough existence, one undertaken out of pure desperation, for Nationalist hit squads were eliminating their enemies, dumping bodies by night in hastily dug graves throughout the region. Apparently Martínazo began sending clandestine messages back to his family asking for food or company, setting up secret meetings with his brother at this or that *majano* boundary marker. Until one of those messages was intercepted by the mayor, Alfonso, and his gang, who went out to the fields one night at dusk, armed to kill Martínazo.

The younger brother of Martínazo—Orel—walked out of town and up the northern hill, finding the sheep path. By most accounts Orel wasn't interested in politics and had no desire to get wrapped into the hot-blooded bipartisan violence. He was a brother doing his brotherly duty, probably delivering some food, cheese and chorizo, some bread and wine. He came across the fields at dusk, stalwart and doomed. At some point he must have heard other footsteps—the *ka-chunk* of boots in the soft dirt. He must have realized he had a problem, that he was *jodido*.

The men stood in a noosed circle with their guns loaded and cocked. Martínazo, coming across the fields, saw the shadows and knew something was amiss. There was yelling, cursing. The circle opened, one man's arms outstretched in surrender. A gun was raised, a shot fired. Then Martínazo's brother fell.

It shouldn't have been surprising that the Civil War had reached Guzmán, for it had reached everywhere else in Spain. Yet for some reason, I was surprised. I'd just assumed that everybody here must have lined up on the same side, or that a village so small and remote had nothing to fight for, or that Guzmán, while rife with internal politics, was somehow exempt from the bigger catastrophes of the world. Maybe I mistook the purity of the cheese for the purity of the place where it had been born.

When Pelayo finished telling me about the murder, he said, "All Civil War stories are nightmares," adding that "people here don't forget grudges until they're settled." After the war, there'd been no prosecutions, no truth commissions. The past, in its own shallow grave, had been left unresolved, with lingering questions like the ones I had now: *What had been said in the moments after the killing, and what was done with the body, and what did Martínazo do, having seen what he saw, knowing what he knew?*

That night, I lay awake until I gave up on sleep and took myself to the roof patio. The sky was hung with faraway suns, and I was a cliché thinking about the enormousness of everything,* about how small we are, but then how consequential, too. Martínazo and Orel, both strangers from seventy years ago, now rummaged inside my mind. I had no idea what they looked like or who they were. I just knew one brother had watched the other die. And now their story was partially mine, too. I leaned back in a wooden chair and sucked in the night air. What was a person to make of all of these stories? Everybody had at least one to tell, and then their own version of the hundreds of others that got told already. Everybody kept adding more story-noise to the clamor. It was dizzying and enthralling and what kept us bound together.

As I sat there, I was thinking, too, about Ambrosio and what Sara had said. Maybe the reason I couldn't seem to move forward on my book was that I'd come here to move backward. This was a special case, wasn't it? Or that's what I told myself. As a journalist, you entered other people's lives, collecting what you could, positioning yourself off to the side, as the ultimate observer. Later, after you wrote the story—*your* story about *their* story—the reaction was never

---

* Cliché until it wasn't: During this same time, in 2003, NASA had programmed the Hubble telescope to photograph what appeared from Earth as a thumbnail of empty, black sky. But what emerged when four hundred images were superimposed as "The Hubble Ultra Deep Field" astonished even the astronomers: Out of that nothing patch came ten thousand galaxies and a thousand trillion stars just like our sun.

predictable. Sometimes you ended up friends; sometimes you never heard another word; every once in a while, you were threatened with a lawsuit. Perhaps this was my unconscious hedge with Ambrosio, then: If I wasn't a journalist, he wouldn't have to be my subject—that is, we'd never have to be anything but friends. If I wanted to be in his world, then I wouldn't have to stop and observe. I could just live it.

When it came to the cheese, it was easier to assume the same avoidance pattern with Ambrosio as everyone else because clearly talking about it made him feel miserable. It would have made him feel even worse, I imagined, if I'd gone behind his back to talk to Julián. In the meantime, there were all these stories, like constellations residing in the same atmosphere, in conversation with each other, by turns connected and disconnected, overlapping and individuated. Perhaps I'd lost my gumption to press Ambrosio about the cheese because I didn't want the stories to end. With the telling of each one, he connected me to Guzmán—and then he connected Guzmán to Castile, Castile to Spain, Spain to the world, and, finally, the world to the stars. He was already telling me everything he thought I needed to know about him and his cheese.

At the telling room the next day—sitting in the cool, late-afternoon shadows with Ambrosio, Carlos, and Ambrosio's father, who dozed off and on at the table—I asked about the murder. We grazed on chorizo, bread, and Manchego. As Ambrosio happily loaded and reloaded the *porrón,* his eyebrows raised at the question. As the keeper of my education here, he seemed genuinely startled to find I'd acquired knowledge—let alone a secret—without him. "I'm not completely sure of this story," he said, "because no one talks about it. I guess in several generations people will forget about it, but now it remains a very sensitive topic because of the grandchildren."

He continued, "Back then, the situation was dire. My own grandfather went to prison because he was a Red. Other members of my family, who were Nationalists, protected him in jail. But not everyone was afforded such protection. Brothers fought brothers. Friends and family became enemies, and because they knew each other so well, they could be the most cruel."

Ambrosio's father roused himself and said, *"Santos cojones!"*—holy balls!—"why are we even talking about this? I don't want to talk about this anymore." He was so good-natured and loveable in old age, but now he struggled to rise, and get away, with a grimace on his face. It took awhile, and he mumbled irascibly as he went, in his blue *mulo*, hunched over a cane. Ambrosio's face filled with boyish wonder as he watched his father maneuver around the table, down the steps, and out into the bright light.

"Papá," he called after him, "do you need a ride?"

And his father said, "Oh, go fuck yourself." Which made Ambrosio laugh with a mix of surprise and pride.

Meanwhile I was working backward, doing the math in my head. Anyone in this village who was eighty-five now would have been about eighteen at the time of the murder, old enough to go to the fields with Alfonso's hit squad. So maybe that's why no one wanted to discuss it. I thought of those angelic, bereted old men on the bench across from the bar, or playing *mus* or *julepe* at the tables by the window. What secrets were *they* keeping? What role had *they* played?

I asked Ambrosio if he knew anyone involved with the murder, and he said no, he was certain that all of them were dead now. But he did remember that Martínazo had eventually returned to Guzmán after the war and lived out his days here. He and Alfonso passed in the street often, but despite everything between them, they never exchanged a word.

THAT SUMMER OF 2003, a number of curious, makeshift settlements began to appear in the Duero region around Guzmán, in spots just off the road, up a nearby hillside, at the fringe of a pine forest. We'd pass them as we took the kids to the public swimming pool in Torresandino or to shop in Aranda, and we'd wonder. They were shrouded from view by opaque plastic sheeting.

In Aranda during the war, Franco's Nationalists had run concentration camps, and the existence of mass graves had been a widely known secret. Someone's father had gone missing—a mother, a son, a daughter. A farmer found newly turned earth where a day or week before the land had lain undisturbed. Over time, as the buried bodies decayed and lost volume, declivities formed. Here was a watch, the eyelet of a shoe, a fragment of bone. No one had the temerity to dig for their relations or ancestors lest they end up in the same hole.

It had recently come to pass, however, that a man from Aranda named Restituto Velasco had gotten fed up and had gone looking for his grandfather. He began digging randomly, and two old women from a local village pointed him to a nearby mountain. They told him, "There's one oak in particular. Dig by that one." Despite the illegality of trespassing on the land, Velasco hired a backhoe and found six pits full of bones.

When the Spanish government showed no interest in excavating the past, a small collective calling itself the Association for the Recovery of Historical Memory took it upon itself to begin the retrieval of remains for proper burial.* Tent cities cropped up in the countryside. With the first unearthing of mass graves came squads of volunteers—a number, it turned out, from England, some of them students wearing bandannas and tank tops—living at the sites in makeshift quarters, driving borrowed, beat-up cars, spending weeks at a time digging in the red clay, trying to forensically piece together the past. Because there was still so much fear associated with these spots—an air of

---

* Signed two years after Franco's death, the 1977 Pacto de la Moncloa, known as "the pact of forgetting," offered amnesty to those who might have been implicated in atrocities. While the pact ensured the transition from dictatorship to democracy, it also had the adverse effect of silencing history. When the Association for the Recovery of Historical Memory began its work, editorials decried the exhumations, and vocal critics lined up to warn about the dangers of going back to the chaotic days when both Republicans and Nationalists alike had committed atrocities. If people started digging, the argument went, who knew where it all might end? What the new generation didn't understand, according to the older one, was that everybody—*everybody*—was implicated.

solemnity hung thickly over the proceedings—they were treated by most like Area 51, to be avoided. Although the mass graves were crime scenes, it was against the law to prosecute anyone, so the sites we'd been passing were designated as archaeological digs. One of those in charge of the excavations was a local archaeologist named Eduardo Cristóbal, a stout, hirsute character from Aranda whom Ambrosio insisted I meet.

In the loud, crowded bar where we convened—and where Ambrosio sat listening for once in silence—I strained to hear Cristóbal, until he raised his voice. He said his grandfather had been branded a Red, while another in his family had been a Nationalist who was shot to death in Madrid. This was not so unusual, these divisions and bad endings within one family. What was unusual was speaking so loudly about it in public, seven decades later.

Cristóbal's task had been to collect records and interviews in order to identify the dead. He'd gone from village to village, living room to living room, talking to old people, listening to stories of cruelty and heartbreak that made you question humanity. "In theory, these bodies were supposed to be the Reds who were taken from these camps and killed," he said. "In reality what we found were innocents: a girlfriend or boyfriend of someone suspected to be a Red. Or grudge killings, people using the war as an excuse to settle old scores: a brother-in-law murdered so the sister could inherit his money. Another man killed for leaving his girlfriend. Family enemies disappeared."

Cristóbal had spent months climbing down into these shallow trenches behind the plastic barriers, examining skulls and skeletons, shoes and clothing. It was trying detective work, but it was also something more: an emotional journey to build narratives. He'd found children and grandparents, two brothers hugging in death. They followed him home at night, haunted him in dreams. It was almost easier to focus on precise details—the bullet hole in the skull, the frilly lace on the shirt—by way of detachment. "Most of the victims were in summer wear, in *alpargatas*"—sandals—"or boots, between the ages of twenty and thirty-five," he said. They were killed in the summer of

1936, in the melee at the beginning of the coup, by German Mausers loaded with Spanish ammo, shells marked FNT, for Fábrica Nacional de Toledo. Astonishingly, Cristóbal found that if somebody had a copper coin in his or her pocket, the coin magically preserved the fabric of the pants, the underwear, the shirt, within a ten-centimeter radius of the coin.

"No one told me about this special property of copper," he said, "but it's been enormously helpful."

The other thing was the hands. If Cristóbal found someone with a limp hand—that is, with the finger bones easily extended—it meant the person had died immediately, often with a precise shot to the head, whereas someone with clawed fingers had died in agony, digging his or her nails into the dirt. Or at least that's what he surmised. "My job is to give the relatives as much exact information about their loved ones as I can," he said.

Given the immensity of the task, the emotion it undammed, and the strenuous, at times threatening, condemnation it evoked in certain pro-Franco quarters, Cristóbal seemed outwardly stoic.* He was compiling a report that would be released through the University of Burgos itemizing his findings, identifying the dead and describing their last moments. He planned to deliver his results in a public forum in Aranda, but he admitted that, judging by his encounters so far with families of the deceased, it would be difficult bringing them back to the precise moment their worlds exploded. And yet nothing could

---

* Later, when I spoke to another association member in Madrid, the researcher José Ignacio Casado, he described the pressure this reclamation work had put on his marriage. His wife's family had been Nationalists, and were displeased with his investigations. His wife's feeling was that for every victim, you pulled up a killer. Which hadn't stopped Ignacio Casado. In another grave near Aranda, fifty bodies had been buried by street sweepers. One man heard that his grandfather had not been properly executed and was found alive near the ditch; the story went that, when he claimed to be thirsty, his attackers urinated on him, then finished him off. Later, some of these killers were seen walking through town in the clothes of the dead. "My wife and I almost split," said Ignacio Casado, "because she knows that I'm a very thorough person, and that if I'm going to do this, I'm going to get to the bottom of it."

stop him now. He had the righteousness of a storyteller, recovering time, reanimating the ancestors, telling the most difficult story, based on forensic truth, in order to set it free, once and for all.

"It's the most important work," he said, "finding the voice of the dead."

15

HONOR THE GRAPES

"There was something in the air above the village. . . . And then it fell."

THE WEATHER OF CASTILE OWES ITS PARTICULARS TO A DYNAMIC known as the North Atlantic oscillation, which is defined by an atmospheric low that hovers near Iceland and a high that does the same near the Azores. The fluctuations in differences between these—in the various collisions of Arctic chill and warm southern air—define the intensity of the winds and storms buffeting Galicia, the piling clouds that gain momentum as they race across the Meseta to Guzmán, sometimes hurling lightning and rock. The seemingly endless, heat-battered days of summer can change to mayhem within minutes, which is why the Old Castilian always watches the sky for signs—and never more so than when the grapes go from being hard pellets to fleshy baubles, when they first come into their nubile own and ripen with juicy guts, and the countdown to harvest begins.

That summer, there'd been little chatter about what kind of grapes the vineyards might yield. Perhaps it was superstition not to talk about them before their time. But the weather had been hot and dry, perfect for the vines. Under Ambrosio's direction, Josué, of the flowing locks, and Kiké, of the Mohawk and many piercings, had lavished care and attention on the vines. They'd clipped and fed and sprayed. And the closer we came to September and the harvest, the more vulnerable it all seemed. In the dead heat of those long summer days, time crawled. The suspense became unbearable.

It was during this time that Sara and I loaded up the kids and headed north to Cantabria for a brief getaway. One evening while we were gone, Ambrosio found himself in the barn, putting up bales of hay, when he first heard a soft pinging over his head, and he thought, *Good, it's going to rain, it's going to rain and clean off the leaves and moisten the dirt a little. It's going to water the vines and the worms and the earth.*

In this moment, he had no inkling that anything might be amiss. He'd spent the day with his sons. There'd been some minor repairs on one of the tractors, which Kiké had handled. Josué was irrigating, adjusting the huge sprinklers that arced water over the dry fields in a thick, cool spray. Another day full of hours to add to the thousands they'd spent already. After stacking the hay, Ambrosio planned to go up and say goodnight to his parents, maybe have a quick drink at the bar, and then be home for *cena*.

Later, when Ambrosio spoke to Kiké, trying to trace the origin of the disaster, Kiké described a strange occurrence. He'd been up on the *páramo* at about 8:30 p.m., when clouds began to gather and a wind picked up, a very dry, hot wind. What surprised Kiké was that behind the wind came a sudden blast of cold air, as if it were pouring from above or from all sides, frigid and directionless. The cab of his tractor was buffeted; branches came loose from the trees, and the dust swirled.

There was no inkling of this in the barn sheltering Ambrosio and the bales of hay, just the benevolent ping-pinging on the roof. With the passing moments, however, the hits became louder, more insistent and tinnier, picking up in frequency. Ambrosio listened in the dark to the tumult of what soon sounded like pots and pans smashing against each other. He frowned and drew air through his nostrils, but all he could smell was the hay, piled high in the open bay. It was a remarkable shade of gold, bright and burnt pale enough to give off a glow in the murk. And when freshly cut like this, it flooded the barn with the scent of Castilian earth. Ambrosio paused and breathed in again, almost tentatively. It was just as he thought: Through an eddy came the smell of ice. The time between realization and physical reaction was a matter of seconds, and sluicing through those seconds were other bitternesses, a lifetime of them, revisited. His voice rose reflexively. *"Me cago en la leche de Dios,"* he said out loud. I shit in the milk of God. "I . . . SHIT . . . IN . . . THE . . . MILK!" The hunting dogs looked up from their bed in one of the stalls.

There was something in the air above the village, above the atmospheric layers of dream-ghost-metaphor that already hovered over the village (the flung birds were revenge; the flying leaves, ancestors). And then it fell: *el granizo,* hail. From the cold ceiling of a massive cloud, the ice guillotined, gathering rime as it hurtled earthward.

The cloud covered a mile and a half, and moved whichever way the wind blew it. Ambrosio followed the hail's pattern across the roof, intuitively marking its path. Following that line, and at that speed, it would strike the family vineyards within minutes. This was something that couldn't be undone. The clouds didn't tally all the hours a father and his sons spent in the fields. The wind didn't know that wine was a religion to these people, as precious as any family heirloom. (Ambrosio used to say that his father always perked up at Mass whenever the wine was being blessed, that he would literally spring from a deep sleep for that promise of a holy swig.) And the hail, the hail struck only what stood between it and the ground. When it hit the grapes—halfway to being ripe, not young enough to heal magically—it ripped and slashed and ruined.*

To Ambrosio, the grapes were alive, and helpless, and being slaughtered. To think about it was nearly too much, even for a man who'd seen it all, who when he'd returned to his village at nineteen—the now tender age of his boy Kiké—had vowed to live his life as an Old Castilian, burdened and set free by the land and its harsh vicissitudes. His pact had been simple: He'd accept what the earth and sky gave.

But why did he have to accept this? Just to consider the intricacies of the vine, especially the older ones, was to confront the intelligence of grapes. The leaves acted as solar panels, tilting toward the sun in the cool of morning, allowing light into the plant, and then creating an altogether impenetrable canopy to survive the heat of midday. Drought was often the vine's moment of reckoning, and the plant would do everything it could for the grape. A stressed vine curtailed its growth and underwent hormonal changes to survive the rest of the hot summer. It became tough and focused, and the oldest were the most tough and focused. As a result, its fruit became more concentrated and flavorful, something to revere.

The cloud crept across the barn, taking the noise with it, then knifed for the field just below, picking up the road and following it to the vineyard. It sprayed hail in indiscriminate patterns, sometimes ceasing for hundreds of yards, only to begin again. Now, it came in rapid fire. The vines and grapes took the blows like bodies at a massacre.

---

* This comes from an eighteenth-century account of a hailstorm in Madrid by one Pedro Alonso de Salanova, who described the hail as the size of "hen's eggs": "It killed many small creatures such as doves, rabbits, hares, ducks, sparrows and other birds. It wrenched the branches off many trees leaving them leafless and fruitless; it wrecked many kitchen gardens, vineyards, olive groves, melon plots and unreaped wheatfields. Some say that this furious cloud was born in the mountain lake of Gredos in the nearby province of Ávila, because that day at 12 o'clock a dense, thick, sulphurous and flame-like vapour was seen to rise therefrom."

Ambrosio sat in the barn, smoking cigarettes. Twenty minutes passed. He climbed into his tractor, drove to his mother's house, and gave her a kiss. His mother didn't say anything to him. She knew what had happened, she knew how her son was. How could you not consider yourself damned, to lose your grapes to hail after all that work? He said good night and drove home in the tractor. The headlights shone on the damage, branches and leaves in the road, trees down at the edge of the fields. And yet by the time he'd made it to his own home and had some food, when it came time to sleep, he slept soundly. He couldn't visit the vineyard until three days after the storm because the thought of it turned his stomach, but that night he remembered the worst and most difficult things done to him—including the cheese—and that perspective allowed him to sleep.

The days after the storm were cool and cloudy, the skies low and leaden: sweater weather. The villagers assessed the damage and once again marveled at how the cloud had left a patchwork of destruction. The Pedrosa vineyards, which occupied the rising lands southwest of the village, had remained untouched, but not more than a mile away, there were vineyards that had lost 90 percent of their grapes. Some quietly rejoiced; others, like Ambrosio's sons, took to the fields in green rain slickers, spraying the broken-skinned grapes with fungicide, leaving what looked to be green paint on the wreckage in hopes of stanching disease, in hopes that something might be saved.

By the time Ambrosio came down to the vineyard on the third day, the weather was sunny and warm again, back to the furnace of everlasting summer on the Meseta. We'd returned from our trip up north, having heard about the storm. Ambrosio was already sweating through his shirt as he made his way through the vines, boots sinking deep in the embankment of loose dirt. I followed as he walked with his sons, then bent down to inspect the damage. He picked a grape, holding it between his first finger and thumb. The skin was punctured and slit, and he grimaced. He picked more murdered grapes, making his way along one row. He broke loose a cluster and held it up in the sun, then laid it down gently. He put his hands on his hips, exhaled.

"It's the way of the field," he said, as much to himself as to the rest of us. "When the harvest is good, you enter the temple. When it goes like this, you're fucked, and must live with it.

"This is what it means to be an Old Castilian," he said, looking out toward Mon Virgo, which levitated above us. "The weight of Old Castile falls on your back in moments like these, and you either have the strongest, widest back or you need to get out of here."

He turned and trudged toward the road, the boys following.

When he came to the tractor, he glanced back at the vineyard, pressing his lips together. That evening he would be up at the bar, in the *bodega,* drinking, laughing, telling stories, singing—the most boisterous of them all, trying to forget—but now he looked once more on the wreckage.

"Honor the grapes," he said in a hoarse voice to his sons, "because they were once whole like you."

16

GONE FOREVER

"Wow . . . wow . . . wow!"

EYOND MY POSSIBLY NAÏVE BELIEF THAT AGRARIAN LIFE MIGHT solve all of our problems, what rooted me first and foremost to Guzmán was Ambrosio's story of the cheese. It had begun with my original deli fantasies, leading to the intensity of that first meeting with the cheesemaker—during which, like the greatest of tellers, he'd drawn me in and ensnared me—and leaving off with this sort of stalemate. There was something lurking behind Ambrosio's tale that I felt compelled to know/not-know, and that hindered its full unfolding. What was it, though? What revelation could ever undo the spell, or undermine the Storyteller with a beautiful-terrible story to tell?

Meanwhile, the clock was ticking. Our summer was vanishing, in seemingly uneventful fashion, discounting the fact that everything felt eventful. Carlos had returned home with his family to get ready for the upcoming school year. My mother arrived for a visit,* and left as

---

* And I was thankful to her for more than one reason: There was finally someone in town who knew less Spanish than I did. When Sara mistakenly introduced her as her *cuñada,* or sister-in-law, my mother would smile and nod, shake hands and

transfixed by Guzmán as we were. We began our own countdown—
four, three, two weeks left—even as my page count in the telling room
slowed to a dribble and then, to my alarm, started running backward
with some ruthless self-editing: sixty-seven pages . . . seventy-three . . .
seventy-five . . . fifty-eight . . . *forty-nine* (!) . . .

Normally I would have fumed and fretted about this, but according to my book contract, I had more than a year left to finish a draft.
More than enough time. We began to pack the plates, lamps, and
knickknacks we'd acquired, and took them in two boxes to Ambrosio's garage. We tried to milk our last moments of escape: in the fields
and telling room with Ambrosio, at the *pantano* and pool on family
outings, at night in the bar* or streets. We'd celebrated May's first
birthday at the *fuente* above town, beneath the shade of huge oaks, the
town bakers—Marcos and Ilena—arriving with their three-year-old
daughter, Lucia, and a gorgeous vanilla-and-strawberry cake. We'd
taken a bunch of family excursions with Ambrosio as our tour guide.

One, to a town called Covarrubias, transported us to a picturesque
valley in the mountains about forty miles east of Guzmán. Famous
for its black pudding, the town seemed to be a perpetual medieval fair
and tourist attraction. Ambrosio led us through a crowd of lute players
and costumed dancers, jesters and knights, chicken grilling over open
flames, to a famous chapel at the end of town. Inside, musicians were

---

repeat the word *gracias,* as if she were a befuddled movie star looking for auto-
graphs to sign. When introduced to the son of one man—*"Es mi hijo, Javier,"* the
man said—my mother said, *"Encantada, Mi Hijo,"* sounding like a wise kung fu
master.

* And I marveled again at the bar at how storytelling was the native industry, a
swarming hive of words in the bright light of midnight, an interweaving of tales
that all spoke to each other, or past each other. The tales, told by a variety of storytellers, often contained the same set of characters, or could be traced at least by
family name, which lent everything an air of authenticity and familiarity. And
some of these were figures from history, the ur-Castilians, who rose from the dead,
from their own legends, the kings and queens, the knights and dictators and lost
souls. The conversations felt more like continuations, stories like unfurling standards over the field of time.

playing ballads with antiquated instruments to a large crowd. The music filled the church, the voices and strings intermingling with clarity and feeling in that space. I had no idea what they were singing, but it was transfixing—and Ambrosio allowed himself to be transfixed by it. He stood for a long time in thought, then, when the concert ended, gestured for me to follow. He lumbered down a side aisle to two stones by the altar, etched with a name, Fernán González, the eighth-century count who ruled Castile, and that of his wife, Sancha.

Ambrosio knelt by the stones and ran his hand over them. "These are my ghosts," he said. "The ghosts who made me. These are my ancestors. And this is one of my holy spots, where I feel most alive."

In the waning days we made our farewells, with last dinners and visits. Fernando the Mute shimmered beneath his tree across from the church; Clemente still ambushed us with advice; the sheep floated up through town, then out to the *barcos*. There was a legendary afternoon when Leo and I were led down into a series of half-collapsed *bodegas*—was it a test of our mettle or a friendly gesture?—led there by loquacious Carlos the farmer and his small son Alvaro. It didn't seem like a great idea, but we scrambled down into the earth, rump-sliding into the breach behind Carlos, slipping on scree and loose dirt until we were emboweled in guana-filled caverns, convinced that one sneeze would bring it all down on our heads, or that a wolf might come charging. Leo suddenly burst into tears, unloosing an orphan wail, and Carlos, who held a small candle as he led us deeper into complete claustrophobia, brushed his dirty hand over my boy's head in reassurance, an act that startled Leo out of his fear while we plunged deeper.

Carlos was an intriguing figure, hyperindustrious, intelligent, and one of the hardest-working farmers in the village. He was an innovator, too, the only one at that time who had turned to organic farming, as much because he believed in its environmental benefits as because he realized there was a ripe global market, and profit, in it. I was often met by Carlos's smiling face, up at his barn, as I returned from an early-morning run. He would begin telling stories even before I'd slowed to a stop, and with my poor Spanish I strained for meaning while using my refined method of serious head nods and the repetition of the word *vale*—a Spanish version of okay—to convey understanding.

One time, as Carlos spoke of the logistics of keeping falcons in his attic, one of his mousing cats was run over in the road by a friend, who slowed his car to a stop while shaking his head, disappointed in himself. Carlos kept on with his story while his friend backed up past the cat, writhing and bleeding in the road, to offer an apology.

"Nahhh, hombre, no es problema," Carlos said. His friend insisted on his sorryness, and Carlos leaned on his car, took up some tertiary matter with him that had nothing to do with the cat, and sent him on his way, beaming goodbye. Then he walked back, grabbed a shovel, and picked up another story—this about an unprecedented event, a four-mile road race held one year in Guzmán, the town innovators thinking this might attract some kind of crowd, or at least a human being who could actually *run* four miles. Regarding himself as the fittest person in Guzmán, Carlos entered the race, but riding in a tractor all day is different from physical activity, and he realized after sprinting the first quarter mile that he'd greatly overestimated his cardiovascular fitness and now found himself on the verge of dying. True to the Spanish character, this fight with death led Carlos to vow that he would finish the race no matter what. In the end, the record would show him finishing in last place among the five runners who had entered, but he still reigned as town champ, given that no one from Guzmán had entered the contest. "Would I do it again?" he mused. "I might." Then, with the shovel, he buried the cat.

On another late-summer evening Don Honorato invited us to his *bodega,* a neatly kept cave halfway up the hill. It was a perfect night, temperate and clear, and Don Honorato, regal with his carefully parted silver hair, told us a bit of his own fascinating story. His mother had disappeared when he was very young (that was the verb he used—*desaparecer*—but he didn't specify whether she'd died), and his father was a delivery man who often went to the pine forests in the mountains of Soria in his mule-drawn cart to sell cattle feed, hay, and cereals harvested from the fields near Guzmán. This left behind Honorato, who at the age of six became a seller of spirits—*aguardiente,* to be specific. He was charged with riding his horse to fill huge jugs with the stuff at a nearby still run by women, who often took pity on him and fed him breakfast. Then he carried on to the fields, sometimes riding ten miles out and ten back, this diminutive child with big ears, selling liquor to the field hands. The teachers at school understood young Honorato's situation and were lenient as he came and went. But Don Honorato acknowledged that he grew up with a tight ball in his belly and a chip on his shoulder.

He remembered once visiting a teacher who played cards with the priest. Honorato had committed some youthful transgression, and for his punishment the men made him kneel, arms outstretched with a book in either hand, holding them aloft. Honorato held the books as best he could, body beginning to tremble uncontrollably, and when both men started to giggle, the boy grew furious, rose, and with his right hand threw one book at the priest and with his left threw the other at the teacher, then sprinted away. He would have been in big trouble, probably beaten badly with a stick, as happened in those days, had the men not, as he put it, "shit themselves laughing."

As with so many instances in the village, I found myself surprised by this excavated history. Here all summer I'd spoken to Don Honorato daily as he stood watering his lawn in two pairs of pants. I'd thought of him as almost erudite, admired his paternal manner and his considered words of wisdom, especially in regard to keeping grass green beneath the Castilian sun. His fixation was almost comical, and at the same time deeply sentimental, for his wife had loved the lawn. I realized I'd come to depend on him for those pleasant conversations without really knowing the first thing about him. My projection of him—faithful—stood in for everything he might have actually been, or wasn't at all. The truth was, I didn't have a clue.

Now Don Honorato broke into song, conjuring the lyrics of his youth with ease. His voice was tinged with phlegm, but his was a sweet, in-tune tenor. The words filled the twilight:

> *Que bonitas niñas que en Guzmán se entierran,*
> *Pues en esta tierra, es de lo mejor*
> *las unas son rubias, las otras morenas,*
> *pero todas bellas, esto es un primor.*
>
> *Tanta gracia como tienen las muy lindas cortearreras,*
> *Se pasean por las cerras en los dias de San Juan.*
> *Con sus motos de Bracete, con de pars de tambori,*
> *y con sus bellezas luciran!**

It was a song that the men of Guzmán once sang to their women, at fiestas, the bar, the *bodega,* to celebrate their beauty. Don Honorato said he'd been asked to sing it by friends and acquaintances from Bilbao to Madrid, everywhere really. It brought people back to another time. He couldn't remember exactly who had written it, but it was indicative of the way small villages self-mythologized, of how they reminded themselves that theirs was the charmed life, that theirs—and ours—right here and now was the magic moment. That was what we'd begun to find out for ourselves, grounding ourselves among the grounded, two feet on this lawn, water glubbing its nourishment.

---

* *What beautiful girls are buried in Guzmán,*
Since in our soil you find the best
Some are blondes, some are brown-haired,
But all of them are beautiful, a lovely thing!

These pretty harvesters are so full of grace,
They walk the hills on San Juan days.
With their Bracete motorcycles, their drums
and beauty, they will shine.

As PART OF OUR goodbye tour I went to see Emilia, the mayor of Guzmán, in her modest home directly across from the palace. Her front door opened onto the road, and the downstairs was dark, with low ceilings, which made it feel burrowlike.

"*Hombre, venga!*" she said, motioning me in. Though by now most people might have seen me as Ambrosio's lapdog—and perhaps rightly so—and though that fact should have meant the poisoning of any relationship between Emilia and me, the truth is that I was fond of the mayor. I'd first encountered her during an early visit to Guzmán, when I'd attended Mass one Sunday. Afterward she'd approached with a big smile, and the first words out of her mouth were, "Would you like to see our bells?" We passed through a door at the back of the church, and spiraled up to the bell tower above. Suspended from open arches were four bells, made of bronze. They'd been crafted by a reputable German bell maker, Emilia said, and were rung only on special occasions: before Mass, to start the fiesta, or when someone died. Back during the war, the bells would sound a warning when bombing sorties flew overhead, and people took shelter in their *bodegas* and basements.

Short and busy, with a raspy contralto, Emilia smoked cigarettes automatically, with zeal. She made tea, brought out a plate of *pasteles;* her fine, feathered pet, a white parakeet, flew through the cramped rooms, eventually perching on my shoulder. Although at this point I could fumble a few questions in Spanish and understand some in return, I clicked on my tape recorder as backup. The parakeet muttered; Emilia lit a cigarette.

"*Que tal, Miguel?*" she said. "Has it been a good summer?"

"Marvelous," I said. "Magical." She smiled and repeated "*Bien, bien.*" Sitting across from her now, I regarded her as one of my *majos*—if I had *majos* here.* And I marveled at how similar she was

---

* I counted Don Honorato as one of my *majos,* too—as well as Ambrosio's father. And Ambrosio's brother Angel. Roberto and Mika, Ambrosio's other brother and

to Ambrosio in her energy, warmth, and decisiveness. Their alikeness made it easy to understand how they'd been friends, and why they might be enemies. The cause of their rift was, as Ambrosio's daughter, Asunita, had told me, "forgotten," but apparently unsolvable now. Had Emilia been behind the flyer campaign that drove Ambrosio from Guzmán? Had Ambrosio started the pernicious gossip that turned public opinion against Emilia's mayoral doings, running his own shadow administration out of the bar? Who knew? But these were the chiseled narrative lines that their enmity ran on.

We started with chitchat, how the children were doing, the shortening days and cooler weather, how soon we would be leaving. She asked about my book; I told her it was going well. *Very* well. And super. I described our field trip to Covarrubias, mentioning that Ambrosio had been our tour guide. If the segue was ham-handed and Columbo-like, I didn't care.

"Una pregunta," I said. "What do you remember about that time when Ambrosio wanted to move his cheesemaking operation into the *palacio?"*

"Hombre," said Emilia, shaking her hand as if she'd just touched something very hot. "It was a long time ago." It was hard for her to speak openly about anything, she said. Her job as mayor required impartiality, for she was often called upon to mediate various land dis-

---

wife, were also my *majos*. Carlos the farmer was one of my *majos*. Abel, the metalworker, was very cool, and though I didn't know him as well, he might have been one of my *majos*. Fernando, deaf and mute—I counted him as a *majo,* for I thought we understood each other at some unspoken level. Pelayo might have been a *majo,* and the bakers, Marcos and Ilena, they were certainly *majos* because of our demographic kinship. I liked Cristian, the sculptor of nude women, so he was my *majo*. There were many old women who smiled at us when we went walking, and they, too, were all *majos,* as was Puri, Ambrosio's mom, just for being Ambrosio's mom. Basically my *majos* included anyone who talked to me, was kind to us, or was affiliated with anyone kind to us. As for the ones who cast wary glances, the ones who steered clear or otherwise shot us the occasional malevolent sneer, they were all just one night at the bar, one rotation in the telling room, away from being *majos,* too.

putes, financial issues, or tensions between neighbors. But she admitted that she was tiring of attacks on her character, most of them related to her handling of the recent state-funded renovation of the *palacio,* which was still in process. If she'd indeed faced off with Ambrosio over possession of the building all those years ago, she'd won. At least temporarily. But it came with a cost. When I told her that I'd heard inferences that she had something to do with the flyer campaign that ran Ambrosio out of town, she looked sad. "No," she said. "It wasn't me."

In the Guzmánian sense of time, Emilia had been an interloper, which made her a target, too. She'd moved here, to her husband's village, almost thirty years ago, while in her early twenties. Together they had two children, a boy and a girl. They were like any other family here. They went to church. They became embroiled in town life, the town had elected her mayor, and now, after working so hard for her family and community, it seemed Emilia was wrung out, struggling to find herself. "I've tried for four years to bring a cultural life to this village," she said, emitting an exasperated puff. "I have two more years left in my term. It's lonely being mayor, hombre," she said.

I could imagine it, especially for someone with her energy. The day we'd first met, she'd pointed out from our bell-tower perch all the improvements she hoped to bring to the village, from gussying up the trash-ridden playground and cemetery to the introduction of streetlights. But there was hardly money in the budget, and change didn't strike everybody as a good thing, though it kept coming in small, personal ways: Someone died, someone went to a nursing home. Someone, like the bright young woman Rosa, moved back to care for her dad, Antonio, the Andalusian.

Rosa was an interesting case study. In her twenties, sweet and funny, she was a good friend of Asunita's. Once she'd worked at Pinto's bar and then at a hotel in Roa, where the gossip mill surrounding her and her possible suitors was always grinding. The rumors were so pervasive that she could barely converse with a boy before there were inventions of a torrid affair. This affliction, for that's what it really was, seemed to place Rosa on the defensive, slowly removing her from some life she might have dreamed for herself, for to have fallen in love, or even let herself go for a night, was to have fulfilled someone else's pernicious prophecy of her, when quite the opposite was true. She seemed to be sacrificing life to be here, not living it.

Emilia's enervation, meanwhile, was the kind that settled into the bones over time. Sameness was Guzmán's charm and curse: Pinto sat behind the bar, grumpy or happy, ignoring or doing his job. The same farmers came and went from the fields, sometimes in a new shirt or with a haircut, sometimes shaven or hung over. The old men gathered for cards and the old women swept out their houses. The sun rose and set. Opinions ossified, never to change. Spring came, followed by summer, the hail, the gathering cumuli of autumn, the crippling blast of winter wind. People were friendly and remote. Grudges were frozen in blue ice. Was this glory or closed-minded obstinacy?

Because Guzmán was so strictly bound by the codes and rituals of its past, because someone in that tight circle of eighty people was always naysaying your actions, it seemed inevitable that defeatism would set in—and Emilia's seemed to reside in the unrealized visions she'd had for Guzmán as a tourist destination. When validation wasn't forthcoming, when the hordes didn't arrive (Castile was never *ever* going to break the grip of Provence or Tuscany) and her efforts at refurbishing the castle were second-guessed, something in her seemed to have broken. And now she echoed what Pelayo had observed.

"Little villages like this have a way of squelching your dreams," she said. In that moment, she could have been speaking for both herself and Ambrosio.

It put me in mind of a story I'd heard about the man who owned our summer rental. He'd retired to Guzmán, his birth village, with his wife. Then he built his dream house, not fancy or perhaps even attractive from the outside, but its virtues were its amazing views, light, and space. When it was finished, they moved in, but his wife was soon diagnosed with cancer and died quickly. In the aftermath, the man—I'll call him Consuelo—appeared to let himself go, didn't wash, developed a host of mysterious physical ailments. The village worried for him in his grieving. They felt they would soon lose him, too. But then something amazing happened, something that should happen to all lonely old people: He fell in love.

The woman was from a town in a different region, but she came to live with him in that house on the hill. And, oh, how they carried on, kissing in public (unheard of!), dancing in the street (*escándalo!*), and, most shocking of all, sunbathing nude on the rooftop patio. Consuelo would go down to the bar with his pals and share certain intimate details of the boudoir. People were titillated, incensed.

The shock of the residents—and worse, his children—wasn't something that concerned Consuelo. Yet he must have been worried for his paramour, for she was the one suddenly branded with a scarlet letter. Guzmán wasn't a stage set for the scene in a movie where two lovers trip over each other in a trance of self-referential adoration, then make out in a fountain. The priest spoke from the pulpit about modesty, restraint. The woman was shunned. Eventually the lovebirds took wing to her town and were rarely seen in Guzmán again, which was cause for some relief, for had they continued with their liberal ways, who knew how it would have ended?

"Gossip is the only activity here besides television," Asunita once told me, "especially in the winter."

"You can count on your enemies," said Emilia now, "but sometimes it's the one who smiles who keeps you up at night."

There she sat, a crucifix on the wall behind her, framed photos all around: the children, a wedding shot, Emilia with her young family at the beach. She looked like a kid, tanned and full of life.

"Someday," she said, sighing, poised with a cup of tea in one hand and cigarette in the other, parakeet fluttering in the air behind her head, "I may move somewhere far away from here." But something in her face in that sallow light made me think that it was almost certain she wouldn't.

NEAR THE END of our stay, in the first days of September, Ambrosio invited us up to his *bodega* for a *merienda*. Though the invitation came as a matter of course, spoiled as we were by him, he informed us that he was also gathering some friends, which added a hint of uncharacteristic formality. What friends—and for what occasion?

When Sara and I arrived, towing Leo in his Real Madrid jersey and May in a red dress and hat that described a big triangle below and a smaller one on top (as if she'd arrived directly from some Paris of one-year-old sophisticates), we found a covey of Ambrosio's best *majos,* all of them in various aspects of enjoyment and inebriation. There were the bloodshot eyes and crooked-tooth smiles, the togetherness that comes from elbow-to-elbow eating and drinking, from conversation that forms a bridge connecting human landmasses, all of it the trademark of Ambrosio's telling room. Even before we were halfway up the hill we could hear throaty laughter pouring over the village.

Inside, the windows were thrown open and a breeze stirred the smoky room. Mon Virgo loomed to the east, and through the casement the roofs seemed lit on fire with their glowing red *tejas,* or tiles. On the table a minor feast awaited: clay pots covered with foil, plates of chorizo, the *porrón* and *aguardiente* going around, bread and olives. We were met by the scent of some sort of consommé—and then Ambrosio, with his great blast of welcome. "AMIIIIIGOS!!" he boomed, drawing out the word, singing it. He pinched May's cheeks and lifted Leo from the ground, swung him, and placed him down gently again, his feet finding purchase in slow motion, like an astronaut first touching the moon.

Ambrosio introduced the men at the table, many of whom I'd met during the summer. Ambrosio Senior was there, ears jutting, that smile on his face, working the *porrón* when conscious, provoking his son to make a familiar joke about how, after years of avid tippling, after thousands of gallons of wine waterfalling from spout to mouth, his father had notched a groove on his front tooth where the liquid pooled before flowing down his gullet. Don Ambrosio nodded at that and slurred something that everyone laughed at—and then, in the moment's diversion, snuck another lengthy pull from the *porrón*.

We were told that there was stew in one pot, and in another, *orejas de las ovejas*. OH-*RAY*-HAS DE LAS O-*VAY*-HAS. Because the words were so sonically similar, this sounded like "sheep of sheep," or "ear of ear." When we asked for clarification, we were told it was deep-fried sheep ears, and that seemed very funny to us, the way Old Castilians might prank unknowing visitors. We assumed appropriately shocked expressions, then moved to the no-but-seriously. *Seriously*—it was deep-fried sheeps' ears. And since they'd only been waiting on our arrival to eat, the foil was unpeeled from the pots, plates appeared from a basket, and then the deep-fried collection of ears—two, three dozen in all?—were divvied up and the sweet-smelling glop was ladled. Before her serving even became a possibility, Sara demurred. She said she didn't eat mutton, then mumbled "*Ears, mutton ears*." Meanwhile, outwardly I showed no fear, affected an expression of joy and anticipation. *Venga! Dame!* I was trying hard to prove I'd passed my summer audition, that I was one of them. I wished I could say something appropriately Ambrosio-like, for instance boom out: *Joder, hombres, I shit in the milk, for it's been three weeks since my last chewy ear.* And then slap someone on the back—or something. Ear of sheep, I imagined, was probably going to be like leather tongue of shoe (potentially manageable) . . . or deep-fried frog (less get-throughable) . . . and then my mind went blank.

I was not drunk enough for this, hadn't had a drop yet, but at the table a place was opened for me, a parting of flesh, and I squeezed between two of the smoke-stained men, where a plate sat with four sheep ears. I smiled broadly, trying to convey assurance. In other travels I'd been occasionally called upon to eat strange food: blood pancakes; rotted, urine-infused shark meat; whale steak. I'd had ants and crickets once in the Burmese jungle, and while not ready for Zingerman's prime time, they were enjoyably crunchy. There was a whole raft of food I took for granted—foie gras, hot dogs, even eggs—food you couldn't think too hard about. So what if back home animal ears were used as dog chews? The Old Castilian recognized a delicacy when it was laid out before him.

Except it was so *chewy,* and it gave a luxury of time for thought. What in the name of Zeus were sheep ears made of, anyway? Ligament? Cartilage?* They didn't really look like ears but like thick, oversized potato chips. And they fought back in your mouth, like a flexed muscle. As I chewed, I began nodding my pleasure. *Wow, this is something . . . something* else. *DO . . . NOT . . . BARF.* After some time, I swallowed hard and started on a second (two left on the plate now, until the pot came around again, and one of the burlies graciously scooped three more on). There was much ribald conversation, but I hardly paid attention. Chewing, chewing, chewing. *Do not . . . do not . . . do not . . . !*

Once the second ear was down, I focused on my stew—quidbits of tender meat (important, I now knew, not to ask from what), carrots, potatoes—and during this time, two more ears were delivered to my plate. *Seven left.* Which is when I took theatrical umbrage, gesturing with open palms to the pile of sheep ears and then at the plates of others that seemed to have three or four at most. No, hombres, this was not fair to those who consider themselves lovers of the sheep ear! As an egalitarian, I demanded *igual* rights for all! Sometimes Castilian hospitality could be its own tyranny. I scooped four back, immediately regretting that I hadn't added two more. And then it went

---

* Later, when I referred this question to the all-knowing Internet, I came upon a website entitled About Chinese Food, with this verbatim prose poem about preparing sheep ears for consumption: "Handbags Gristle constituted may, alone or in middle ear apex, and the roots. Net primary scraper before cooking, the root of the ear pull a knife, into the clear water pot Cook for use. Dishes such as Tianjin 'quick-boiled wind from Afar' Henan 'Coriander cuisine wind from Afar' Shaanxi 'Braised wind from Afar,' 'halal cuisine' double Feng Chui '(middle of sheep ear),' fan '(sheep ear Apex systems)' and 'gantry angle' (sheep-the root of the ear). Sheep ear may also cut shredded, FRY quickly, or soup. Sheep ear practice guidance: Ear can be baked or grilled inlay filling cooked in sheep. In China, the pig's ear is often added spice conditioning."

on again, between my molars—*Handbag gristle, middle ear apex*—
somewhat excruciatingly as I tried to get down another, and then another. As soon as our collective focus turned back to stories and wine,
bawdy joking and ribbing, I exchanged a set of hand signals with
Sara, the dirty-diaper hand signals, my pointing, her shaking her
head no, me shaking my head back *yes!*—an attempt on my behalf to
create confusion and parental alarm so I could excuse myself, which I
did, to attend to the dirty diaper that wasn't dirty at all but would save
me from the sheep-ear imbroglio.

I carried May outside and breathed deeply, letting my lungs fill
with clean air, my queasiness resolving in purification, in that vision
of high clouds carrying away to the east in wisps and floating feathers
over Mon Virgo, the mystical mesa. Everything dissolved then. She
was nearly fourteen months old, this little girl with fine strawberry-
blond hair and round eyes who had blossomed from that fleshy,
swollen-eyed, wailing lump to this burgeoning nymph, this shiny,
ever-alert creature who seemed to miss nothing. Even her squalls were
fantastic, fits of tears and high emotion. She was still light, but heavier
than when we'd arrived.

If I feared anything, this is what I feared: We were all growing so
fast. And here was my daughter, her limbs reaching farther, her eyes
focusing higher. Now her mind sparked and glimmered, her mouth
motored on. Her gaze was so intent, it seemed to belong to an old
woman from another time who had seen it all, and was seeing it all
again. She wiggled and giggled, shouted her *holas* and *aguas,* burst
into tears, and waddled with such determination and brio as to have
earned a new nickname, Goosey. When we inevitably brought her
into our bed during the night, she slept between us, plugging fingers
into both of our belly buttons, then falling fast asleep.

Gazing out over the ancient Meseta with the gruff, worn voices of
the *majos* in the background, I was arguing back, telling myself we
had so much time, and that even if she was a gift more than a possession, we still had a while to offer her these landscapes and people,
these adventures and epiphanies, these molecules of parental awe and

humility. Someday, of course, she would light out on her own, following her own riverbed, and though we'd follow as long as she allowed, and though we trusted she'd come and go from our lives with regularity, she would also be half memory, always the little girl here in my arms, or the five-, ten-, fifteen-year-old she was yet to be.

In this reverie, I felt a meaty paw grip my shoulder, and, thinking my ruse revealed—or my tender thoughts—I turned to meet Ambrosio's inquiring gaze. "My-kull!" he said. "Come in, I've something more for you."

Something more? Pig schnozzle? Hobbit toe? I'd already been given *more,* was trying to escape their wretched regime of *more.* However, I followed obediently, and when we entered the telling room again, he went to the corner next to the window, with his broad back to me. While the men carried on around the table, oblivious and louder by the minute, roaring with wine fumes, Sara stood off to the side holding Leo's hand, pointing at whatever it was Ambrosio busied himself with, mouthing the words, *"Come look!"* When I leaned in, I saw that Ambrosio had lit a Sterno can that flashed a blue flame. He had a can opener in one hand, and lifted a white tin with black lettering in the other, that of the cheese known as Páramo de Guzmán.

He took the can opener to it, punctured the seal, and cranked the metal into a jagged edge, peeling back the top. Then he stared down at the wonder he held in his hands. It was his offering, the last tin of cheese he would ever open, more than a decade old, and he pushed it with a finger, in a sort of methodical way. The cheese, the stunning, alluring, beatific, mind-blowing cheese, glorious source and cipher that it was, the original, undead, soulful cheese, redounded in its soft amber glow. And it lit Ambrosio's face, too.

Had he planned this as our goodbye present?

Ambrosio seemed pleased by what he'd found, as he'd been pleased all those years ago, on that Christmas Eve when the cheese spoke to him and said, *Get that son of a bitch.* But if the cheese said anything to him now—*What's taking you so long?* Or: *Forgive.*—it was between the two of them. Given the enormousness of the moment—the last tin opened—I'd say that what followed seemed to verge on sacrilege. Everyone at the table ignored Ambrosio. Or perhaps it was very Castilian to downplay it all. Ambrosio himself called no attention to the cheese. He took a pair of pliers and held the tin over the flame, allowing that it was important to heat the cheese, to open it up, let the pores and veins breathe, let the oils and herbs mingle and genie forth. This was one simple part of unlocking the great secret. The olive oil in which it soaked began to bubble, and Ambrosio bent over the cheese while he rejoined the conversation, adding his own commentary to the gossip. On he talked as the room filled with the aroma of warm milk, and at some point, he pulled out his pocketknife and jabbed one wedge of the cheese—the knife tip sinking softly inside—carried it through the air and pinioned it on a plate, then began slicing carefully.

Watching his thick fingers grip the knife and delicately work the blade, watching as the cheese gave, mini-slab by mini-slab, I couldn't help but imagine those wedges as emblems of a lost purity. Before genetic modification, before the inundation of windblown spores and superspores, there was a time when the land was discrete and parceled into its own ecosystems, tucked in its own valleys and canyons, containing its own idiosyncrasies and bursts of inspiration and originality. When Ambrosio spoke of the "old tastes," this is partially what he spoke of: the taste of the Meseta, or this patch of the Meseta, as it once existed, and as it coursed through the blood of the animals here and sprouted from the earth. The wheat from these fields, *el trigo,* tasted different from the wheat of Burgos, fifty miles away; the grapes, *las uvas,* were heartier here than the grapes of Rioja. The *lechuga*— lettuce—of Castile, celebrated for its succulence, was worth twice that found in the rest of Spain. Even the water of Guzmán was different from the water of Roa just down the road. "We need to preserve the tastes of this magical place for our children," he'd once told me.

Arrayed on the plate now were a dozen or so slices. Ambrosio offered the cheese to us first, and I took a piece, then Sara took one, our eyes meeting briefly as we mirrored flickering smiles, and together we slid them into our mouths.

Yes, this was really happening.

How do you begin to describe a moment for which you've waited a small eternity, thinking it was never to be? How do you downplay such a consummation? Inside, I was turning cartwheels, doing the watusi, soft-shoeing with a vaudeville smile, while outside, my ersatz Castilian stoicism crumbled.

"Wow . . . wow . . . wow!" I repeated, as Ambrosio watched and grinned, saying nothing.

Oh, it was a strong cheese, a Herculean cheese, you could tell that immediately, tangy and tart, melting and then flaring again. With the first crumble it spread slowly, in lava flow, across the palatal landscape, tasting of minerals and luscious buttercream, of chamomile and thyme. It tasted of flower and dirt, manure and nectar—and perhaps of love and hate, too. A gustatory alert went up and my whole mouth was watering and alive, awakened from Van Winkle slumber and emergency-ready. This was a cheese that, like its master, sharply caught you unawares, lovingly provoked you while assuming your submission, and then its richness overwhelmed all previous thoughts, tastes, memories. I now understood, if vaguely, how the cheese must have created a conduit to the past, for its concentration was a force, an energy, a momentum, the psychic drill bit boring a wormhole in this Castilian space-time continuum.

I had no past with this cheese. My past lay in those individually wrapped slices of processed Kraft American cheese, or cheese so alien that it was spelled C-H-E-E-Z (Cheez Whiz, Cheez Doodles, Cheez-Its), fromage facsimiles that conjured school lunches and our seventies suburban kitchen, my mom flipping grilled cheese sandwiches, punching open can after can of Hi-C for my brothers and me, until our purple/orange mustaches glowed with a Sharpie permanence. Eating Páramo de Guzmán now, I realized that *this* was the memory. That is, I was *having* the memory as I was *making* the memory. That this cheese could compress time. And yet it was just cheese, right? So what was it that I tasted now?

Ambrosio leaned over and dropped the plate on the table among the chattering men, who reached out greedily and grabbed what there was to grab. Had anyone asked, he might have said: *Oh that? That's just some old cheese we had lying about.* But no one bothered. They gobbled the slices, carrying on as they did, not once remarking on what they ate.

Perhaps Ambrosio wouldn't have had it any other way. It seemed like an age-old Castilian transaction, homemade food delivered to guests, like the sharing of family wine, but with wine also came conversation about the wine, and debate about the wine, and expositions about the wine, histories and tall tales and smack talk, and here, with Ambrosio's cheese, there was none of that. What didn't occur to me at the time, what never crossed my mind, in fact, was that perhaps the event was significant only for us, that maybe we'd made the cheese mythic—or I had, sucking in everyone behind me—and Ambrosio, flattered as anyone might be by an interested visitor, and gifted in the art of mythmaking himself, had gone right along with me, pumping helium into my balloon while I ran around urging everyone to look at the beautiful balloon. Meanwhile the men in the room took the cheese for what it was: *cheese.* Besides, why would they willingly revisit Ambrosio's bad luck with it?

And yet here were Sara and I, transfixed and under a late-summer spell, now with a second piece of the original Páramo de Guzmán in our mouths, tasting the specific land and animals from ten years earlier (the Churra sheep grazing in the Barco de Valcabadillo), the essence of a lost place unlocked for us by Ambrosio, the giant on his witness hill. What did the cheese taste like? I'd like to pretend it tasted like love or history or God—if those things possess a real taste—that its molecules reshaped my own and created a flash of insight, but you know, it tasted like . . . *really good cheese.* Sublime cheese, though in this context, it didn't matter what the cheese tasted like.

The children cooed and squawked. We were bursting with gratitude. Ambrosio placed the last of the slices on the table, and one by one, the men with hairy fingers and raspy laughter picked them from the plate and popped them thoughtlessly into their mouths, until the much-heralded and ballyhooed Páramo de Guzmán cheese was gone forever.

III

"This is Castile, the land that makes men only to waste them."

Alfonso Fernández Coronel

17

HALF-TRUTH LIES, AND OTHER MISDEMEANORS

"Egads . . . is this what I'd done with my life, then?"

Imagine the deaf painter Francisco Lucientes Goya near the end, living beyond the city gates of seventeenth-century Madrid, by the lazy Manzanares River, rising each morning to his lover, Leocadia Zorrilla, who putters in the farmhouse where they live, movements he can't hear so much as sense in vibrations through the timbers. In the first light of day, the deaf painter shifts off the bed, hikes on his trousers, tucks his shirt over his paunch, looping leather suspenders over sloped shoulders, and reaches for his badger-hair paintbrush, a habit of his seventy-two years.

I picture the view from the deaf painter's window as it once must have been, before Madrid sprawled to devour its outer edge: meadows and farmland rolling to some local infinity. An arid breeze stirs, carrying a faint whiff of manure. Flashing through that window, too, are the apparitions of Spain: its kings and queens, marauders and plotters, victors and jesters. The wooden-handled brush records it all, is the deaf painter's hoe, his ax, his pen. When he paints, he holds history in his hand. Now, near the end, the images appear to him from some dark dream-river: witches and monsters, the wretched and doomed. And he paints them without a canvas, in a frenzy it seems, directly on the plaster walls.

As a feckless, brawling young man, Goya had a fantasy: to paint the king. It seemed absurd, for he was twice rejected from the Royal Academy of Fine Arts, had no contacts at the royal court, grew up in a relatively obscure, lower-middle-class family of artisans in Zaragoza, and seemed an erratic womanizer who enjoyed song and drink as much as art. He went away to Italy in 1770, where he traveled from town to town with a *quadrilla* of bullfighters, placed second in a painting competition sponsored by the city of Parma, and returned home to marry the daughter of his art teacher.

In Zaragoza he found work painting a church cupola, then some frescoes, and eventually won a commission to paint designs woven by the Royal Tapestry Factory, some of which were hung in the royal residence at El Escorial, which is how he came to the attention of the royal family. At the age of thirty-seven he did a portrait of the Count of Floridablanca, a chief minister to the king, then painted Crown Prince Don Luis. Within three years he was named court painter, a position he held for nearly four decades, until his death in 1828. He painted canvas after canvas of the king and queen in various aspects: posed in drawing rooms, eating, seated on horses, if not comely people then surrounded by the finery and glamour of wealth.

One of his most famous paintings, entitled *The Family of Charles IV,* depicts the royal couple, inflated by arrogance, striking a weak-chinned, toadlike pose with their brood. From our vantage, it seems an almost merciless rendering, the frog who became king without first having transformed into the handsome prince. The nineteenth-century French writer Théophile Gautier saw in Goya's handiwork a royal couple who could be "the corner baker and his wife after they won the lottery." And yet as Goya's biographer Robert Hughes points out, the king was lucky to have Goya's talents—for perhaps Charles was even uglier in real life—and asks, "Did ever so dim a monarch deserve such virtuoso treatment?" He describes the painting as "a free, spotted, impasted crust of pigment that keeps breaking into light," and "an exciting defense of kingship."

It is indeed stunning, on many contradictory levels, but what always draws my eye is that figure in the shadows at the back of the room: Goya, paying homage to Velázquez's *Las Meninas* by painting himself into the scene at his easel, grinning as if to say, *I alone consign these people to history.*

When I imagine the deaf painter in that farmhouse at the edge of Madrid, that's who I see: the storyteller who's lived a teeming double life, remunerated for trying to glorify a drab king in his portraits even as he takes to the streets and fields with his sketchbook to paint the king's subjects. One moment he's worrying over the fabrics and dispositions of his royal subjects, the next he's drawing the lowly and defenseless (children and women in rags, the insane), as well as the repugnant (murderers, pederasts, and rapists, in full pillage). He paints massacres in war, and on one canvas of a mother and child on the verge of falling prey to a vengeful mob, he scrawls the words "I saw it," placing himself at the scene of the crime as a documentarian.

I picture the dabbed paint on the walls of the farmhouse that will make twelve images known as the Black Paintings. In one, two boys flail at each other with cudgels, lumped up to their knees in Iberian earth, as if sprung from it like stalks, doomed to bash each other to bone and viscera. In another, Saturn, huge and monstrous, gray haired and bone colored, appears possessed by a carnality so overpowering that he seems shocked to find himself gnawing on his son's headless cadaver. Here are witches in icy blues, the devil in dark shadow, the Fates in dun-colored ugliness. And then the head of a helpless, wide-eyed dog, just above what appears to be rising water. Here near the end, Goya paints the most terrible reflection of his home country, and the most truthful. The deaf man, who usually signs his paintings with his name, leaves these allegories blank.

Soon, after a quarrel with the king, Francisco Goya flees to France for his safety, leaving everything behind, including the Black Paintings. Whatever his disenchantments, he paints on. In one of his last works, that of a milkmaid reflecting youth and beauty, he eschews his brush altogether, using only his fingers, his palette knife, and rags. Before his death at the age of eighty-two, before his body is transported back to Spain and interred in a chapel a short distance from the monsters on the walls of the stone house, he pens a letter to a friend. "Pardon me infinitely for this bad handwriting," he scrawls. "I've no more sight, no hand, nor pen, nor inkwell, I lack everything— all I've got left is will."

Is that what drives him, then? The will to express truths he's already found, or has left to find? Does the younger man, ecstatic to be painting at court, worrying over the gold silks and orange velvets of his king, have an inkling, even then, that he will come to see his king as flawed? And if the king is flawed, why did he paint him so beautifully in the first place?

WHEN I HAD FIRST broached to Ambrosio the idea of my book— a book about him and his cheese—he seemed to take it all in, nodding with understanding, and said that he would do whatever he could for me. I'm sure something in the project appealed to his grandiosity, as it might for all of us. He appreciated the idea of being memorialized, but also perhaps of finding a bigger megaphone for what mattered most to him: his *grandísima filosofía* and setting the record straight about the cheese. (Did storyteller's revenge factor into it, too?) Thereafter, when he found himself making an important observation, or thought I needed the correct spelling, he'd remove the notebook from my hand as if it were half his, and jot down the necessary information.

Thus, the book became known in Guzmán as AMBROSIO'S BOOK, eventually having little to do with its author, who seemed to take forever in writing it, who seemed to be a hindrance, actually. On occasion I'd be asked by some random townsperson: How's

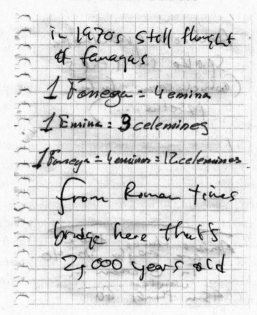

in 1970s still flought
of fanagas

1 Fanega = 4 emina

1 Emina = 3 celemines

1 Fanega = 4 emines = 12 celemines

from Roman times

bridge here thats
2,000 years old

AMBROSIO'S BOOK going? Or: When will we see AMBROSIO'S
BOOK? Or: Did AMBROSIO'S BOOK get a lot of attention in
America?

It was difficult to explain that AMBROSIO'S BOOK was really a
pile of half-finished drafts moldering on my desk in the attic back
home. In the year after our return, I sequestered myself and wrote, always concluding at those same end-of-the-summer scenes, shipwrecked
in that vineyard after the hailstorm with Ambrosio among the bleeding grape-corpses or sharing his last tin of Páramo de Guzmán, and I
couldn't bring myself to push on. What held me back wasn't exactly
writer's block, because I kept writing, amending, adding pages.

Perhaps it was some underlying complex: I didn't want to go any
further because I didn't want to add time to the story, to Ambrosio's
or mine, to life itself. (*Add more time and the boy becomes insufferable;
the king is made a fool of. Someone calls for everyone's head.*) At dinner
with a friend in Manhattan, I laid out the whole problem, and he suggested taking a page from Philip Roth's *Operation Shylock: A Confes-
sion,* creating a doppelganger in hopes that this might release the

book, that by halving myself, half of myself could stay and half of myself could scout the territory ahead. This made perfect postmodern sense. If not Rothian, I did contain multitudes, didn't I?

Thus, I embarked on a draft featuring myself and my alter ego, nicknamed Possum, a draft that caromed and cascaded for a couple of hundred pages, and should anyone suggest that the writer's life is nothing but glory, I'll never forget a meeting with my editor, who had just returned from Japan, jetlagged and more than slightly irritated by Possum's impossible megalomania, saying, as she patted the pile of paper that represented months of work, "I think you need to start again."

And so I did. I wrote the Speed Draft and the Footprint Draft, the Here We Go Draft and Almost There Draft, the I'm In Hell Draft and the Kill Me Now Draft, all of them—*again!*—breaking off at the finale of our Guzmán summer, with May in my arms and the taste of Ambrosio's cheese on my tongue.*

What was my problem?

I missed my first deadline, and was given a new one. *Don't freak,* I was telling myself. *You're freaking.*

I tried to work up my own *grandísima filosofía:* Time is irrelevant—and writing a book is like building a house that will be a hundred years old (in book years) before anyone is allowed to inhabit it: entire rooms have to be rewallpapered; wings added and torn down; the chimney clogged with ash swept clean, billowing with smoke. The roof needs repair, the windows need cleaning, and when it comes time to put it on the market, you hustle to create the illusion that it has always been perfect, of a piece, that it was born into the world fully formed—or, at the very least, habitable.

My book advance spent, I traveled for magazine stories—Australia, Ukraine, Afghanistan—living on that familiar adrenaline rush of perpetual deadlines. What made matters worse was that I'd stopped

---

* Was this to be my midlife crisis, then, a book forever stuck at the end of the summer of 2003? If you could order such a thing from a catalogue, mine would have been called "The Miss Havisham," the world frozen at twenty minutes to nine, wedding cake melting on the table.

talking about the book altogether, stashed it away like the obscure tomes in my backpack, as if they were CIA case files: *Gatherings from Spain, Fields of Castile, A Romantic in Spain.* When someone asked after this book of mine and I actually admitted I was writing about cheese, the most common response was, "You mean like *Who Moved My Cheese?*" At first I thought nothing of the analogy, knowing nothing about it, but eventually I visited Wikipedia to find that the book in question was a "business parable" with two mice characters, "Scurry" and "Sniff," and two miniature humans, "Hem" and "Haw," who meet at a place called "Cheese Station C" and gobble cheese until it's all gone, at which point the mice move on to "Cheese Station N" while the miniature humans begin arguing, and hurling recriminations about how the cheese disappeared at "Cheese Station C."

After that, when people came around and said, "Like *Who Moved My Cheese?*, right?" and started guffawing, I would join them (A-HA-HA-HA . . .) until they stopped (. . . HA-HA-HA . . .) and moved away (. . . HA-HA-HA . . .) or, with a look of concern, said they were sorry. And I would say, Oh no, this is not a book about the conceptual, perceptual whatnot of businesspeople and how to build an empire thing: I'm writing the epic history of the ingenious Ambrosio Molinos de las Heras, visionary cheesemaker, witch doctor of human truths, and storyteller extraordinaire.

And that usually put an end to the conversation. Occasionally someone would exhibit the kind of bewilderment reserved for the platypus tank at the aquarium, and would raise the question that frightened me most: Why?

Why? Because something that started as a lark to a broke grad student—to go to Spain and someday try THE MOST EXPENSIVE CHEESE EVER SOLD!*—turned into nearly two decades of my life, thus conflating said lark with love, loss, birth, and death.

---

* With Páramo de Guzmán at $22 a pound, this claim couldn't be verified, of course, and it would have to be qualified. Most expensive cheese sold at Zingerman's up until 1991? Yes, Ari had said as much. Most expensive cheese in Michigan? Maybe. But certainly not the world. As an example of cheeseflation these twenty-odd years

Why? Because I was born into a family, like others, that had once left Europe behind, and so here, I thought, was my chance to regain everything lost by my ancestors, to reclaim the virtues of the abandoned, agrarian past.

Why? Because I could see those of my generation who were increasingly made miserable by their acquired bitterness, and—this will sound terribly naïve—I wanted to go backward and find innocence again.

Why? Because in Guzmán, nothing was ever disingenuous or ironic. In talking to Ambrosio once about the nearby convent named St. Domingo de Silos, one of the places where the Spanish language was first written down, he became animated, describing the spot as *"impresionante"*—amazing, astonishing, impressive—with signature emphasis on the word, the same emphasis he would have given it were he describing an old well or vineyard or lamb cooked over an open flame. "It has one of the oldest cypress trees in Spain," he said, "and the church—you can feel the music in your body. The sound becomes your body. It rises to the cupola and crashes back down, a *choca de física*. That is divinity. That is what real sound should do."

Why? Because Ambrosio seemed right so much of the time, and he forced his prescription for a better life on me—and I felt honored to receive it.

Why? Because in the end I saw this whole business as a learning moment of some sort—and I was waiting to see how he might resolve the ending.

I said none of this to those people who asked why I'd squandered so many precious American hours writing about a piece of Spanish cheese. In the end we were too busy for the long answer, which re-

---

later, one of the most expensive cheeses on the market today is a white stilton made with edible gold leaf and gold liqueur that sells for $450 a pound. Allegedly the priciest cheese in the world, however, is a smoked cheese called *pule,* made from the milk of Balkan donkeys, that costs between $500 and $700 a pound. It was reported in December 2012 that the tennis player Novak Djokovic had purchased the global supply of white, crumbly *pule* for a chain of restaurants he planned to open.

quired time and concentration, eye contact and the negation of our
personal, handheld self-reflectors for more than a minute. No, outwardly I shrugged, while inwardly the answer came in the piles of
puzzled words and half starts, the drafts that became my own figura-
tive quest to make cheese, none of the batches tasting quite right, but
still, I told myself, in pursuit of *something*.

DURING THIS EXTENDED PERIOD of drafting and redrafting, hallucina-
tion and hard work, we had another child, to make three—towheaded
Nicholas, born an exuberant bundle of motion. Now there was no
containing anyone or anything. The children grew of their own accord, long unfrozen from the fleeting dream of timelessness in
Guzmán. At night while I wrote in the attic, they slept on the floor
below, mumbling in sleep, their bones elongating. They lost baby fat,
grew complex emotions. Their sleep-talk evolved from the single
bleats of "Why?" and "No!" to actual sentences, like one our daughter uttered: "You are *not* cookie-worthy, sir!"

Now—between her assignments out in the world (India, Portugal, Ghana)—Sara urged me to return to Guzmán, to ask some
direct questions, to remind myself that this cheese drama wasn't
all just a figment, that it was real and deserved resolution. "You
need to put an end to this," she said. Drive a stake through it. Kill
the bull, *estoque* to the hilt. For some reason this is what I seemed
to dread most, the path that led to the end, to a knock on Julián's
door, like some muckraking journalist. Would it be opened wide
or slammed shut? Was he a despicable snake or someone else
altogether?

"No more digressions," she said.

"*Everything* is a digression in Castile," I replied, adding a scholarly
addendum that Castile itself began as a footnote, a buffer between
pages in the master plan of the northern Christian kingdoms against
the Muslims.

She thought for a moment. "You're not Castilian."

"Well, Ambrosio's story is," I protested.

"But this is *your* story."

If it was my story, then, what did it mean that I still didn't have the answers to some incredibly basic questions? For instance: What was the status of the various lawsuits? Or: Why couldn't Ambrosio go back to making a slightly different cheese without Julián? And what responsibility, if any, did Ambrosio bear in all that had happened to him? Could he really be guilt free?

So I packed my bag, bused to Logan, was lifted over the ocean by airliner, and found myself in Guzmán again, the beautiful village on its witness hill, the familiar sights and smells flooding my senses—the grain and loam, the wine and homemade chorizo. Ambrosio was Ambrosio, all-enveloping in his welcome. I'd resolved to start simply, by asking him for the name and number of his lawyer in Madrid. But even that left me fumbling in the telling room, mouth turning cottony with nervousness. For some reason the question suggested mistrust, that I would now be double-checking him. Asking it felt like its own kind of betrayal.

When I looked at Ambrosio seated there in the crepuscular light, beneath the blue china plate painted with saints, I saw a good man, one of generosity and compassion. I saw someone who'd done something remarkable with his life, furthered the cause of the past by resurrecting his family cheese, by telling stories. And he'd been, in all those pages of writing, the necessary myth I somehow needed to tell myself. *Egads,* thought I, *is this what I'd done with my life, then? Told myself a story?*

When I worked up the gumption to finally ask after his lawyer, I did so as casually as I could, but the shift was awkward and palpable, a lurching curve in the road. He seemed to hesitate, looked down at his fingernails, which he made a show of inspecting, then said his name: Pascual Llopis.

"And his number?" I asked.

And this time, when he said it out loud, he didn't reach for—nor did I offer—my notebook.

I wrote the phone number down in my own hand.

18

BEGINNING OF THE END

"He understands nada."

"AMBROSIO IS A UNIQUE CHARACTER," SAID HIS LAWYER, PASCUAL Llopis, triangling his fingers into a steeple and pressing them under the tip of his chin, striking a pensive pose. He sat behind a large leather-topped desk in a beige suit and brown-striped tie, with a neatly trimmed salt-and-pepper beard, while I sat on the other side, admiring the pastoral paintings on the wall, depictions of a grape harvest, a rabbit hunt, haystacks. He proclaimed that a man like Ambrosio was a bit of an endangered species in the new Spain, "a bohemian, an artist."

In coming to see Llopis—this was December 2005—I felt something break loose, some winged bird take flight. I'd spent five years vacuum-sealed in Ambrosio's world, and now I would find that there wasn't a question Llopis wouldn't answer, as he led me through the obliterated cheesescape of Ambrosio's dreams.

Llopis (pronounced yo-*PEACE*) was maybe sixty, with a kinetic, busy manner. He conveyed a shrewdness ostensibly built on a bedrock of experience and professional success. He admitted that he was very fond of Ambrosio, even protective, and that he'd first heard about the cheesemaker from another client, which seemed to contradict Ambrosio's version that they'd met through Ambrosio's father.

The trouble began, Llopis said, after the *palacio* debacle in 1989, when Ambrosio went looking outside of Guzmán for more space. While Páramo de Guzmán was a darling of caseophiles and the international cheese cognoscenti, while world leaders and celebrities consumed it, and while it was sold in some of the world's finest stores, it remained an eccentric cheese. It was one of the first sheep's milk cheeses on the market, and one of the first artisanal Spanish cheeses to find a larger audience. And yet one friend and would-be investor gave Ambrosio this advice: Keep it small. " 'This is a niche product,' " said Llopis, quoting the friend's message to Ambrosio. " 'Just because it sells well to a predetermined group of people doesn't mean the whole world's going to buy it.' "

"What he tried to tell him was: everything in moderation," said Llopis. Meanwhile, Ambrosio had fallen under the spell of two local investors—Pedro Tallos and Teodoro López—who were hungry to expand their portfolios and whose sales pitch, according to Llopis, seemed to match Ambrosio's vision for his cheese operation. All three were taken with the idea of buying property in Roa in order to build a state-of-the-art factory complex with a large cellar, a tasting room, and land to expand. "Ambrosio began to dream bigger and bigger," said Llopis, "and it was easier—and in some ways, lazier—to go with the yes-men."

Right from the start, with their initial contract, the fraud was in place, claimed Llopis. "Even in that basic arrangement, you already have the trick"—*un engaño*—"because the investors promise to be Ambrosio's partners, but have majority control of the company"—two board votes to Ambrosio's one—"and no legal or monetary exposure. Meanwhile Ambrosio has staked his entire *patrimonio*"—his inheritance, including all his land and money—"on the company." In other words: While the investment of Tallos and López was in fact minimal, while they offered Ambrosio the presidency of the company, paid him a salary, hired his wife, and allowed him to keep running the business, they had majority control. At the same time, Ambrosio carried all the financial exposure, since it was his name on the contracts with suppliers.

It wasn't until the company was drained of funds and unable to pay its debts—the moment when the board members, seeing the writing on the wall, began scrambling to protect their own assets—that Ambrosio realized the implications of his signature on that initial partnership agreement and the supplier agreements he'd signed. "My client let himself, or got himself, tricked by a couple of guys without shame. *Sinverguenzas.* And he was fooled for, like, two years," said Llopis, drawing a hand through his full head of silver hair. "So the problem—and huge danger—for Ambrosio, and his wife, Asun, was that they were the only ones who had contracts with the providers, the shepherds and all the people they had to pay monthly to keep the business going. The investors had no obligation."

And the debts piled up with astonishing speed.

But, I wondered, how in the world would Ambrosio allow himself to be so duped, unless led into it by Julián, who was supposed to be checking such contracts?

"What gave Ambrosio confidence from the start," said Llopis, "was that there was tons of cheese in the *bodega,* stored and cured—and it was essentially cash, money in the bank. Knowing Ambrosio, you kind of get the feeling that he was like, 'Don't worry, I got it. I'll pay the shepherds.'* After all, he's the Guzmán guy, it's what he wants to do. He *wants* to be the one who's up there dealing with the sheep and shepherds, because that's where he's most happy and alive."

Even so, without having parsed the intricacies of the contract, and suspecting Julián's hand in what he took to be a conspiracy, he sought out Llopis. "Ambrosio came to me, and at first he was very angry. He was in a bad state. And he said, 'Can we still save this company? Can

---

* This wouldn't have included the Basque-brother shepherds and their Che Guevara T-shirts, as they came to Guzmán well after Ambrosio had lost the cheese.

it still be mine?'" Llopis said that, if the company hoped to avoid bankruptcy (an act that would relinquish control of Páramo de Guzmán to the bank), there was no option but to freeze all cash outflow, to stop payment to the shepherds and other providers. But in order to go ahead with the plan they needed the approval of the other two investors—the *accionistas,* as Llopis called them.

"So one fine August day, I went with Ambrosio to Roa to meet with them, and they laid out the same plan, to stop payment." But then, most strangely, according to Llopis, the two *accionistas* said they weren't going to vote for it. They didn't care whose family cheese it was. Once they realized there was no upside, they wanted out. Or so it seemed.

"I was there with Ambrosio, as his attorney, but they didn't have any lawyers present," said Llopis. And Julián, in his auxiliary role, wasn't there either. "These guys were pros; they knew exactly what they were doing," he claimed. What they said, in essence, was that Ambrosio bore the obligation of those payments, and if he couldn't raise the money, the company was headed to bankruptcy. Realizing his powerlessness, offended by their ruthlessness, Ambrosio immediately renounced his board position. Páramo de Guzmán was an artisanal cheese, and Ambrosio had been its creator, curator, and head artisan from the beginning. Perhaps he never expected them to call his bluff; perhaps he overestimated his importance; perhaps he could already see the outcome. But the two *accionistas* seemed pleased, according to Llopis, like, "Okay, you're going to resign? Perfect!"

In Llopis's telling, the two men sat blankly while Ambrosio exploded. He raged and called the men bastards, yelling, *"Me cago en todos . . ."* I shit on everything.

"I've been doing this a long time," said Llopis, "so I wasn't surprised by the outburst; I was more surprised by the *accionistas.* They kept their calm with an iciness that was chilling."

The *accionistas* insisted they should go immediately across town to legalize Ambrosio's resignation from the board before a notary. The new board would consist only of Tallos and López, while Ambrosio was relegated to employee status. Five days later the board fired Ambrosio—and Asun—outright.

Listening to Pascual Llopis relate his version of events, I found myself confused. Where was the big showdown between Ambrosio and Julián, the standoff in Julián's office, the *puta* clutching his dissembling throat and emitting the liar's choking giveaway, *huh-huh-huh* . . .? Then Llopis said something with a bluntness that surprised me, as if stating a universal truth. "When it comes to the law and business, Ambrosio is a big zero," he said. "He understands *nada*."

It hadn't ever occurred to me before this moment that anyone would use those words—*big zero*—to describe Ambrosio Molinos. And this was his lawyer speaking. I'd taken it on faith that the cheesemaker was without glaring weakness, even if he hadn't made it past high school. If he was gullible—if that was what had led him into the whole mess with Julián and these newly introduced *accionistas*—then wasn't that still a virtue more than anything? A sign of his nobility and deep-seated trust, a belief in the goodness of people?

Llopis carried on, the bright December light slanting through the windows at his back, finding the gold flecks in the worn oriental rugs. Distant street noise rose through the window, too, the oblivious masses moving from appointment to appointment in the fancy Retiro barrio without, as Ambrosio would have had it, time to shit.

"This is when we get to the big problem," Llopis said. "Ambrosio was still the third shareholder in the company. He's been fired, he's not an employee, he's resigned from the board, but he's still an owner of a third of the business. This is when he really gets into trouble. Because all of a sudden, all of the shepherds, all the people who are delivering the milk, they aren't being paid, and they start to go after Ambrosio *solo,* because he's the one who pays them."

Llopis explained that in 1992 and '93, "there was a lot of aggression flying around. It was Kafkaesque. And worse in a tiny town." When I asked what he meant, he said, "Death threats."

"Death threats?"

"Yes," he said. "Very serious." Shepherds were knocking on Ambrosio's door and "threatening acts of barbarity."

What, exactly? I pressed.

Like the killing of his wife, Asun, said Llopis.

This seemed impossible. What did Asun have to do with it? It was Ambrosio's signature on the contracts. But then I reminded myself of what had happened during the war, of what Eduardo Cristóbal, the archaeologist, had said about the victims in the mass graves: "What we found were innocents." The shepherds didn't want to kill Ambrosio; they wanted him to pay. Under the pressure of such a threat, he might pay faster.

"Ambrosio's a big, strong guy," said Llopis, "but this is Castile, and when someone threatens you, you listen. The most painful part was the loss of honor. Some of these guys were friends of Ambrosio's from childhood, and he had committed to paying them, and couldn't, and the whole thing drove him crazy."

Llopis helped Ambrosio reluctantly prepare the bankruptcy papers, which were filed with the court in Burgos at the beginning of 1994. According to Spain's laws, a company filing for bankruptcy must gather willing creditors—those to whom they owe money—to vouch for and approve any potential judge's ruling. At first most of the aggrieved parties were, as Llopis said, "at the door threatening death," so they were not exactly in the mood for "a bankruptcy party." Therefore, the first filing was rejected that March.

Meanwhile, the two *accionistas* had one more surprise up their sleeve. "In the midst of working out all of this bankruptcy stuff," said Llopis, "the guys sell the whole company, all of the assets of Páramo de Guzmán, for so cheap that the cheese in storage was worth more than what they sold it for, which was eighty million pesetas," or roughly $850,000. "Not only do they sell off the assets, but twenty tons of cheese at market to pay off their debts, and the first agreed-to sum goes to the bank, which is the first creditor in line. After that"—and here Llopis clapped his hands together—"they're clean. No more

Páramo de Guzmán, no more assets left to pay all the day-to-day guys who are coming after Ambrosio."

But, I wondered, as an equal and third shareholder in the original company, wasn't Ambrosio entitled to one-third of the money from the sale?

"No, he was the third owner of a company that had nothing," said Llopis. And that company was gone now. He had no stake in the new company, the one making Páramo de Guzmán cheese without him. The only legacy left to Ambrosio Molinos of his beautiful family cheese was now the nearly $3 million of debt that was his alone to repay.

HEARING ALL OF THIS, I felt the need to speak up, to defend Ambrosio. But then I realized it wasn't that Pascual Llopis was blaspheming or disparaging my friend. Quite the contrary. I understood that the lawyer was summoning his truth as best he knew it, based on logic and facts, on certainties and the exact color of the shirt worn.[*]

It's not that I couldn't imagine Ambrosio's defects once they'd been pointed out. Of course, he knew nothing of the law. (Who understood the law anyway? That's why the world is populated with lawyers charging $1,000 an hour for their services.) As for his business acumen, evidence suggested another lack. Yet, to my mind, Ambrosio Molinos wasn't driven, in the end, by money in a way that made him careful with money. He was ambivalent about it, at times oppositional toward it. He appreciated a modicum of comfort, but his ideal was that sculptor in the nearby village, Santiago of Sotillo, hammering at his rock with no regard for how food came to be on his table or a roof

---

[*] So read the lines from *Don Quixote,* which seemed to point up an important difference between how we—Llopis and I—were inclined to tell Ambrosio's story: "It is one thing to write as poet and another to write as a historian: the poet can recount or sing about things not as they were, but as they should have been, and the historian must write about them not as they should have been, but as they were, without adding or subtracting anything from the truth."

over his head. Let others be the moneylenders and profiteers while Ambrosio made his poetry!

His mind was rife with visions, and having lit upon one, his assumption was that you, too, could see it, through the power of his words and convictions, that you could cross some imaginary threshold with him—for Ambrosio Molinos rarely traveled anywhere alone—breaching this wonderful frontier, this new ideal, in the same stirrup. He was a rare believer in this collectivity. And if this was the nature of his gullibility, then he was guilty as charged. He was animated by others, by their companionship and a sense of shared trust. That he gave of his own trust and company so freely was his greatest downfall in the new Spain. And he'd paid his price.

At least that was my thought in the moment, followed by a second one more self-damning. My downfall, it was dawning on me, had to do with these delusions I seemed to perpetuate in my own mind: How, when I found myself deeply in the throes of a story-spell, everything gleamed with gold leaf where a much duller patina existed. I felt thrill amid boredom, saw angels in the twig tree and secret hieroglyphics instead of fried worms in the road. Where this village of Guzmán might have been considered shabby, disintegrating on its rise of land that surveyed the Meseta, I had come upon it as an intoxicated explorer and saw a lush paradise. Where its eighty or so inhabitants were all dying their own slow, in many cases painful, deaths—lung cancer from smoking, failed livers from drinking, bodies beaten by farm labor, psyches weighted with sin and grudges—I'd seen a compelling tableau: kindly old men wearing black berets, cane-clomping with dignity, concealing light-filled truths within their secret hearts. If a man coughed up half his lung, graphically cursed the Creator, and spit out some foamy substance at the side of the road, I conceived of it as a sentimental gesture full of hidden meaning. In this world I'd found dusty-booted Ambrosio, and fallen in love with the ideal for which he stood.

How could you not? And this was what angered me most about the Julián I hadn't met: As he'd once basked in the glow of that ideal together with Ambrosio, how did he now justify having thrown it all away to be in cahoots with the *accionistas*?

Llopis held up his hand, signaling *patience*. There was more. Páramo de Guzmán, the first company, was now dead. But its debts were very much alive, which meant that Ambrosio still had to go through the effort to declare bankruptcy. When the first petition had been denied by the judge, more creditors warmed to Ambrosio's predicament, in part because they realized that he, too, had become an aggrieved party. In a separate ruling, the court had decided that the *accionistas* had fraudulently driven the company toward bankruptcy and owed Ambrosio a penalty payment—roughly 250,000 euros, according to Llopis, in part for his client's illegal firing. So Ambrosio had taken his place in line with the shepherds and other suppliers for remuneration that would never come.

For the second bankruptcy petition, twenty creditors agreed to join, since they had no options left. Ambrosio was broke, in debt, having lost the totality of his inheritance—including his farmland—to the bank. And this time the judge granted the bankruptcy.

Llopis rose from his desk and disappeared, in search of some document he wanted to share. Outside, eternal Madrid: the blue sky, the skeleton trees of winter in Retiro, the hushed sound of traffic and a stray voice rising from the street that sounded like a squawk of distress. In a 1620 book, *Guide and Advice to Strangers Who Come to the Court in which They Are Taught to Flee the Dangers that are in Court Life,* the author, a prolix titler named Antonio Liñán y Verdugo, wrote that "of every four things one sees, one cannot believe even two," because in the end, the court was a stage set of "fabulous appearances, dreamed up marvels, fairytale treasures, and figures like actors on a stage," all conjured, in part, to devour the novice. The "strangers" in the title also historically went by another name in Madrid, *forasteros,* new arrivals tinged by a sort of naïve bumpkinism. And this, too—the illusion, the stranger, the bamboozlements—all could have been true of modern Madrid, or Castile, or the story in which I found myself, as well.

Llopis returned with an unruly accordion file under his left arm and a single, fluttering piece of paper in his right, set it on the desk, and barely referred to it again. "Among his debts, Ambrosio owed a large amount to the Bank of Bilbao," said Llopis. And what did the bank do? It did what banks do in Spain: It took everything, in order to hold an auction to make that money back.

"No farmer in Castile is going to buy a farm because his neighbor went under," explained Llopis. "It's more than bad taste. You can't do it. The benefit of buying that farm cheap would be far overshadowed by the problems of taking over his destroyed neighbor's property and then making money off of it. So the bank holds three auctions for Ambrosio's land. No one steps forward, no one takes advantage of this cheap deal. After three tries, the bank says, 'Okay, well, we'll keep the property.' Its value is sort of undetermined, ultimately, as you can't say anything's worth anything, really, until somebody actually pays for it."

Llopis sighed. "All this stuff that we're talking about right now," he said, "if I were explaining this to businesspeople and merchants and economists, this is all normal. They understand all of these machinations. But, the problem is, you take a guy like Ambrosio who knows planting, he knows farming, he knows how to make a really good cheese—by the way, the cheese was *fantastic*!—and he knows about local honor in a small town. And you start talking about this stuff to him, and you might as well be speaking Chinese."

There was something tragic in his tone, a resigned nostalgia. Even Llopis seemed to recognize the glories of the bygone world embodied in his rather hopeless client. "When Ambrosio first came to me, I said, 'You were the owner and creator of Páramo de Guzmán. Are you telling me you didn't put any guarantees in that contract, nothing to protect you?' And Ambrosio said, 'My lawyer was my friend.' But what a friend! Like, *vaya, amigo*—wow!" Llopis then elucidated how a basic contract with protections might have read: "Say you were bringing in outside investors who wanted two-thirds control for giving a million. If they've only put down twenty-five percent in the beginning, well, up to now, you only have twenty-five percent control of two-thirds. And if next month, you've put down fifty percent, okay, now you've earned your fifty percent. And so on. You might also stipulate that they never have administrative control of the company, so they can't make decisions about selling assets. There are all sorts of simple protections like this."

But none of them appeared in the contract. The *accionistas* were immediately granted two-thirds, but according to Llopis, only delivered a small portion of the money they had pledged.

So who was to blame? That was the question suddenly on my mind after assuming for years that the answer was simple, and exactly as Ambrosio had delivered it to me. Llopis thought for a moment, then surprised me again with the blunt force of his answer. "In large part this is Ambrosio's fault. For being the bohemian he is, for being disconnected from everything legal and financial."

I tried to see Ambrosio in this new light, but couldn't quite manage it, and continued to admire him, and caught myself admiring him again. Yet some part of me then forced the other part of me—the part of me that lived inside these stories—to recognize that there'd been a real cost to this deficiency of Ambrosio's. What first enraptured me had been Ari's newsletter riff, one that had set my imagination whirring, followed by Ambrosio's telling of a legend that blew my mind. But these had been story versions of a real life in conflict with a real world. And this conflict hadn't been spurred by just "the bohemian" coursing through his veins, but a little of the hubristic hidalgo, the nobleman, too. Llopis confessed that, yes, it was likely that Ambrosio's grandiosity might have had something to do with it. As a member of one of the richest families in town, being in charge of a renowned cheese company may have fulfilled the hidalgo's role he fancied for himself as provider and benevolent, principled patriarch. Certainly, Ambrosio saw his own rise as a validation of the past.

In literature, however, the fictional hidalgo was often also a figure who had somehow squandered his family wealth while holding weakly to the title of his nobility, the prototype being Don Quixote, whose delusional meanderings in attempts to fulfill his dream of being a knight-errant also made him a subject of ridicule. ("Finally, from so little sleeping and so much reading," writes Cervantes, "his brain dried up and he went completely out of his mind.")

"It's true," said Llopis, "Ambrosio was blinded by this microcosmic vision of himself in this world that's disappearing. But hold on! He didn't *become* Don Quixote. Don't forget that principally behind this is his best friend."

Finally—Julián! But when I asked him to describe Julián, Señor Llopis surprised me again. He praised Julián for being "a very smart attorney," for having a "magnificient" reputation. "One thing is what Ambrosio supposes happened, and another is what the evidence is," he said. "And we never had anything to go after Julián." Llopis spoke of certain "coincidences" that might look dubious from a certain point of view. Yes, the *accionistas* had been conniving and clumsy, for once they'd fired Ambrosio, once they'd removed him from the company's board, and sold Páramo de Guzmán, they weren't done. Llopis alleged that they'd sold it to other friendly investors, who resold it among this growing group of *accionistas,* and in this way, it was passed on, creating iteration after iteration of Páramo de Guzmán, to distance it from the legal obligations and debts of the first company. One matter of suspicion for Ambrosio—one bit of evidence of an unholy alliance between Julián and the *accionistas* that he substituted as proof of a setup—had been the fact that Julián's name had appeared on documents associated with one of these later companies, as someone who'd been paid for services. But even here Llopis held a contrary point of view.

"It's a small world up there, so the fact that Julián might have ended up representing or being in business with some people implicated in these complicated sales of Ambrosio's former company isn't so far-fetched. You know, a lawyer in Aranda has access to only a small pool of clientele, and so ultimately you have those kind of coincidences a lot, much more so than in a city like Madrid or Barcelona.

"Here's how I see it," said Llopis. "There were these guys who saw this cheese business as a way to make a lot of money by putting only a little down. They were businessmen, outside investors, and Julián maybe knew these guys and presented them to Ambrosio. They started doing their thing on Ambrosio. There are a series of coincidences later on, when you connect the dots in hindsight. Did these guys trick Ambrosio? Yes. And did they scramble over a series of years to get themselves out of this jam by creating one company after another, and transferring the assets? Yes, they did it badly, they got caught to a certain degree, they were convicted of fraud. But to say that there was something totally planned from the beginning? Against Ambrosio? It's highly unlikely."

It took another moment for these words to register. *Highly unlikely.* What I heard seemed to raise the issue of Julián's actual culpability, the question of percentage, the exact pie wedge of his guilt. If Julián's blame was minimal, or even if he had allowed for a contract that disadvantaged a friend—and this too now seemed in question because it was a bit unclear how events unfolded, how carried away Ambrosio found himself with the idea of the new factory, how integral Julián really was to the negotiations—Llopis suggested that instead of being an act of intent, his might have been a mistake.

That, too, seemed impossible at first, but if so, then why hadn't Julián gone straightaway to Ambrosio with an apology? Wouldn't honesty and supplication have solved the matter between dear friends? "It's one thing making a mistake, and another making amends," said Llopis. "Remember, this guy's got his balls, too." Llopis started making a series of gruff, snorting noises meant to characterize a certain Castilian machismo.

"Admitting the mistake in front of Ambrosio would've been hard," he explained, "admitting the mistake within that society, too, as a lawyer who'd royally fucked up, would've been even worse in terms of his career, his credibility, his honor, his dignity, his pocketbook, his *everything*. If you never admit to having done anything wrong, people eventually forget. Julián got out of it by admitting nothing. The other guys got the company, and Ambrosio got screwed."

Yet wasn't this Castile, I insisted, still clinging to some petrified notion of honor, the land where all threats were to be taken seriously, and justice, however it was meted (or metered, in those epic poems), must prevail? Ambrosio, for one, hadn't forgotten any of it. And what about his plot to murder Julián, then? Llopis nodded with sagacity. "Julián took that into account, this physical threat against him, and he was very prudent. According to what people say, he carried a gun."

By now the light in the room had shifted, lifting off the floor and oriental rugs, bathing the walls in clean pools of luminescence, the faint scent of tobacco lifting, too, though the lawyer did not light the pipe that sat on the desk. Llopis wanted to rephrase the story one last time, to put a final fine point on it, for it seemed apparent that I didn't understand. "At the end of the day," he said, staring at me intently, bringing his knuckles down on the documents before him, "these two guys pulled a fast one on Ambrosio—and in a sense they pulled a fast one on Julián, too, knowing that he was Ambrosio's friend and lawyer. Essentially they duped both of them."

He stroked his beard, shook out his tie, sighed one last time. "Ambrosio had it all," he said. "He had a great design, an extremely well appreciated product in the marketplace. It was all going beautifully for him, but it was like caviar—and not everyone eats caviar."

Ambrosio, he said, was more like a caballero, a gentleman on horseback. "Here in Castile," he said conclusively, "we're all gentleman riders, but somewhere along the way we lost our horses."

19

FORGIVENESS (PART I)

"Anyplace, anytime."

THE NEWS FROM ENGLAND WAS, WELL, BOLLOCKS—but, I supposed, inevitable. "The manuscript is already almost six years overdue," read the e-mail to my agent from the British publisher. "So sadly, we must terminate our agreement and request repayment of the advance already received." That was 18,000 pounds sterling, which I didn't exactly have buried in a jar in the backyard. So the cheese had racked up more debt that was going to be hard to repay. Meanwhile, here in America, the publisher kept cranking out riders on my contract, establishing new due dates that I kept missing, submitted as evidence here:

RANDOM HOUSE
BERTELSMANN

September 18, 2008

Mr. Michael Paterniti
███████████████████████
███████████
Attn: ███████████

Dear Mr. Paterniti:

Reference is made to our agreement of June 18, 2002, as amended by letters dated July
26, 2004 and September 28, 2005 (the "Agreement"), for your two novels provisionally
entitled THE TELLING ROOM ("Work #1") and Untitled ("Work #2").

Further to discussions between ███████████ and your agent, ███████████ this letter
shall serve to confirm that Clause 5(a) of the Agreement is hereby deemed amended to
specify that the complete manuscript for Work #1 shall be delivered to Bantam Dell not
later than March 15, 2009.

It was no longer eccentrically charming, this tangle I found myself in. I had a family, college educations to fund. Part of the problem
was that I'd used up whatever resources, time, and gemütlichkeit
granted to me as a book writer, and I was again bog-hopping full-time
between magazine stories—Cambodia, China, India—with hopes of
stealing back to Guzmán, which became harder and harder to do. If
I was honest, the book was dying a slow death. But as dire as things
seemed, the more resolved I felt. A voice from the ether said, "Miguel
Ricardo, it's your time to kick some ass!"

My next trip back to Guzmán came four months after my meeting with Llopis, just after Ambrosio's father, Ambrosio Senior, passed
away. It'd been a long, slow decline, and he'd told stories until the
end—funny, bawdy, outrageous. No one was more entranced, no one
laughed harder, than Ambrosio himself, forever the child at his father's knee. At the funeral, the villagers turned out to pay their respects and listened to the priest usher him to an afterlife that one
hoped was less a matter of fluttering angel wings than wild rivers

flowing with red wine. In the cemetery, where the bodies were buried east to west, Ambrosio had his father buried with his head facing south and feet north, so the old man could keep an eye on the family bodega, and all the wine being drunk there.

I found Ambrosio in the house he was renting in Roa (or perhaps, in his financial ruin, his brother rented it for him). The property abutted the Duero River, a silver thread through his backyard. Ambrosio seemed older, hunched ever so slightly by the mantle that had been passed to him in his father's absence; his eyes, already mournful, seemed to flicker with a new awareness, as if he spied his own mortality approaching with sharpened sickle. There was a brittleness, too, that I'd never seen in him before, a hollowness in the cheeks, a wattle at the neck. If he'd once played the role of Falstaff, willing to make a comic figure of himself, to pass his hours with wine and song, he now seemed preoccupied by some bigger, cosmic account settling. Which is how we ended up in his Pathfinder, hurtling toward Aranda.

We'd been talking, talking about everything: his dad, our kids, the news from Guzmán. To the horror of some, the new streetlights had been installed, and, predictably, Ambrosio said, "I liked it better when the stars and moon were our lights." He pulled out some pictures of his father as a young boy in the streets of Guzmán, in the army in Morocco, on his wedding day. He seemed lost in thought, the photographs fanned over his lap, grazing his fingers over his father's face, then began to weep. So I waited to bring up my conversation with Llopis.

In many respects I was still confused by it. How was it that ninety minutes in Madrid with Ambrosio's lawyer had jumbled the story I'd spent years writing, or should I say, gilding? I believed in Ambrosio Molinos de las Heras, for he, as much as Spain, or Castile, or Guzmán, was both the real person, and abstract idea, to which I felt most committed. To see him so vulnerable, so diminished now, made me want to believe in him again twice as much.

Finally, after Ambrosio had put the photos away—and clapped his hands, saying, "*¡Venga!* What's our plan?"—I blurted out that I'd met with Llopis during my last visit, on my way home through Madrid, and had been struck by one thing Llopis had said: that there wasn't evidence to prove any wrongdoing on Julián's part. Therefore he hadn't been named in the lawsuits against Páramo de Guzmán. If Julián were guilty of fraud, I asked Ambrosio, wouldn't he have been front and center in a civil, or even criminal, prosecution?

And with that little push, we were talking about Julián again, after a multiyear boycott. Ambrosio stared at his hands, speaking in his low gravel but without the venom I was accustomed to when his archenemy was invoked. It seemed to fatigue him to have to sort through all of it again, but Julián was still a dissembler, according to Ambrosio—and had played the whole thing so brilliantly that his name was hidden from any illegality. But this time he wasn't a *puta,* exactly.

I swallowed hard and said, "I'd like to speak to him."

Ambrosio took a moment to respond. There was no swearing, or crashing of fists on table, no drawing of knife from sheath, no telling me to get out. He exhaled deeply, and after what felt like years of resistance, he said, "Fine. Let's go find him, then."

WITHIN MINUTES, WE WERE speeding across the Meseta—"sad and noble high plains, wastelands and stone," wrote the poet Machado—in Ambrosio's Pathfinder, Ambrosio gripping the wheel, his mouth set in a grimace. He made a phone call as he drove, speaking quickly with stentorian authority. "Julián's at the courthouse," he reported when he hung up. "But not for long."

This struck me as astounding. The two men had studiously avoided each other for fifteen years, and with one quick call to a random source, Ambrosio had zeroed in on him with pinpoint precision and was hurtling toward him, like a black bat or punched-up drone. We rocketed through Quintanamanvirgo, Anguix, Olmedillo, then turned at Torresandino, passed a couple of big winemaking operations, and came to the industrial quarter on the outskirts of Aranda.

It was 1:50 P.M., approaching the time for *comida,* and Ambrosio was certain Julián would leave the courthouse by 2:00 P.M. He called again. Still there. This was our best shot, for who knew where Julián would go afterward, or whether we could reach him?

Ambrosio passed slower vehicles, maniacally accelerating. The car leaped and swerved. Who was doing the ambushing here, him or me? And what was I supposed to say to Julián if we did find him? After all, he was a bugaboo, a foil, not a person. To my mind he had no heft, threw no shadow, was a noxious vapor. Despite the firing of certain journalistic synapses, I hadn't exactly prepared for how an interview might go, how we might move past his inevitable denials to something scratching the truth. That I wanted to talk to him didn't mean that I was prepared to talk to him.

As we drove into the center of town, skirting the high, limestone wall of the old city, Ambrosio reminded me to watch for Julián's tic, reaching to his neck to demonstrate again. Pinching the skin below his Adam's apple, he made the sound—*Huh-huh-huh-huh-huh-huh.* "That's when you know he's scared," he said. "That's the sound of betrayal." We screeched to a halt before the courthouse, and Ambrosio said, "Wait here," then stalked across the lot and through the glass doors.

I sat in the car, engine running, picturing Ambrosio's expression, the odd mix of calm and grim anger, his strange disembodiment this day, and his hand reaching into his coat pocket for an object—perhaps a firearm? Was this how it promised to end, with a shooting at the courthouse and a headline on that evening news carried by Radio Cinco?

This was a little nuts. What was he going to do? Drag him out here by his ear?

Having lost his dear father, the only one he'd ever idolized, and the senior half of the entity known in Guzmán as "the Ambrosios," Ambrosio Junior was now a rune. I'd seen him light and rambunctious, theatrical and scatological, at work and at play, but I'd never seen him like this: unraveling in grief. This state of mind, I imagined, must have mirrored his disposition after losing the cheese, for the cheese had been made for his father. The two were twinned. So we were going backward again, prisoners of memory, even while beating forward. And I was thinking of Julián's last name, Mateos, which now, to my mind, evoked the word *matar*—"to kill"—and also the sobriquet for that vineyard that always haunted me, Matajudío, or Jew Killer. I thought of these childhood images that haunted Ambrosio's daughter, Asunita, who'd shared them with me over hours of conversation: old hunting dogs, past usefulness, hanged from trees; dead crows slung from antennas on the roofs over Guzmán to frighten off the flocks of other crows that descended on the village one summer like a plague; the innards of a rabbit gutted by something, or someone, in the fields. Suddenly, everything abounded with violence. I couldn't tell whether Ambrosio was acting as an agent on my behalf, or for himself alone, searching out the confrontation he'd darkly dreamed of for fifteen years, to get his revenge at last.

Five minutes later Ambrosio reappeared in the windshield, making his way back to the idling car. It was cold outside, his breath crystallizing in clouds, as if he, too, gave off exhaust. The door flew open; he dropped into the driver's seat, tilting the vehicle with his bulk. "Missed him," he said, "by minutes." He seemed beleaguered, as if someone had siphoned the air from his body, then he fumbled for a cigarette, lit it, shifted the car into reverse. "To his office, then."

Ambrosio drove at a reasonable pace this time, no more breakneck theatrics, back through Aranda to a point near the city wall we'd passed earlier. He parked the car at a square. "Julián's over there," he said, gesturing across through the flat-topped *plátano* trees to a nondescript office building. "I'll wait in here." He pointed upward to a sign that read BAR PEPE. Then he took himself inside, leaving me on the sidewalk.

I gathered myself and went across to the copper-colored façade of Julián's office building, moving through a bolt of sunlight between the other structures of the downtown. The portico lay in shadow, however, and my eyes needed to adjust before I could read Julián's name on the directory. And there it was. *Julián Mateos.* I rehearsed my lines: Friend of Ambrosio's? Journalist on a story? Strange, obsessive *americano* with a funny thing for dying villages and slow-food relics? I have a few questions about the cheese, hombre. . . , *How could you?*

I could feel Ambrosio's eyes on my back. What was his play in all of this? To remain true to his word and facilitate my book in any way he could, be it giving me the key to his telling room, or showing me everything there was to show of his world, or delivering me here to the doorstep of Julián? This again was the curious thing about Ambrosio, his willingness to live fully inside the moment, whatever its virtue or folly, without regard for the future. I again remembered something Asunita had told me, how, as a kid, she'd been shielded from the details that surrounded the demise of Páramo de Guzmán, though later, when she was nineteen and had moved away from home, her parents explained everything.

"My father has tried every kind of thing," she'd told me, "driving lorries, working in agriculture, making wine, having chickens. There's a saying: He has a lot of 'forest and stream' to do things, a lot of resources and power, but the main thing is to have the spirit to do it. The worst of what happened to my father when he lost the cheese was that his spirit was stolen away." Could her father have started again, made the same cheese or one that was similar, one with that same care, one that when tested against the "soulless" cheese might have reminded the world of a higher way of eating—and being? "I think he's run out of time," she'd said.

On the street, I pressed the buzzer, and a woman's voice said hello. *"Ta' lo,"* I responded. Then, in English, "Is Julián in?" There was some confusion on her part. *"Soy americano,"* I said. A few excruciating moments passed, Ambrosio somewhere back through the light and shadow at the café, and then the door buzzed open.

Upstairs, I was shown in by Julián's secretary, seated, and abandoned when she disappeared through a door. The office suite had that typical, antiseptic nondescriptness of hushed law offices everywhere, binders and briefs, bound collections of the Law on shelves. There was some muttering through the wall, and then after an interval she returned and said, "Julián will see you now."

In retrospect, Julián must have thought I was an opportunity of some sort, and his curiosity must have been piqued. Otherwise, how would I have made it through that door? Perhaps that was one of the pleasures of the job: You never knew what problem or proposition might blow in on the day's breeze. A real estate deal? A new company needing incorporation? At the very least, it wasn't often that a foreigner showed up in Aranda. I could count on two fingers the Americans I'd heard about in town (one was a veterinarian; the other ran Aranda's English-language school); most expats could be found in the warmer, more sybaritic climes of Spain, attending language schools or taking advantage of tax havens like Gibraltar, living on the beach or partying in Seville, where the sangria and good cheer always flowed and orange blossoms and jasmine filled the air with sweet scent. As it was, in the old days of unforgiving Guzmán, foreigners—meaning anyone not from the village, not just those from abroad—were taken up to the fountain and dropped in the stone basin. They got their asses kicked. And an element of that Castilian wariness persisted. Strangers were sometimes still greeted not with "Who are you?" but "*Whose* are you?" As in: To which family do you belong?

Julián was a tall man with a full head of hair and firm handshake. His handsomeness was disarming, for even in that symmetrical face with its square jaw, small, tilted ears, and shy brown eyes, there was a boyishness that came through, someone capable of friendship and enjoyment. He was neatly dressed, in white collar and red tie, dark slacks, a verdant blazer. The office was a large room with a window full of sky. His black lawyer robes hung in the corner. A colorful poster commemorating Old Havana hung on the wall behind his desk. He held a piece of paper in his hand and at first affected a sort of distraction, as if still drawn to whatever was on the page.

I apologized for arriving unannounced and thanked him for his time. He was, as Pascual Llopis had said, impressive, commanding. And he was curious now, gazing intently at me as he sat in a green swivel chair. I realized almost instantly that my anger toward him was really just Ambrosio's anger, that I harbored this tumor of hate on his behalf, and yet not knowing Julián but face-to-face with him now, I bore him no ill will. How could I? He was just a lawyer in a tie. Besides, Llopis's words played again in my mind—*He was tricked, too*—and a sort of pity anesthetized me.

"What brings you in?" he said, smiling.

I told Julián I was visiting the region for a book project. "It's set in Guzmán," I said, and then I added that I'd become good friends with Ambrosio Molinos, and at those words Julián seemed to recede. Literally seemed to roll back in his chair. Or had I imagined it? His smile reflected a cocked curiosity, but his fingers didn't grab for his throat and no strange sounds came out, no whimper for mercy. Did he think I'd come to kill him? If so, he never reached for his supposed gun, either.

"I'm writing a book," I said, "about Páramo de Guzmán. Of course, there are many stories about this cheese, and I thought I'd better come and hear yours."

"Yes," he said, gathering himself. He stood up, removed his jacket, draping it over the chair. He seemed quite thin, and I noticed a blotch of dry skin, eczema or something, on the side of his face, the back of his hand. "Yes, Ambrosio is an old friend. Or *was*. There's been a misunderstanding. Are you—do you speak with him often?"

I assumed he was trying to gauge the depth of my friendship with Ambrosio, but here my cynicism was met again with surprise. "We were best friends," he said. His hand tremored almost imperceptibly. "And I've been hoping to have a conversation with him for years." He asked me if I'd be seeing Ambrosio soon.

I looked toward the window, knowing that down below sat the man himself at Bar Pepe, that we could have easily gone down and had that conversation right here and now, if Ambrosio wouldn't tear him limb from limb first.

"Yes," I said, "I'll be seeing him tonight."

"Would you convey a message, then?" he asked. His voice was

soft, polite, cordial, but almost pleading underneath. "Anytime he has time, I'd love to meet—at his *bodega,* in the telling room, in a bar—to try to mend our friendship." He reiterated that there'd been a mix-up in the past, a confusion, and that it was time to set it right.

As for his side of the story, Julián said it would have to wait. He gestured to the piles on his desk. "There are pressing matters that need attending to today," he said. And with this, his air became a hint more officious. Underneath this initial exchange, I detected something else at play: He wanted me out of his office so he could regain his footing.

"But I'm not at all averse to meeting and talking to you," he said, adding that he'd welcome the opportunity. No, this week was bad—but later, yes, absolutely. Could I meet him in Madrid, in a month's time? He was there often, in court. There was a bar he liked. He consulted a calendar: 5:00 p.m. on a Tuesday?

I said I'd be there, affecting nonchalance, making the unspoken point, I thought, that I cared only tangentially about his version of events, that he should be worried not for any physical threat I posed (zero), but for those "myths of observation" that I might carry away from this place to employ in the making of my own story. That his would have to be the mother of all closing arguments.

But there was suddenly something more. In the coliseum of the adversary who didn't seem much like an adversary, this was no longer about Ambrosio, or Julián for that matter, about versions of events that had transpired fifteen or twenty years earlier. This, I now realized, was about *me,* my version, wasn't it—and why I'd thrown over everything for it. No, this wasn't Ambrosio's book after all. It *was* mine. And I was gathering my breath to say something. But what?

"I'd like to hear your side," I said.

He came around his desk and we shook hands. *"Vale,"* he said. He averted his eyes briefly, his vulnerability making him sheepish again. Then he scratched the dry patch at the side of his face.

———

ACROSS THE STREET, BENEATH the *plantano* trees in the square, and then through the glass door of the café, sat Ambrosio, smoking, drumming fingers on the red tabletop. I wondered as I walked whether Julián's eyes were now on my back, gazing down from above. These oscillations between poles left me feeling like Boutros Boutros-Ghali trying to solve some intractable diplomatic crisis. About cheese.

How had this happened?

"Hombre," Ambrosio said. "Sit down. *Una caña?*" We'd been apart for twenty minutes, max. He ordered me a beer. *"Dime,"* he said. Tell me.

What was there to tell? "He misses your friendship," I said. "He wants to meet, at your *bodega,* whenever you say the word."

Ambrosio fell back in his seat, ran a hand over his whiskers. "Did you ask about the cheese?"

"Yes," I said, "we're going to meet again to go over all of that. But the main thing is that he'd like to talk with *you.*"

Ambrosio descended into thought for a moment. Gazing upon his face, I noticed something. It looked as if he'd been crying again, or, at the least, as if his eyes had been irritated by emotion. Was I imagining this, too? I didn't think so. Somewhere out there, the church bells sounded, seeming to ring for Ambrosio Molinos de las Heras. And now this—an old friend reaching from the past. For a moment he reached back, to that protected, idealized place of their early friendship.

I'd once seen faded pictures in a photo album at Ambrosio's house, and in frame after frame, Ambrosio and Julián appeared as they were in those years, best friends. They were seated against a wall mugging for the camera, maybe twenty at the time, Ambrosio tall and thin, in a work shirt and black beret, hunched and making a silly demonic face, while Julián sat upright, in a heavy wool jacket, holding his beret as if it were a steering wheel, that head of thick, curly hair, the two more identical than Ambrosio and his own brother Angel, who sits to his left, short by comparison, less instigator than neutral musketeer.

In another from that era, the camera captures the people closest to Ambrosio. Taken in someone's telling room, Ambrosio's mother,

Puri, appears to the left in profile, abstemious, nibbling on bread, ever regal with a thick swirl of dark hair, wearing earrings and a bracelet. Then comes Asun, Ambrosio's wife-to-be, a kid with long black hair, holding a cigarette between tapered fingers, looking fresh-faced and coltish. Next is Ambrosio, his wavy hair worn over his ears, that imperial profile, the strong nose and the heavy brow. A Herculean mass, he sits with one hand in his lap and the other casually holding a cigarette. To his left is, of course, Julián, affecting nearly the same pose as Ambrosio, elbows on knees, one hand holding a half-eaten apple—even the point of his collar is the same as Ambrosio's, as if each acts as a reflection of the other. And finally, there's Angel again, in too-tight white shirt and blazer, *porrón* set before him as he looks somewhat lugubriously at a pot apparently empty of its stew. What's noteworthy is how they listen—especially Ambrosio, who seems more intent than the rest—to someone just out of the frame, and here I imagine Ambrosio's father stage right, telling a story.

A last photograph, my favorite, features the familiar three—Angel, Ambrosio, and Julián, plus a friend, Pepe—all four in a man-hug on the streets of a fiesta somewhere, clad in white shirts and black berets. In a strange way, however, this feels like a photograph meant only for Ambrosio and Julián, with the other two added as an afterthought on the left of the frame. In fact, Pepe is caught sidelong, gazing adoringly as the best friends look directly into the camera, big and unafraid, at the height of their physical powers. Ambrosio wears an unruly, Fidel Castro beard, his white shirt unbuttoned to just above his belly button, revealing a spray of chest hair, while Julián, clean shaven, with his lantern jaw and good looks, has his shirt unbuttoned half the distance but with a thicker mat of chest hair and what appears to be an expensive watch on his wrist. Ambrosio's arm is draped lazily over Julián's shoulder, his paw of a left hand hanging there, and Julián's left hand, clutching what seems to be a cigar, reaches up to it. Whether he's about to grasp it or already holds it isn't clear, but what's most arresting isn't their physical comfort with each other, which is very Spanish, but rather the way the two possess the world together, how they form a locus, or sun—one hydrogen, the other helium, locked in their magnetic sphere—that seems to propel other planets around.

In the café now, Ambrosio was talking about those old times once more. "I loved him like a brother," he said. Family: It was hard to imagine it had come to this. Then a tear sploshed on the tabletop—and another. Ambrosio wanted to know: *What had he said again?* I told him: Anyplace, anytime. *What does he want?* To make it right, I said—to mend this rift, to stitch back the lost eras until everything becomes whole again.

Ambrosio pondered. He looked beyond me out the café window, across the street to the front door of Julián's office building, doing some internal calculation. His face reflected a deeper spasm of pain. Then he let out a sigh.

"*¡Venga!*" he said, clasping my shoulder, "let's go home."

20

MON VIRGO

"Before my gentlemanly giblets could take on the pallor of hoarfrost . . ."

O F COURSE, I WASN'T THE FIRST. THERE'D BEEN A DUTCH GUY who'd come to Guzmán for a number of months—but no one ever quite figured out why. They thought he might have been studying agriculture—writing a dissertation?—yet he never asked any questions. Then disappeared. There were the Basque brothers who came, settled, and were still here. And there'd been some other guy everyone remembered from the eighties, a cultured, city personage, a Spaniard who'd renounced his privileged life and declared himself a shepherd. He bought six sheep and gave them full human names. "People shit themselves laughing," Honorato's daughter, María, told me one day. "I remember taking in the laundry and I could hear him over the wall, talking to the sheep: 'Hey, Little Fred, get your nose out of the tomatoes.' "

People said that his transformation had been a capricious stunt, but María disagreed. "He was very poetic, and very nice to the children," she said. "He was having an experience. Until winter came, and he realized the house had no heat. So he left."

I remember having had a good, unself-conscious laugh with María about Little Fred. God—what a goof! I saw no connection whatsoever between me and this man who talked to sheep, whose innocent belief had led him to seek a simpler way of life even if it had also led him astray. My blindness to this seems all the more absurd in retrospect, given what I had up my sleeve. I'd harbored a secret idea, a self-initiation, that I knew must be performed to enter that exalted circle of Old Castilians.

And so I waited—and waited.

And then my body said it was time.

I'd just left Ambrosio in Abel's barn, where the two were working on a new invention, a tractor attachment of some sort. Ambrosio had sketched it on a bar napkin, and now they were sawing, soldering, and hammering huge pieces of metal. Outside, the day was cold and gray, wind scraping bits of earth. I drove east out of the village, past the bar, hairpinning below all the hillside *bodegas* with their telling rooms— smoke from a single chimney the only sign of life. The *coterro* settled below, traces of snow blown beneath the bare grapevines, like bone-colored shadows.

Driving on days like this, I was hollowed by the seeming nothingness of the place, by the wordless silence and grandeur of that nothingness. I was carried over that limestone-strewn pitch back to a world that predated language. In that season, there was an isolation one might have felt on the lava flats of interior Iceland or the empty veldts of southern Sudan. That feeling of utter windswept aloneness. But never had I felt more resolved.

As I traveled deeper into the fields, the nothingness filled with silhouettes and signs of life. There was an improbable owl perched on a rock pile, the same dark color as the stones, with the same dapples of white. Rabbits bolted from the scrub brush and retreated back again. There were ruins, too: an old shepherd station, called a *choza,* half collapsed, and the piled *majanos* marking out the field boundaries. The dirt tracks on either side of the road split into more tracks, veining to more piles of stones and fallow fields. This was a landscape constantly touched not only by human hands, but by happenings. Had the earth a voice, the murmur rising from it now to tell all the stories would have been deafening.

I drove past the field that had once held all those bright sunflowers from that summer long ago. Now, ragged stalks stood in their place—wrinkled and brown, tattered paupers in sad rags—and I drove on to the town of Quintanamanvirgo, past the bar there, which was shuttered and closed, down past the *frontón,* where there was a dirt turnoff. The car accelerated over a rocky track that slowly began to climb. With one more sharp right, the road canted to a steep incline. The tires spun to find purchase, and I was shot out onto the mesa, up over the world, into space.

Up here, the wind was something fierce, an exhalation of anger. I got out of the car, sucking in the cold, and walked the circumference of Mon Virgo, hands stuffed in my pockets, tottering against the icy gusts like a penguin. You could see it all from this vantage, the towns and villages of this world, including La Aguilera, where Ambrosio's mother had been born. I remembered Ambrosio's stories of arriving here in the dark of night, in the time after losing the cheese, playing Lear on his heath, swearing an oath of revenge on Julián. Mon Virgo was the kind of platform that invited the dramatic, a long fall of land dropping away, rocks piling to make a treacherous downward staircase. Out to the west, Guzmán was a pile of limestone on a hill, and the other villages, down on the flats, seemed like fragments of the same broken rock. No cars or bodies moved below.

I'D BEEN WAITING FOR this—the perfect confluence of bowel readiness and free time—since first meeting Ambrosio years earlier, to prove that I could be as Castilian as the next Mr.-Take-a-Shit-on-a-Mesa. *In this moment,* Ambrosio had said, *it's as if you're seeing God.* The wind was a battering ram, and there was no scent of the highland herbs, just the mineral smell of winter. I looked around, but everything was open and exposed. Where were you supposed to do your business up here anyway?

My chosen spot was slightly protected, down off the lip of Mon Virgo. I'd done some backcountry camping, but this was rock and hard ground—steep, too—and it didn't even occur to me to try to dig a hole. I glanced behind to make sure a shepherd wasn't creeping up on me, and then I just crouched and fumbled with my belt. Almost immediately, it was all wrong: My fingers were numb from the cold, and as I tried to lever my pants off my hips, I began sliding down the hill, picking up speed, until I self-arrested. *¡Puta madre!* I re-set myself and resumed pulling my pants down. With my jeans now bunched at my ankles, I hunkered into a crouching position . . . and began sliding again, a ski jumper accelerating down a track, unpeeled from the waist down.

Eventually I clawed to a stop. Before my gentlemanly giblets could take on the pallor of hoarfrost, I had to admit this was preposterous. Whatever auspicious internal conditions had led to this moment were now frozen by inhospitable external conditions and a case of unmitigated stage fright. Before I knew it, I was fully down and sliding again, my naked butt on cold stone, tugging at my pants as I went, trying to maintain some shred of dignity in this fraudulent moment meant to be my coronation as a Castilian. Ambrosio's voice returned: *Look where we are! Look at how incredible this is! Look how happy!*

I came to rest on the scree thirty feet from where I'd begun and, looking up at the sky half-clad, I had a thought: *What the hell am I doing here?*

My kids were back at home, and my wife, and there were bills to pay, and I owed England a bunch of money. And then I had another thought: *I'm really not Castilian, am I?* Sara had said as much, but I hadn't believed her—hadn't wanted to—for in that moment, I'd felt myself so close to a breakthrough. I'd desperately needed a breakthrough. Why couldn't I be the guy in the poncho, herding my family to a slower way of living? Why couldn't I settle in here and embrace the

simple life, its quietude and old-world charms? What was so wrong
about wanting to sit by the fire with your family, telling stories?

But no. It was like the boy raised by wolves, who realizes he likes
raw rabbit innards less than pepperoni pizza, and begins to ask some
hard questions. I heard a voice in my head singing my lonely
hallelujah—and it now seemed as plain as deep-fried sheep ears when
it spoke: *You're an American, dude.* I had long ago pledged my allegiance to Starbucks and microbrews, to stupid TV shows and those
fluorescent Slurpees. I liked to order food without always hearing,
"Como?" I couldn't invent attachment-apparatuses for a tractor, let
alone drive one. When I was away from home, I missed vegetables
and the phone ringing with some new assignment to somewhere I'd
never heard of. Or a friend around the corner who wanted to grab a
beer. I pledged allegiance to the ideals of our oft-flawed political system, for, at our best, we seemed less haunted than other countries,
more protean, less grudge holding, even if the world seemed more so
toward us (and sometimes for good reason). As much as I loved that
vision of Guzmán on its hill, I don't think my heart had ever soared
higher than the first time I drove cross-country and, in an adrenalized
rush, saw the Rockies, carved in indigo, before my eyes—nor was I
ever more taken aback by pure, random friendliness than, when first
walking into a Waffle House after hours of driving, I was greeted by
the woman behind the counter with, "Hey, shug-ah, anything I can
get you?"

Yes, American life was messy and maddening, overwhelming and
aggressive, supersaturated and plaque plagued, but it was deeply com-
forting, too. In the blur of our digital times, we may not have been as
in touch with our inner Daniel Boones as Ambrosio was in touch
with his El Cid, but this America was who I was.

As I lay there, no longer able to feel anything below my waist, I
realized that whatever legacy I gave my kids, I wanted them to know
what it meant to be close to the land, close to history, close to the song
of stars at night. I wanted them to feel close to me, too, and to Sara, by
finding unfettered time that was so hard to find unless you flew far

away from the madness. But it hadn't occurred to me to try to tame that madness rather than escape it, to bring the lessons of Castile back to my American life.

I tugged up my pants and clambered as best I could back to the top of Mon Virgo. When I found the summit again, I assumed the attitude of conquering mountaineer, as if none of what had just happened had happened at all. I again peered at the sweeping vista below, just to make sure I was still alone in this desolate world, while I re-buckled for good.

The clouds piled gray in the west; the wind buffeted. The land was pocked with its settlements and histories, its vineyards and rivers, but I left no impression there "in the cold country," as the poet Machado had it, "more moon than earth." Her indifference was palpable: Castile didn't care what road I took, or what nonsense I might be getting myself up to on a winter Thursday afternoon. In her hinterland, I was another gypsy, a gadabout, a hobbledehoy. To enter eternity here, you had to let Castile break you and put you back together. For years and decades. Like, really—for life.

Until she buried you for good.

CHAPTER 21

DEAD MAN TALKING

". . . worse than a killer putting a bullet in my head . . ."

HE ARRIVED AT THE BAR AROUND 7:00 P.M., SPORTING A JACKET and tie and dark pants. The bar was situated down a set of steps, half underground, with a low ceiling and windows that provided a view of Madrid's below-the-knee fashion scene on the twilight street—of cuffed slacks and shimmery stockings and shiny, pointy shoes clicking on the sidewalk outside. Julián was accompanied by a fellow whose name I didn't catch, another attorney, originally from Cuba, where Julián also did business. Having been to Cuba, I tried to break the ice with the stranger, but this fellow, barrel chested and imposing, didn't seem amenable. When he grunted, we agreed to let it go, and from that time forward he sat with his arms folded over his girth, yawning to punctuate his indifference. Was he there to fill the role of bodyguard, or was he merely second-seating his colleague at the defense table?

I never asked.

Julián wore his hair neatly parted, his face and hands unblemished by the flaking, dry patches of our first visit. He struck a more confident figure. His phone kept warbling, which required his constant attention, living as he did in lawyerly minutes more urgent than our merely quotidian ones as he triaged the emergencies of the day.

The waiter took our orders, vanished briefly, and returned with beer in tall, chilled glasses, along with silver plates of mixed nuts and *quicos,* roasted corn kernels. After checking his phone again, Julián looked up, sighed, and said, "Yes, Ambrosio and I were very, very close friends, from when we were very small—and as a result our families were really close, too." He sat with one leg folded over the other, stock straight, and at first he seemed at a remove, as if he were there to watch the rest of us play a card game. "Ambrosio, as you know, was always a farmer, he was working the land, but he had bigger ideas. He was a restive fellow, *inquieto,* scattered, always playing music. But incredibly imaginative. Once he read an article about worm farming and bought a million earthworms because he had the idea that their excrement was a good fertilizer and would help the plants grow in his garden."

Julián's tone was even, flatly factual, a baritone the same as Ambrosio's. If he was presenting his opening argument, I was rapt, inordinately so, especially for someone who, upon first hearing Ambrosio's story those years ago, had vowed in outrage that I was "going to find this Julián," and "ask him some questions." Now Julián's fingers grasped the *quicos,* brought them to his mouth, while in my mind's eye I saw those same fingers wiggle from Ambrosio's flickering blade. He talked about other Ambrosio schemes: There'd been a long-ago attempt to make goat cheese—a sudden trip to Basque country to buy a bunch of goats—that had failed. "But the sheep's cheese," declared Julián, "that was the one thing he had great success with."

Julián recalled the first time Ambrosio had mentioned it. "He told me two things: One, he said, 'I remember my mom used to make this incredible cheese, and that cheese doesn't exist anymore. There are no artisanal cheeses like it on the market.' And two, he said, 'I want to produce this cheese from Churra sheep.' " Normally, according to Julián, Churra were meat sheep found in Extremadura, in Castile, even

in Australia, a breed that lived off small sprouts rather than lush veg-
etation and thrived in the more extreme climes. He went on briefly in
this vein, while my mind processed what he'd just said. Was Julián
suggesting that Ambrosio's cheese had been a business proposition
first and foremost? If it had been an offering in the name of Ambrosio's returned-from-the-dead father, wouldn't *that* have been what
stuck in his best friend's mind?

Julián said he couldn't recall Ambrosio saying anything about the
cheese as an offering. "There's much I've forgotten, so it's possible," he
said. "But he brought it to me as a way to make money." Yes, it could
have been both at once, I reasoned, for why did they have to be mutu-
ally exclusive? Everyone had to make a living, didn't they? Some were
just better at it. Like Julián, who might have stood for everything
Ambrosio wasn't: orderly, well dressed, a disciple of logic and facts, a
success by the standards of the new Spain. His credibility came not
just from experience or money or even a touch of vanity—all of which
he seemed to have—but rather the low, rumbling reasonableness of
his vocalized mind. He remembered a Saturday when Ambrosio,
Angel, and a couple of investors had shown up to tell him that they'd
signed papers in front of a notary to form a corporation with the sole
purpose of manufacturing cheese. It had been a fait accompli. Julián
recalled that the operation was going to be run out of a stable across
the street from Ambrosio's parents' house with a little *nave* on the side
for the sheep. What they'd wanted from him were some ideas on how
to procure aid from the state for starting an agrarian business. Julián
had pointed them to an expert.

"My role was occasional in the beginning," he said. "They might
ask me to look at a contract when they were buying some sheep, but
that was it. I remember they started off with very few people; even
Ambrosio's mother worked on the cheese. The idea was: high quality,
small amounts."

As an intimate, Julián was invited to the first tasting. "It was fantastic, exceptional cheese," he said, growing animated. "It was like a
bomb going off in your mouth. It was really strong and salty, which I

loved. And had an authentical taste of milk. You could only eat a little at a time.

"In the beginning the cheese wasn't soaked in olive oil," he continued. "Rather it had a lot of fat in it from the pure milk, and it would sweat and dry out very quickly. And this was producing losses in production. So Ambrosio thought to immerse it in oil." Ambrosio's other smart, if absolutely bold, idea, said Julián, was to export Páramo de Guzmán. So he began visiting food festivals, and, given the force of his personality and his cheese, he seduced a lot of people. Soon, Páramo de Guzmán was carried by El Corte Inglés and Harrods, in countries from France to the United States. "The result of his success was that he gained more fame," said Julián, "but then his fame was bigger than his production capabilities. He couldn't keep up with the demand."

Julián took a sip of beer, glanced at his phone. I'd grown so accustomed to the chaotic wires and sparks of Ambrosio's tales—the digressions within digressions, the footnotes and annotations—that I was relieved by Julián's methodical efficiency as a storyteller. "Now that I've established these two facts," said Julián, "about the fame and prestige of the cheese and its actual production, I need to express my opinion that, in the beginning, the outflow of cash wasn't controlled very well. No one had a good handle on the movement of money. And Ambrosio was the guy running the show. His partners were just pure investors."

Julián claimed that, when the original investors realized they weren't likely to make any money, that the company was running up debt, they sold their shares to Ambrosio's two brothers, which for a short time made Páramo de Guzmán a strictly family-owned and -operated business. But the problems persisted, and then became dire: too much demand, too little cash flow, limited means of production. The brothers bowed out. For the company to become profitable— which would allow Ambrosio to pay his growing pile of bills— Ambrosio believed that Páramo de Guzmán needed to expand, which required an influx of cash. After the village had rejected its prodigal son with a flurry of flyers—*Don't let him steal the palace!*—this was where Julián could help, wrangling the new investors Llopis had mentioned: Pedro Tallos, the local businessman with whom Julián already had dealings, and Teodoro López.

The company now incorporated as PRESA, the new investors facilitated the move to the Roa factory by pledging money and outfitting the facility with the latest cheesemaking equipment. Soon, however, they found themselves at odds with Ambrosio. Despite the popularity of Páramo de Guzmán, despite a full warehouse and trucks transporting containers of it at all hours of the day, the debts multiplied. At some point, according to Julián, everyone began looking for relief.

"This is the period when things went south," he said, leaning in. He seemed in the card game now. "I don't know what happened. And obviously I haven't ever had the chance to talk to Ambrosio about it." He reminded me that, again, he wasn't involved in any of the day-to-day business operations, but acted as a friendly adviser for which he claimed he was never paid a cent. But he remembered offering a piece of advice to Pedro and Teodoro. "Ambrosio's not a businessman," he told them, "but he's the salesman, the public relations guy, the controller of the quality of the cheese, the face of the company—he's brilliant at that. He's just terrible with numbers. If you guys keep control of the numbers, you'll be fine."

But, according to Julián, they didn't listen.

Meanwhile, sales couldn't keep pace with expenses. *Not everyone eats caviar.* So the three shareholders—Ambrosio, Pedro, and Teodoro—came to Julián yet again in search of new investors. Julián enlisted two more local businessmen, who formed an entity called ESCOSA that pledged nearly $1 million to Páramo de Guzmán. I asked Julián why anyone would have invested at this point, given the realities of Páramo de Guzmán's balance sheet. "They were friends of mine, and trusted me," said Julián. "The factory was state of the art, and everybody loved the cheese. We all believed in it. It was so good, you know?"

But even with an infusion of cash, Páramo de Guzmán continued on its downward spiral. It was at this point that Julián saw "less and less" of Ambrosio, while Pedro emerged as the one keeping him apprised of developments, assuming the go-between role. "One day Pedro came to me and said there's a problem with the company, a split between PRESA and Ambrosio," Julián said. Ambrosio wanted to declare bankruptcy, while PRESA was in favor of trying to sell the company.

"I've thought so many times about what happened," Julián said, tugging the cuff of his dress shirt, seemingly agitated. "I think one possibility is that Pedro pulled a fast one on me. I remember clearly saying to him, 'If you have this conflict, why don't I call a meeting?' And in that moment, Pedro said, 'Forget it. Don't even think about it, because Ambrosio doesn't want anything to do with you. He's already got a lawyer in Madrid who's trying to get a bankruptcy thing going.' At the same time, I think Pedro might have told Ambrosio, 'Guess what, your old friend Julián doesn't want anything to do with you right now,' thus creating a rift. In retrospect, I made a big mistake in that moment: I should've called Ambrosio just to say, 'What's up, what's going on?'"

According to Julián, the urgent issue for Ambrosio was his own personal debt, which Llopis had calculated at that dizzying $3 million figure. "This idea that he wanted to save the company doesn't jibe at all," Julián said, "because, at first, Ambrosio wanted to sell his interests and just stay on as an employee. Pedro and Teodoro were the ones who insisted, who strong-armed him to keep his part of the company—and gave him a salary, too. I mean, in some ways, he never lived better: he was getting paid; he had benefits; his wife and aunt were employed. But he wanted to sell the whole thing. He wanted out."

Again the words came in a rush that needed deconstruction. *He wanted out.* The heretical sentence echoed in my head even as Julián kept moving his mouth, low-volume jazz playing in the background. Really? Could it really have been that Ambrosio Molinos, rather than fight the malevolent forces that sought to unfinger his grip from the cheese he loved, had come to such a desperate impasse that he wanted—indeed, *needed*—to dump it instead?

The idea of this was like a full-body Rolfing, the sudden readjustment of some narrative spine. I needed to let it settle and to rearrange the architecture of my thoughts around it, for I was thinking about all the years I'd let myself live in this stupor of belief—that Ambrosio was so heroic and principled that he could never be tied to venal concerns, that, aside from being magical, from being a cheese of lost memories, Páramo de Guzmán symbolized a kind of lost purity that needed to be ferociously protected at all costs, that only Ambrosio could have made, nurtured, and guarded a cheese such as this. How many times, in how many drafts, had I written it so? The way Julián described Ambrosio's toxic finances led me to realize that, with each passing day, the cheese must have broken Ambrosio a little more because he owed more and more—and lost a little more of his dignity in the process, which was the thing that mattered most to him. Only bankruptcy, in the end, could have stanched the hemorrhaging.

In this alternate telling, Ambrosio appeared in Julián's office, lamenting that Páramo de Guzmán, his company, was "crashed, gone, dead." Ambrosio confronted Julián over the bankruptcy issue, and Julián told him that he didn't advise going the route of bankruptcy because, in the end, it would be a financial mess for everyone, that the banks would go after personal assets.

"I told him that it's better to find buyers, because the product is good, and you can keep this business alive," Julián said. "Otherwise, the banks don't care: They'll try to take everything."

As a man with nothing, perhaps Ambrosio thought the banks could take nothing more. He just needed an ending. And yet in Ambrosio's version, he'd arrived at Julián's office waving a spurious contract as the flag of his betrayal, papers he said he'd signed unwittingly that gave away his cheese. And Julián had retreated in fear. *Huh-huh-huh-huh-huh-huh-huh* . . .

Never happened, said Julián now.

Rather, in Julián's account, it was he, Julián, who argued to keep Páramo de Guzmán alive. The last meeting in Julián's office, the one Ambrosio had described so graphically as that final showdown in which Julián, hoist with his own petard, in a puddle of fear, clutched his throat, whining out his mercy song, seemed a very different encounter from what Julián described now. Julián mentioned nothing about cowering before Ambrosio's anger, though he admitted his friend's anger was real.

"He was really stirred up," said Julián. "While he's usually so friendly, he was extremely unfriendly. It was clear he'd just come to give his little talk—his speech—and get out. I said, 'Why don't we get everyone to sit down and find a way to harmonize the situation and move on?' And Ambrosio said, 'It's too late, there's nothing for us to talk about.' In that moment there wasn't some deep moment of reflection on my part—and perhaps that was a miscalculation. Dealing with people with big problems every single day, I think maybe my alarms didn't go off. I didn't first think that there was some bigger problem between Ambrosio and me. I said to myself, 'Okay, everyone has problems, I deal with problems every day, we always work them out, we'll work this out.' "

But that's where Julián had been wrong. They hadn't spoken again, and now nearly twenty years had passed. "There was one more coming apart which probably served to piss off Ambrosio the most," Julián acknowledged. "The actual sale of the company." Again, Julián painted himself as an adviser more than a player. If anything, he'd lost one of his biggest clients, a Spanish bank, for refusing to go after Ambrosio as the bank tried to recover its money from defaulted loans in his name. "But the truth is, I brought all of these Páramo de Guzmán investors to the table, and I couldn't just walk away," Julián said. With Páramo de Guzmán on the verge of collapse and "the banks descending like wolves," everyone wanted to protect their interests, so they formed a new company and bought the cheese operation.

"They make the sale, and this new company, they renegotiate the debt, and sit down with all their creditors and say, 'We're gonna pay

this, and that. We're gonna pull some money from here, and there.'
They hired me to be secretary of the board of directors. What is that?
It's their lawyer. But this is where Ambrosio got the idea that I'm the
guy who ran off with the company."

Surely it wasn't all altruism, was it? I wondered whether Julián
could understand how Ambrosio might have gotten that impression,
how he might have drawn certain conclusions when he found his best
friend on the other side of the fence.

"No, impossible," said Julián sharply, his open palm meeting the
table for emphasis, "because he's not ignorant. He knows that the secretary of the board isn't the owner of the company, he's an adviser.
Okay, probably he would have preferred not to see my name associated with the company, but you've also got to stand in my shoes. The
last investors, who put up their half million each? They're in this mess
because I brought them in. Because I did Ambrosio's bidding. So I
had an obligation when both sides came to me and said, 'You be our
financial guy, because we're in trouble.' I brought these guys to the
table, so I couldn't just abandon them. Imagine if I'd said, 'No, I can't
help because I have this history with Ambrosio.' That's not their business. Also—*this is my job*. I make a living doing this."

At that moment I found myself, despite myself, being persuaded—
and feeling something unconscionable, really: that maybe, just maybe,
Julián possessed his own kind of decency, daresay honor. "This was
about the sale of a company that Ambrosio hadn't been a part of for a
year at that time," he said. "And no one made any money from this.
The banks got all the money."

Julián wasn't done yet. He seemed to be revving up. I had never
forgotten—for it was so hard to forget—one of the central dramatic
scenes of the Ambrosio narrative, the Judas betrayal in which he and
Julián crossed the plaza in Roa, going to sign the final agreement with
Pedro and Teodoro, the conspiracy to steal his cheese already supposedly in place with Julián's active collusion, and Ambrosio turning to
Julián to ask if the contract protected him, and receiving the devious
assurance that it did.

"Totally false," said Julián now. "I wasn't there. I had one lunch with Ambrosio and Pedro—Teodoro wasn't even there—that's it. But look, at that moment Ambrosio was in an extremely desperate position. He needed money. He'd just returned from Bilbao, where he was trying to talk up some other economist, and he wanted other people to buy in. This whole tale of him wanting to keep the company like it was his pride and joy, bring in some investors but be protected, was never the case. He wanted out."

Julián continued. "It's important to go back if we really want a snapshot of who Ambrosio was in that moment. He considered himself ruined, and he was ready to give away the company in exchange for having his debts erased. And therefore, he didn't want to—nor could he—put any conditions down."

The whole affair didn't come as a surprise to Julián either. "Look," he said, "I just told you he once bought a million worms to put in his garden for fertilizer. And you know what he forgot to do? He forgot to put a plastic tarp at the bottom of the worm pit, and they all escaped."

The story was meant to illustrate how Ambrosio the Discombobulated couldn't, or wouldn't, connect the dots. Julián had more proof. "How many trees are there in Guzman? Twenty, thirty?" he asked, his aggrievement aroused now. "When Ambrosio was eighteen, there were four trees in one of his family vineyards. He had to cut down these four trees, and he said he was going to go out and buy this giant chain saw. The chain saw was going to cost more than what the wood was worth. Our friends said, 'What are you doing? You don't need this chain saw. Invite us to a *merienda* up at the *bodega,* and beforehand we'll each come with an ax, and we'll cut down the four trees.' Nonetheless, he bought it and cut the four trees down, and the chain saw never got turned on again."

Julián pushed himself back from the table, slightly jostling a couple of errant *quicos* from their silver tray. "*That* is Ambrosio."

Here was Ambrosio the profligate son, afflicted by some sort of attention deficit disorder. Here was Ambrosio the creative soul who'd given birth to Páramo de Guzmán but whose mind, when confronted with gnarly details, turned to Swiss cheese. Here was Ambrosio the genius marketer but haphazard CEO, and Ambrosio the flamboyant friend and wasteful dreamer. Here was Ambrosio, who still possessed the innocence of a child although he was very much an adult, looking at the proverbial stars as he slipped on sheep shit. But if Julián's story was true, then why had Ambrosio turned so vociferously on his best friend, the one who had played only a peripheral role while suggesting a solution for keeping Páramo de Guzmán in the hands of its creator?

"I don't have an explanation for this," Julián said. "It just seems like Ambrosio launched this huge battle, and he made me the responsible person."

Had Julián felt physically threatened?

"Was I ever afraid, physically, for my being? No. Never. You know, I crossed paths with him in the courthouse, and he'd say 'Hello' to me. Not in the most friendly way, but he'd say, 'Hola.' But you train yourself not to be afraid in life in general."

Hadn't he heard the stories about the candle, rope, and knife in Ambrosio's trunk? Hadn't he heard that Ambrosio planned to torture him to death? Julián didn't flinch at the question, but his eyes widened. "Umm—I never received any direct threats, but it started with *columbria,* this spoken slander that would reach me through other people in our circle." He offered an example. "In Aranda there was an attorney on trial for heading a prostitution ring and smuggling cocaine. In Spain they won't mention the name of someone who's been accused of a serious crime until they're found guilty. So it just said 'Attorney X.' Eventually the rumor going around was that *I* was this attorney, and later on I found out Ambrosio started this rumor."

Julián detailed another incident, before the first bankruptcy hearing, when Ambrosio had called an impromptu press conference in a café in Aranda, during which he announced to the local media—and this included reporters from the radio station owned by Julián—that Julián had stolen Páramo de Guzmán from him. Julián had been in his office at the time, and taped it. It was, he said, the only explanation he had from Ambrosio for the end of their friendship.

"Look, I've known him since he was a kid," said Julián, "and when he used to talk about other business failures of his, this was his thing: justifying. But with this big one, with the cheese, instead of just saying, 'I made a mistake again, I messed up,' and just accepting responsibility, he had to say, 'Somebody pulled a fast one on me.' Now, if you're saying, 'I'm a smart guy; I'm not an idiot,' who can you blame? And Ambrosio says—and this is a direct quote—'Who can betray your honor? The person who's closest to you, your best friend, that's the definition of betrayal, right?'"

Although he had not spoken to him in twenty years, Julián mimicked Ambrosio's exact words now. And though in our time together Ambrosio had called his blood brother a slew of names and alleged certain inflammatory character flaws, Julián seemed to be describing Ambrosio's weaknesses only to explain his character, and did so without brio or satisfaction. As Julián laid out the evidence, his Cuban friend never indicated that he was listening, never moved except for the drawbridge-lowering of his mandible to emit those leonine yawns.

Here Julián shifted in his chair—and winced. "Everything comes and goes," he said. "Problems come and go, even slander and perjury, but losing Ambrosio's friendship is the thing that still hurts the most."

The statement sat for a moment on the table. Julián took a long sip of beer. Having spoken in a voluble stream, he fell silent, eyes downcast. I posed a hypothetical: What if Ambrosio walked in right now? What would Julián do or say? The Cuban's eyebrow inched up, and his eyes scanned the door sleepily.

"Listen, I'd offer him my hand," said Julián, "and I'd say, 'I know that everything you said about me is a lie. But if you ever need anything from me, I'm here for you, it's obvious.'"

Julián choked a little on those last words, and I said something I wasn't sure about later, for perhaps I'd betrayed Ambrosio's trust, or my own allegedly objective place in the order of things. But Ambrosio had recently sat across from me shedding real tears, and here sat Julián seemingly trying to keep his own pain at bay. "When Ambrosio spoke of you last," I said, "he became very emotional, remembering all the time you spent together."

"I can tell you the same," said Julián. "He was one of the best friends I ever had, and he's one of the people that I continue to appreciate."

He pressed his lips together, fumbled for his phone. It was suddenly so immediate, inescapable. "We all make mistakes," I said without thinking, not even sure what I meant.

"But what did Ambrosio *say*?" Julián wanted to know.

I was trying to remember the exact words in the café that day a month earlier, after I'd seen Julián for the first time. "It was hypothetical," I said. "He said he didn't want to go on like this."

At this Julián sat up as if plugged into a wall socket, eyes glinting. "Is that what he said—exactly? Tell me what he said, *exactly*." It was strange to have Julián's full attention like this—and a little heady, too, for here I was, finally needed by Castile to right the wrongs of its past. I didn't want to overreach my authority. "He said—I *think* he said—that if you had this conversation and there was some reconciliation, it could be forgiven."

"Hold on," said Julián, "let me see if I understand, because for me this is very important: Are you saying that he's willing to talk to me?"

"Reading between the lines—I think, yes," I said. I couldn't speak unequivocally for Ambrosio, but it was true, wasn't it? Isn't that what he'd said in his distress? That this all needed to end now? And wasn't this what I really wanted, for it all to end now, and what I needed, too, an ending of some sort, in order to find a way to end my book? A murder, a reconciliation, a climax, a denouement, something dramatic and fitting, definitive and final that made it *a story*.

Julián looked stunned. "I have two things to say, and then probably need to ask a question, if you don't mind." I nodded, put out my open-palmed hand to signal that the floor was all his, since the moment seemed to require something theatrical on my part. *Please*.

"Okay, years ago now," said Julián, "I sent Ambrosio a message on three occasions. Once via one of Ambrosio's cousins and once via a client of Ambrosio's. And then once through another attorney who's a good mutual friend of both of ours. To the first two, Ambrosio's response was the same: 'There's nothing for us to talk about.' With the third, Ambrosio passed along a new number, but said, 'Don't trust him. You're a lawyer, he's not trustworthy.' So under those conditions, even though I didn't really feel welcome—I called once. Asun answered the phone, and said Ambrosio wasn't there. I said, 'Okay, tell him I called.' And he never called back. The gates weren't really open, so I never tried again. But of course, if there were an opportunity now, it would cost me nothing. As I told you, I'd meet him anywhere, anytime."

What if it could be finagled? I could imagine the scenario, in the telling room, some wine and chorizo on the table, the awkwardness at first, a chilly distance, an opening gambit, some random chat—about shared friends, or the fields, some innocuous point of interest. Would it be Ambrosio who spoke first, muttering, *Dime?* Tell me. Then it might begin. The conversation for which they'd waited two decades, the crux of the matter. I could imagine one talking while the other listened, and then the other explaining his side. Or would Ambrosio take offense at Julián's version, would it be a call to arms? Then would they quarrel? Would it trigger an ancient anger? And what then? Perhaps, knowing the delicacy of the situation, they wouldn't discuss it at all. Having seen each other again, with all those memories in the balance, they'd agree to let bygones be bygones. In the best-case scenario, they would embrace—and then would come the flood of relief on both sides, the freedom and eventual joy of being set loose from the past, of having put an end to the cheese affair.

"I always felt that Ambrosio had this desire for reconciliation," said Julián, "but you know, on some level, it became impossible after he built up his legend, this History of the Betrayal of the Best Friend. To reconcile would essentially undermine the very legend of my betrayal. But now I'm beginning to suspect that time is undermining the legend of its own accord."

Julián kept on. "The other day an uncle of Ambrosio's, one who wouldn't say hello to me after all this happened, stopped me on the street and said, 'Give me your hand.' We shook, and he said, 'How is it that you and Ambrosio still aren't talking? To think of the friends that you once were . . . such a tragedy.' Just the fact that this relative broke the ice made me think even more that time is having its way with the story, that maybe there's a chance."

Listening to him, I wondered whether time was the only truth-teller, the trickle that over aeons formed the honest canyon. Once I'd let myself believe that it curdled a story. *The boy becomes insufferable; the king is made a fool of.* But perhaps adding even more time forced new shapes to emerge, new possibilities and intimations of other worlds behind the assumed one, maybe it freed the boy of preposterousness, made the king more dignified.

When he reflected back now, did Julián feel angry that the cheese had come between them? "It's not the cheese's fault," he said. "In some way, Ambrosio grabbed on to this story—this idea that I was the betrayer—as a way of saving face in front of the whole world, of justifying what happened to the outside world."

Could he be forgiven?

"In fact, I have forgiven him," said Julián, "because I've understood his situation. This is a guy who never planned, never really got too far ahead with anything—party, good times, here we go—then all of a sudden he finds himself sanctioned, embargoed, without a company, no money, at a loss with his family."

"It was their legacy, this cheese," I said.

"Yes," said Julián.

"And when he lost it, maybe he kind of lost his mind," I said.

"I understand that," said Julián, "and for that reason I don't harbor any rancor. You asked before if I feared Ambrosio. I know at the end of the day he's not really capable of violence. I know that he wouldn't send someone, or allow someone who might come of his own initiative. There's too much beautiful history behind it and too many friends in common, too much *enlace,* intertwining."

What was "worse than a killer putting a bullet in my head," said Julián, was something that had actually happened. "I was having lunch one day in Aranda with some clients, and by total coincidence there was a large contingent of Ambrosio's family—his parents, some cousins, nephews, nieces—but Ambrosio wasn't there. We finished eating and were leaving at the same time, and Ambrosio's mother approached and started screaming, 'Julián, how could you steal our business from us, how could you rob us? How could you do this to us?'

"If someone had tried to kill me, it would have been over quickly: I would be dead, or I would have killed the killer and been arrested. But this was my best friend's mother, the head of the household where I practically grew up, screaming at me, screaming something that I believe wasn't the truth, in front of Ambrosio's extended family and in public, in front of my clients. It was just so painful, all I could bring myself to say was, 'Puri, you're mistaken. Puri, you're mistaken.' I couldn't say anything else.

"A nephew of hers, who is a local judge or a magistrate, told her, 'Aunt, calm down, don't say these things,' but the damage was done."

When he finished, Julián looked a bit ill, wan, a hank of hair bobbing loose from the controlled follicular landscape of his head. He seemed to have reached the conclusion of what he had to say, and started fiddling with his phone again. What a terrible moment, I said, to have your surrogate mother berate you publicly. He heaved a deep breath, looked up, and said that obviously he'd never returned to that restaurant. "I had my friends back then. I still have friends today. Obviously I haven't gone back to Guzmán in many years." And then he asked me one last time: Can you ensure that Ambrosio wants to talk to me?

"Ambrosio's aware that I'm talking to you," I said, "so in a way I'm a bit of a messenger, even though as a journalist I want to make sure you get to answer these charges."

Julián nodded. His phone was squawking. He took out a roll of bills, left a few on the table, reached for his briefcase, and stood. The Cuban, startled from his reverie, struggled to his feet. Julián extended a hand across the table. We shook, firmly, as if we'd made some sort of agreement.

"Remember," he said, "I'll be there tomorrow if he says yes."

ALL SHALL BE RESTORED

" . . . his blood flowed from the same river."

WHERE ONCE I'D COME OFF THE OVERNIGHT PLANE FROM the States bleary but on a speed-walk to the rental car desk, and after procuring my *coche* I'd gun that mini-car and merge onto A-1 headed north, driving full of expectation, trying to skip minutes forward into my *campo* paradise, my double life, to get to Ambrosio's house with its abandoned pool next to the Duero River, to visit the fields and village bars with him, chugging Cokes to stay awake (so as not to miss anything)—now I devised what excuse I could to loiter a little, to steal a night or two in Madrid, walking the barrios (La Latina, Lavapies, Huertas), visiting new friends in the city (including Ambrosio's brother Roberto and his wife, Mika), inevitably ending up at the Prado to see the Goyas. On one trip, I went to the museum no fewer than four times, muttering at the canvases.

It'd become a rite of sorts: I'd visit *The Family of King Carlos IV,* my eye drawn past the toadlike king and his brood to Goya in the shadows, painting at his canvas. Then I would stroll around the corner to stand in awe before his Black Paintings, before *The Colossus* showing Saturn in full devour, and the drowning dog, and the two boys in *Duel with Cudgels*. I'd stand there and wonder: What caused those two boys to turn against each other with such fury—the cudgel cocked and ready to slice the air with whistling indignation toward the skull—for they seem nearly the same in body, dress, and disposition, just like mirror-imaged brothers, shoulders turned toward each other? What result could possibly favor either?

I saw Ambrosio and Julián in that painting, of course—and the intractable human condition, the seed of all civil war. But did that really warrant all the time I spent standing before it? What was up with me standing in this spot, like Fernando in the shade of the tree across from the church in Guzmán?

Afloat before the Black Paintings, I was reminded of an alternative legend about the paintings brought forward in recent years by a Spanish historian, Juan José Junquera, best known for his writing on eighteenth-century furnishings. When he was commissioned to write a book about the Black Paintings, he combed the archives in Madrid, stumbling on a trove of documents about Goya's farmhouse, Quinta del Sordo. In Goya lore, it was believed that the Black Paintings were completed sometime between 1820 and 1823, and covered the walls of the first and second floors of the house. But Junquera was astonished to find one salient, undermining fact: At Goya's death, in 1828, there was no second floor. That came later. "If the upper floor does not exist in Goya's time, then of course [the Black Paintings aren't] by Goya," Junquera was quoted as saying in a 2003 article that laid out the entire imbroglio.

The drowning dog and the boys with their cudgels, among others, were allegedly found on the missing second floor: So how did they come to be? It was a mystery, according to Junquero, but to his mind, the myth of the painter lost in some spirit world, desperately trying to keep pace with the images haunting him, was flawed by fact. None of Goya's intimates ever claimed to have seen the paintings, and those who wrote about the house described its walls covered with artwork but of a more rustic nature, scenes from country life, friends. It doesn't quite have the same ring, does it? Goya at the end, in a frenzy, painting . . . *picnics and stuff.*

The writer of the article, Arthur Lubow, claims that our ability to judge the authenticity of the Black Paintings is also partially clouded by this "biographical mystique." "In addition to bearing a great-artist sticker, the Black Paintings come with a narrative of the most compelling sort," he writes. "Like van Gogh's crow-haunted fields and Pollock's twisted skeins of paint, Goya's Black Paintings are popularly believed to be the outflow of a tormented great soul. A reattribution would strip away their pained sincerity along with their authenticity."

There are also indications that the Black Paintings don't entirely belong to Goya: the crude, clawlike hands, the heavier use of black, the fact that X-rays reveal other images beneath. Every canvas contains its own story—and mystery. Adding to the confusion are photographs taken at Quinta del Sordo in the 1860s that show some of the paintings in a form very different from what would eventually appear on the canvases at the Prado.

Junquera's theory, however shaky, is that Goya's only son, Javier, may have been the auteur, painting them for pleasure, and when he passed away and his son, the profligate Mariano Goya, thought to sell the property, he saw a greater financial upside in calling the paintings his grandfather's rather than his father's.

You can imagine the cacophony raised in opposition to this theory, but does it make it less valid? And if not Javier, then couldn't one honestly say that the curator and painter Salvador Martínez Cubells, who took the images from the walls of the Quinta, restored them, and then transferred the Black Paintings to canvas—perhaps for the worse—deserves a credit, too?*

* On the Prado wall next to *Duel with Cudgels* (here it's translated as *Fight to Death with Clubs*) is the following clarification: "X-rays of this work and comparisons with mid-nineteenth-century photographs reveal substantial modifications dating from after it was detached from the wall [at Quinta del Sordo]. Both young men were originally standing in a grassy meadow." When it comes to *The Colossus,* the Prado has reattributed the painting to Goya's friend and follower, Asensio Juliá, whose initials, AJ, appear in the corner of the canvas.

No, we're enthralled by the story, the biographical mystique. Even when Lubow visits with Manuela Mena, the Prado's head curator of eighteenth-century art, she claims *The Dog* is one of the most revered paintings of our time and tells the story of Joan Miró's last visit to the Prado. He wanted to see two paintings: Velázquez's *Las Meninas* and Goya's dog. And so go the last lines of Lubow's article: " 'For [Miró], *The Dog* and *Las Meninas* were of the same level intensity,' " Mena said. She looked at me challengingly. 'We cannot send *The Dog* to the museum basement because it was on the apparently nonexisting second floor of the Quinta.' "

So was that to say that mystique won out over the truth every time? All the best stories and strangest dreams metaphorically seemed to exist on the apparently nonexisting second floor of the Quinta, didn't they? In the end, it wasn't so much that there was an alternative narrative—there always was—but it came down to belief: Which one did you *want* to believe. Which one suited you best? Or, perhaps most to the point: Which one told the story you were already telling yourself?

I WAS TELLING MYSELF a story, too. So who was I kidding? This whole business had long ceased to be journalism. It was mythicalism, the making of and suspension in something mythical. This was encouragism, the telling of a story to remind yourself of your higher angels. Before it became discouragism. Or discombobulism. Before it became implicationism and possessionism.

After meeting with Julián, I'd needed to process. And yet in the space of twenty minutes, Ambrosio had called my phone repeatedly: five, six, seven times. Why? More than anything, I felt as if I'd been had. Or I'd let myself be had. Or that I needed to think about whether or not I'd been had, and by whom.

Eventually I returned the call and said that the meeting had gone well, that there were contradictions of course, and that we'd cover it all when we returned to Guzmán in a couple of months. I had a plane out the next morning, to Portugal for a story. I was glad for the space. And soon I was back home, sitting in my attic office, watching the squirrels as they ran on their power-line highway to nowhere and back, as I turned it all over in my mind. 311 pages now, and here's what I knew:

1) Julián the *puta* didn't seem like a *puta* at all.

2) Ambrosio the heroic suddenly seemed grasping and flawed, like an actual human being.

3) I'd somehow entered the drama as the Negotiator.

So wasn't it finally time to force the issue? What if I could find a way to mend their friendship? We might repaint Goya's *Duel with Cudgels* (for if one were to erase the cudgels, the two men appeared on the verge of falling into exhausted embrace), or unbury the dead in their mass graves. Yes, this *was* all about cheese. And now by resolving it, we could begin on the road to world peace.

This was my muddled thinking when I returned to Spain about eight weeks later and found myself killing time in Madrid, visiting the Goyas again. But then I had a nervous feeling in my gut. I'd always been the tide to Ambrosio's moon. He moved me as he pleased, and it had never been the other way around.

I went north to find him in the family room of his house, a fire in the fireplace. He wore a sweater vest, and boomed hello, that wonderful way he had of saying my name—MY-KULL!—as if discovering it for the first time. We embraced. I stepped back, and looked upon him with the fire lighting his face. The mournful eyes, the mirthful mouth. How many years had it been since we'd first met? Almost ten? He was aging before my eyes—and I before his. And how I loved him—and depended on him to say the right thing now.

He motioned for me to sit. There was the usual rundown: my kids, his family, Sara and Asun; the latest news in town, the first plantings and vineyard prep, and so on. And then there was silence, a highly unusual thing in Ambrosio's presence. He was rocking in his chair. He looked askance at me, then at the fire. Had he ever waited for something I had to say?

"I want to tell you about my meeting with Julián," I said.

"Yes," he said, "tell me." He dragged a forefinger over his lower lip.

"He had a lot to say," I said. "And some of it sounds different from your version." I could hear a little quaver in my voice. Crap. This wasn't the Negotiator; this was the guilty ex–altar boy. I felt as if I'd jumped sides, right before his eyes. Speaking of Julián with such intimacy had the odd effect of putting Ambrosio on the defensive, something that seemed impossible. "The most important thing," I said, "is that he'd still like to meet with you if you were willing to meet."

Ambrosio went to speak, but I raised a halting hand. I'd thought through a short speech, and I intended to deliver it. "I've been thinking a lot about El Cid—" I said, and then I regurgitated his story, unraveling it slowly, describing El Cid's loyalty for his friend the king Sancho, detailing how Sancho's brother, Alfonso, and sister, Urraca, conspired to have Sancho killed, and after they did, how Alfonso took the throne, and how then, after some other nonsense, El Cid, the most loyal Castilian, was banished from Castile. "When El Cid was turned out by King Alfonso, he marched south," I said, "and for every town he sacked, he sent the spoils back to his betrayer, the new king, all in hopes of seeing his homeland again." Was I being presumptuous? Annoying? Was I striking a chord? "This is also the legend of what it means to be Castilian," I said.

Ambrosio sat and listened. He considered deeply. The Cid alone was capable of this saintly sort of majesty. The rivers of Castile pulsed through his veins, the mountains and Meseta made him mighty and unshakable. Deprivation had made him all-powerful. He marshaled the wind, the hail, and lightning—and unleashed it on the world. He turned his betrayal into a righteous force for good.

Surely Ambrosio could understand such a tale, for his blood flowed from the same river. He saw El Cid as kinsman and life source.

He saw him riding alongside his car, on his horse, Babieca, wielding Tizona, his sword, as we drove home from Haza on a stormy night. He spoke to El Cid when he saw his face in the clouds. To appeal to Ambrosio through the legend of El Cid seemed in some ways fool-proof, for it gave Ambrosio the ultimate chance to save face: Be the legend. "As much as the story of El Cid is about courage and strength," I said, "it's about striving for a certain kind of forgiveness, too."

Ambrosio rubbed his lower lip, averted his eyes to the fire. "Julián wants to meet," I said. "He'd like for you two to put the cheese behind you, as you told me you'd also like to."

I remembered the last time I'd seen Ambrosio, in the immediate aftermath of his father's death, when the world seemed cracked open, when—perhaps struck by a thunderclap that he was next in line, that death was hurtling toward him, too—he'd laid himself bare, weeping openly in the bar across from Julián's office. But now as I spoke I couldn't read him, and when I came to the end of what I had to say, his mouth fastened in a hard line.

I waited, entertaining one last image of vanishing cudgels, two men embracing. Then Ambrosio issued his final decision.

"No," he said. "It's not possible to forgive that fucking *puta*."

In February 2008 I received an e-mail from Angel, telling me that he and Ambrosio would be coming to New York for a few days. "We will have plenty of time to meet, in fact we have almost nothing to do, only look around," he wrote. The reason for the trip had to do with Angel's desire to invest in Manhattan real estate. He'd sold a finca he owned in Patagonia for $2.5 million and was looking to reinvest the money, given the favorable exchange rate and the burst U.S. housing bubble.

One evening, while Angel went off to see a few apartments, we—my buddy Carlos, Ambrosio, and I—met for dinner at a steak-house, Keens, on West Thirty-sixth Street. We sat beneath a collec-tion of clay churchwarden pipes hung from the ceiling, surrounded by ephemera—paintings, photographs, notices—on the walls. In Spain, I'd always been at Ambrosio's mercy, in restaurants and bars, on the road or street, navigating a language I couldn't completely grasp, but here, when he sat down in the dark-wood booth and opened the menu, Ambrosio seemed utterly lost and out of sorts.

Carlos translated for him, running through certain features of the menu: appetizers, sides, main dishes. Ambrosio ordered an aged, prime T-bone and nothing else but beer, because he appeared confused by the concept of "sides." He fiddled with his stylized steak knife as if he didn't know how to work it, as if fascinated by this fancified tool meant to slice his well-marbled piece of meat. I remembered a meal at his *bodega,* at the end of the summer we lived in Guzmán, to which we'd invited the whole Molinos clan as thanks, as if inviting them to their own telling room was an invitation at all. Knowing that *ternera* was normally a can't-miss, Sara and I relied on a memorized recipe from an old *Bon Appétit,* one we often trotted out for our mignon-loving friends back home, that included a delicious, buttery sauce with roasted peppers. The result could be sublime, the char-grilled meat achieving succulence, the sweetness of the peppers, the butter of the sauce carrying it forward across the tongue in sumptuous sparks. On that special night of thanks at the *bodega,* when we were pretty sure many Castilian minds were about to be blown, everyone seemed to be scraping that amazing sauce off their meat, or if not, swallowing less than enthusiastically. Only much later, when I asked him about it, did Ambrosio admit, as politely as possible, that Castilians didn't like "their meat hidden."

At Keens, however, that was not the problem. The problem was that the spell was broken. In Manhattan Ambrosio didn't seem to have the energy to talk about Guzmán, for it didn't seem pertinent or resonant here, dwarfed and bewildered as he was by the city and its upside-down stalactites. He ate with gusto, of course, voracious with his appetite and appreciation, but in the end found it hard to say much of anything.

Afterward we wandered up toward Times Square, to the hotel

where he and Angel were staying. We paused, beneath a five-story, lighted billboard showing M&M's as characters of many colors and expressions, doing cartwheels because it was somehow important for the Mars corporation to spend millions to have us believe that M&M's are alive and incorrigibly spunky. Once a monumental figure, Ambrosio was trying to be heard above the din, but all I kept seeing were yellow, green, and orange orbs doing cartwheels over his head, winking and saucy. In the capital of commerce, in a place where everything moved so quickly, Ambrosio seemed small and demeaned somehow, in need of protection.

We left him there, melting beneath the lights, half expecting he'd turn yellow, green, or orange himself, maybe throw a backflip with the other M&M's. When I turned to find him one last time, though, he was gone—to his hotel room, to the airport, eventually to solitary, dying Guzmán again, where he might don his farmer's *mulo* once more, and everything that was good and right about the world could reestablish itself under his two feet.

IV

"The imminent awakening is poised, like the wooden horse of the Greeks, in the Troy of dreams."

WALTER BENJAMIN

CHAPTER 23

LEGENDS AND CHEESE

". . . I could feel the goose bumps rise again."

SARA COULD HAVE MARRIED A DIFFERENT GUY. SHE HAD A DIFFERent guy, whom I'll call Mark. They backpacked across Europe after college and ended up in Madrid, at the Prado, looking at the Titians and El Grecos, Velázquezes and Goyas. Afterward they lounged on the museum lawn, in the heat of a June day, and fell into a philosophical conversation. How it started Sara couldn't remember—perhaps they were comparing the orderly realism of one artist to the chaotic dreamings of another—but eventually it boiled down to a simple question: What does one plus one equal?

Mark said two. *Obviously.*

One plus one equals *one,* Sara said.

Mark was adamant. It was an inviolable truth: One plus one equals *two*!

Pfffft, said Sara. One man plus one woman equals one child. One family plus another equals a village. One point of view plus another might equal consensus.

Following this line of argument the world itself—and everything in it—didn't need to be a fixed thing, and one's progress through it might be guided less by grid than by random Etch A Sketch, guided more by possibility and impulse than forethought. That is, one plus one could be whatever you wanted, leading you wherever it led.

So the question itself was a litmus test, a decider of what kind of person you happened to be. The world needed both, of course—the grid-bound and the Etch A Sketcher. But in that moment on the lawn, under the hot Iberian sun, Sara had another thought: Who you are is defined by who you gravitate to, who surrounds you, who reflects you back. Mark, she now could see, was destined for a life of absolute logic: law school, law practice, law-abiding citizen in an American city, perhaps following an unchanging daily routine, while she, the Etch A Sketcher, thought herself destined for a life of squiggly lines. As great as their friendship was, the love affair was over.

I'd never heard that story until a day when we were discussing my/Ambrosio's book—specifically, why I couldn't, or wouldn't, finish it—and she observed that Ambrosio was a "one-plus-one-equals-oner." And then she said: "You are, too—and maybe that's it: You can't finish because you think it will prove everything really *is* finite."

Like all parents, I suppose, the ache of this finitude was something I increasingly felt as our children grew. With the passage of time, Leo, May, and Nicholas had learned to negotiate and outwit, to throw tantrums, then curl up on our laps or snuggle into our sides, gangly limbed. We lived the familiar cycles of parenting, dressing the kids until they dressed themselves, reading to them until they could read for themselves, driving them until they wanted to walk or bike, chaperoning playdates until those playdates became pickup games at the local field or epic video-game sessions in the TV room, which parents were asked not to enter. At night they could be found behind the half-open doors of their rooms, reading their books or playing with their Legos—and later, doing homework while binging on hidden cookies—lost in worlds that had nothing to do with their mother or father. And we understood this to be a good thing, which isn't to say we didn't both miss and not-miss the days when they had needed us for everything.

So time was moving, and, contrary to my fears as a younger man, there was much that gave hope. I had been certain that the erasing speed and noise of modern life would consume and separate us, that we would occasionally text each other from adjoining rooms. I wasn't alone in this fear, of course. As early as 1936, Walter Benjamin had written that "the art of storytelling is coming to an end," that this oral tradition, which was "the securest among our possessions," had been taken from us, that we'd lost "the ability to exchange experiences."

But as our kids grew and acquired more sophisticated language, they became fondest of stories told out loud. At first they loved to hear about the recent past, which for them was deep history, the funny, outrageous things they had said and done when in diapers or as toddlers. Our telling rooms were the car, the kitchen, the dinner table. They were the moments after turning out the lights, when we lay next to each other in bed, in whatever combination of parent-child, in tangles of arms and legs, and poured out the last tales of the day in a hush meant to coax sleep but that often provoked the admonition "One more—*please?*" These were mostly simple entertainments on our part, detailing the way Leo had been generous with his affections at the age of two on an early trip through Spain (so he became "The Bediapered Kissing Bandit of Seville"), or the way May had enthusiastically celebrated big occasions ("The Girl Who Wore Her Birthday Cake") or could never be held without trying to squirm away ("The Baby Who Wanted to Fly"). They knew they'd briefly lived in Castile at some murky time before their own memories could access those memories, and they wanted to hear those stories—about the giant named Ambrosio, about the little village at the top of the world—while Nicholas ("The Boy Who Visited the Emergency Room Too Often") might scuff the floor with a kick of his socked foot and burst out, "Aw, why didn't *I* ever get to live in Spain?"

Soon they wanted to hear stories about the juvenile failures and humiliations of their parents, to take comfort in the golden oldies while they were sorting their own ups and downs. We trotted out "The Swimmer Who Thought He Won a Blue Ribbon, but Ended Up in Fifth Place," or "The Girl at Cotillion Who Wore Such an Amazing Poncho She Was Asked to Dance by the Girl-Who-Thought-Mom-Was-a-Boy." It turned out that there was a very long list of these sorts of stories, and they often contained what Benjamin called "the nature of every real story," the inclusion, whether "openly or covertly," of "something useful," be it a moral or some shred of wisdom, assistance, or warmth. Some way of saying, "History repeats." And: "You're going to be all right."

Next they wanted stories about their grandparents. They wanted the entire story, in exact detail, of their Grandma Peggy, Sara's mom, who had passed away in a scuba diving accident before they were born. They wanted to know what she was like—and it was hard to remember anything bad, for she was remembered as someone good and generous. Leo, obsessed with war history, wondered if we had any "old heroes" in our family, and while he had two great-grandfathers who'd fought in the First and Second World Wars, respectively, and while we told him what we knew—that tale of my grandfather escaping from a prison camp and riding to safety under a train; Sara's grandfather landing on Omaha Beach on day two, then marching with Patton across France to the Battle of the Bulge, garnering three battlefield promotions, and on into Germany where it all ended in the most horrible secret of all, the concentration camps—I wondered if we were furthering certain inaccuracies inadvertently passed on to us, all harmless enough but meant in subtle ways to transfigure normal people caught up in events beyond their control into minor deities, to connect ourselves as the righteous ones to the larger river of time and meaning. The stories became legends of history, and at the same time they became explanations about who we were and what we believed.

In this small exchange, our family kept each other alive and close. This is how we stitched the golden thread that connected the past and present, to make the collective coat we wore, how we passed along all the things that mattered most to us, and hoped to hold the world at bay for the moment it took to tell these stories, our heirlooms, for who knew what awaited beyond the locked doors of our night house, what other errant, whisky-breathed story lurked out there in hopes of undoing ours?

FOR OUT THERE, IT was still madness. Never-ending violence. What the pictures showed, what the generals said, how the mullahs responded—war was its own war of narrative. Then came a financial meltdown at home: Americans lost a quarter of their net worth, housing prices dropped 20 percent, foreclosures skyrocketed. And a new narrative: the greedy bankers, the victimized former homeowners. But unlike the boy I'd been in 1991, taking my news from Bill Bonds and his spun Incan-silver toupee, I now wrote about some of that breaking news myself (an earthquake in Port-au-Prince; a revolution in Cairo; torture at Gitmo). If the chimera of objectivity melted in the mouth of the teller, I, too, wondered at myself and the stories I told. The greatness of America, the country perched on its own witness hill—I believed in that legend. Until I realized with some pain that it, too, was flawed.

I'd like to say this is what kept me away from Guzmán after seeing Ambrosio in Manhattan: chasing the big stories of the day and trying to write them. But this was only partly true. Though it was easier to make narratives out of what didn't leave me stuck, I'd never stopped working on the book. I'd retreat to my attic office and listen to Ambrosio's recorded baritone over endless hours as if he were a mystic poet, Ambrosio of the Mill and Field, describing the planting process, or the history of wine, or the perils of overwatering. It was a meditation, like the aging of cheese. Hit Play, and I could hear the clatter of a glass or the glubbing of a bottle into a *porrón,* and it all came flooding back: the quenching power of the red wine, the scent of burning grapevines, the taste of grilled lamb, the hard benches in the telling room, the wisps of cigarette smoke. I read and reread the

transcripts I'd collected and had bound like a holy text, poring over
the stories he told—the legends, farces, and folktales*—until I'd in-
ternalized them. I interleaved everything he'd said about the cheese,
trying to square it. Because old habits die hard, and I still needed to
believe in the cheese's purity. Because it was so easy to find myself
under his spell all over again.

At the end of my last visit to Guzmán, Ambrosio had dedicated a
few days to explaining once more—in technical detail—how Julián
had duped him, rebutting Julián's version, alleging that for his efforts
Julián had been enriched to the tune of $100,000 by the ESCOSA
partners. He claimed that a check had been written, but it was impossible to prove. On the outskirts of Aranda we sat in a trencherman's
restaurant—a place frequented by truckers and factory workers—as

---

* This one is called "The Witches of Peñafiel," and should be told slowly, in the
fields at midnight. Though this is its most condensed form, and has been altered
slightly, the spoken version can last, according to Ambrosio, an hour or two:

At the time of the Inquisition, the witches fled to the woods just across the river
from the village of Peñafiel to avoid being burned at the stake. There they hid,
covered in leaves, chanting, stirring their cauldron with sticks and bones.

Now, in the village itself lived two hunchbacks: one good and one bad. And
they'd both fallen in love with the same woman, a dairymaid of startling beauty
who seemed unapproachable, given their condition. The good hunchback took this
particularly hard, and pined after her until he was sick with heartache. The bad
hunchback hid his desperation, spreading false rumors to undermine his rival. He
suggested to the good hunchback a visit to the witches, because they were the only
ones who could help him, though the bad hunchback knew full well they would
likely eat him, hungry as they were in hiding. The good hunchback, understanding that he would otherwise die of a broken heart, decided to risk it and left that
night for the woods.

As he did, the wind picked up and a full moon rose, lighting the world silver.
He crossed the river and came among the oaks, which clattered and whipped in
the high wind. The good hunchback could feel a rhythmic beating, and he began
to quake. Slowly, voices rose until they were chanting loudly: "HUNGRY, HUN-
GRY, HUNGRY WE ARE!" The chanting continued as he hid behind a thick
covering of bushes, parting them to see a circle of black-cloaked crones covered in
leaves. There was a throne upon which sat the Queen, and before her the black
cauldron that bubbled and steamed. The chanting continued—"HUNGRY,
HUNGRY, HUNGRY . . ."—until the good hunchback mustered his courage
and leaped from the bushes, yelling, "STOP!"

Ambrosio pulled out a pen, exasperated now by my questions, and scribbled madly on a wine-stained paper tablecloth, boxes and arrows and swirls leading in all directions, showing various iterations of the cheese business, until my head was spinning. Then he tore the paper and handed me his jottings as if delivering the Magna Carta.

"*Mira,*" he said. "It's as clear as day."

But it wasn't. At least not to me, who was not great with numbers, either. Eventually my monomaniacal fixation on gathering facts gave way to a sense of stalemate and resignation. Or succumbed to biographical mystique and clashing myths of observation. (It boiled down to the statement: *We cannot send* The Dog *to the museum basement because it was on the apparently nonexisting second floor of the Quinta.*) And yet there was evidence of doubt in Ambrosio's story, for as his various lawsuits rose through the courts, then flickered and flamed, Ambrosio lost all but one of his cases—and even with that

---

The witches stopped, mouths agape, and the Queen rose from her throne. The wind, the moon, the silence now of the witches, until the Queen shrieked, "WHO DARES GO THERE?" Bowing, the hunchback moved forward and said, " 'Tis I, the hunchback of Peñafiel. I'm in love and come asking to be made whole again." The Queen assessed the poor beast and cackled, then called her witches into a huddle while the hunchback prepared for his death. After an interminable passage of time during which the witches stole furtive glances at him, the Queen came forth again. "For coming here you should be eaten, but for your bravery this once we will grant your wish." The witches took the hunchback into their circle and began chanting—he could feel their hot breath on his face—and like that, he was transformed into a man of perfect posture and health. He then fled back through the forest, over the river, and into the village, where he immediately met the bad hunchback in the street.

Once the bad hunchback saw what had been done, and realizing that by morning light his rival would woo the dairymaid, the bad hunchback took off, over the river and through the woods, where he came upon the same circle of witches chanting "HUNGRY, HUNGRY, HUNGRY . . . " And he, too, burst through the bushes and yelled: Stop! The Queen came forward cackling, gazing upon the bad hunchback. He spoke his wish, and the Queen convened her brood, stealing furtive glances. This time, when she stepped forward, the Queen said, "For your foolishness, we have decided to eat you!" And before the bad hunchback could flee, he was taken and roped, then boiled to be eaten in a stew. The good hunchback eventually married the dairymaid, and lived happily ever after.

single favorable ruling, he was never able to recoup the court-awarded money for his lost wages. In the end he'd been left not only with his previous mountain of debt but also a new hill of legal bills. Meanwhile, the bank, with the help of the *guardia civil,* kept hauling away his belongings.

How could you not feel damned? How could you not wonder: Why go on?

The only thing Ambrosio Molinos had left, then, the only thing they couldn't take from him, was his story: the offering, the betrayal, the murder plot. Each time he told his legend, it was as if he indeed *was* amputating Julián. Each time he told the story Ambrosio Molinos became the righteous one again, the chosen one. He stood once more for something great, the immortality of the Old Castilian.

As for me, I probably realized deep in my gut that something terrible had happened to Ambrosio, that by flaw and hubris and other people's trickery he'd let down his family while putting himself in the mother of all holes, and he'd needed a story that allowed him to live with himself, to reassemble and unshatter himself, to get up and reenter the world. (*We are trying to reanimate Ambrosio.*) Wasn't it true that there was a place in all of us where we kept our secret under lock and key, vain animals capable of strange, petty, sometimes violent unpredictabilities? It wasn't just Ambrosio: We all had our secrets, and maybe the most terrible of them was that we weren't exactly who we thought we were, who we said we were, who we dreamed of being, that we were divided and at war and half made of self-mythologies, too. Sometimes on that staircase spiraling up from the darkness, we met ourselves coming up into the light, not recognizing ourselves or what we might do next.

After so much time trying to uncover the truth, after searching for the cheese and finding it and tasting it at last, I didn't care who was right or wrong, just as ultimately I didn't care if El Cid was a rapacious condottiere, or whatever he was. I still liked the poem about him. I would *always* like that damn poem! And if we couldn't believe in legends, and a hopeful piece of cheese, then what the hell was left in this world?

ONE FINAL STORY: ABOUT how Manuel flew one night. It seemed to be another communal secret. I heard about it at the bar—in yet another congregation of men drinking beer, wine, and spirits—by that Guzmánian tic of identifying a major happening by its proximity to a past weather event. It might have been Carlos the Farmer, it might have been Angel or Pinto or the eight-fingered old man, who said something like, "The storm ripped part of the roof right before the night that Manuel flew."

"Wait, Manuel *did what?*" And everyone clammed up.

Manuel was a fixture at the bar, a walleyed man in his mid-forties afflicted with mussed hair, persistent blinking, occasional muttering. He sat with his legs crossed and shirt untucked. There weren't enough beds in the house for everyone, or so it was said, and the family took shifts. Manuel was the late-night guy, waiting for a mattress to come free sometime in the morning hours.

When the bones first began haunting him, the voice came in distant whispers, as a passing presence. Over time the presence grew more intense. Even Manuel's brothers felt it. A shadow would fall against the wall. Someone would seem to sit at the end of the bed. But no one was there. Manuel became convinced that the spirit was his grandfather—Orel—the man murdered in the fields by Alfonso and his gang during the Civil War. It was Orel's bones that seemed to be speaking to Manuel, making some sort of indecipherable plea.

At least this is what Manuel told me, in his shy, halting manner. We'd never spoken before except for a passing hello, but when I asked if he'd join me one evening in Ambrosio's telling room, he agreed. Ambrosio was working late in the fields with Josué, and while I waited for Manuel, I sat with Ambrosio's father—this being the year before his death—and he told what he remembered of those long-ago times. He said that even though he'd been a small child, he could remember the sound of the gun that Martínazo, Orel's brother, had fired, killing the bride's father at that wedding gone awry. Then there was the war, which started when he was thirteen. And the revenge.

"Of course, I was afraid," he said. The bombing sorties, the hit squads striking indiscriminately. As for Orel's murder, he heard about it the August morning after, from field hands employed by the Molinos family. "But it was in everyone's best interest to stay quiet," said Don Ambrosio. It was a situation where "they may have killed one of yours, and three of mine," but there was no real justice to be had. And eventually people had to get on with their lives. "We just tried to forget," he said, then praised Franco as "the man who eventually fixed everything."

Manuel arrived, sat nervously, took some wine from the *porrón*. He didn't make eye contact. By now I'd heard at least six different versions of the story of his grandfather's murder—and he soon added another. With reluctance. Not everyone in Guzmán was a natural storyteller, and Manuel's soft-spoken reticence, combined perhaps with fear, meant that I found myself asking question after question, trying to pry loose something he didn't necessarily want to give.

In his pieced-together telling, both Martínazo, the outspoken Republican, and his brother, Orel, the apolitical nice guy, had fled Guzmán at different times, to different locations, unaware of each other's whereabouts. There'd been a woman who brought food to Orel. Alfonso and his gang had followed her up into the fields, then killed his grandfather as, by coincidence, Martínazo watched from a far hill.

Manuel claimed that his family had known where his grandfather's remains were buried, and eventually, they'd purchased the plot of land and put a special stone there. But then Manuel's mother—Orel's daughter—had approached the church to see about burying him in the cemetery. It was very important to her that he be buried there. According to Manuel, the priest, for reasons of his own, said it would be complicated, too much paperwork.

And that was that.

Until the night in question. It was Holy Week, just before Easter, two or three in the morning. Manuel said he felt antsy as he headed west out of town, walking the road, then veered into the fields. Suddenly he felt something pushing him from behind, shoving him until he began to run, or "some kind of running—I don't know—because my feet didn't touch the ground and I traveled three kilometers in two minutes," leaving him off about five hundred yards from his grandfather's bones. He heard the words "Get me out," and then a great peace fell over him.

He said he went to find his brothers back at the house and told them of the amazing happening, and they hurried to the spot where the words had been spoken, to see what else needed saying, but the spirit was gone. So in the morning they found the priest and told him in no uncertain terms that they would be bringing their grandfather for burial that day.

And that's what they did. Dug up his bones, put them in a box, and carried them to the cemetery, where the priest waited.

When Manuel had finished with his story, he looked nervously at the door, and said, "Can I go now?" But Ambrosio burst in, bringing a night chill that clung to his corpulent body. His cheeks were ruddy, and he blew on his hands. *"Joder,"* he boomed. "It's as cold as a witch's tit out there."

When he saw Manuel, he said, "Hombre, have you had enough wine?" He clasped Manuel's shoulder, pinning him, reached over to the table, took up the *porrón,* and thrust it back into his friend's hand.

Now Manuel looked absolutely trapped, uncomfortably shifting on the hard bench. Ambrosio sat, listened for a moment, picked up the thread, and started grilling him as if I hadn't spent the last hour doing just that. He wanted Manuel to walk him through the incident again, and seemed to correct little details. "You said it was cloudy," Ambrosio declared, "but then you could see the land. We'll have to presume it was a half moon that night." He went on in this vein, interrogating, reformulating, expanding, until he seemed satisfied.

By now we'd been in the telling room for more than three hours, having seen Ambrosio's father off to bed. It was after midnight, but Ambrosio wasn't yet done. He'd read my interest in this matter, and he wanted a satisfactory outcome. And since it seemed that every story in Guzmán was sooner or later delivered by its Storyteller-in-Chief, he declared that we would now drive the route by car. Manuel said he thought it was too late, but Ambrosio was hearing none of it. Soon we were all stuffed into Ambrosio's Pathfinder, Manuel in the front, me behind, leaning over the seat back as Ambrosio narrated while following the path of Manuel's peregrinations:

"This is a story from the recent past. It was a half moon, maybe quarter—and Manuel couldn't sleep. He started out on a walk from his house right here, on this road out of town. *Arriba*. To the *páramo*. He was walking, smoking a cigarette, thinking his own things when he veered off onto a royal road, the dirt sheep path. He'd walked this path hundreds of times. It was familiar. There were rabbits everywhere, like there are now, breaking in all directions. I shit in the milk: Why are there so many rabbits? The ground was very muddy, the path impassable, really. This is where the event began: Manuel feels the spirit of his grandfather pushing him, saying, 'Come, son, you will learn something now.' He feels something shoving him, and he begins to run. He jumps over rocks, never tripping, and then leaps the fields. He's transported over the streams and rivers. He never tires. He sprints, then flies from this moment to another, three kilometers apart, back past the village. He lands at this crossroad, a place known as Cañada Bola, not so far from the edge of the village. His feet are dry, not muddy. His legs are fresh and nothing on him is soaked from sweat. See, he's flown. And standing here, he understands the message: His grandfather wants to be buried in the cemetery *this* day. He's filled with peace, and walks calmly down this trail, back into Guzmán, the tower of the church coming into view. And now his shoes get wet and muddy. He finds the priest, who is an idiot to the core—and Manuel is reduced to threatening him to get permission to disinter the bones and rebury them in the cemetery. Manuel takes a wooden box up to the field, and a shovel, digs up his grandfather's remains—all that's left are the rags, bones, and decayed shoes—and brings them to the cemetery where the priest says a prayer. The box is put in the ground, and Manuel shovels again. He's never revisited by the spirit, the shadow or presence that came to his bedroom and haunted him. He walks home, up through the village, and tells his mother, 'It's done, he's buried now, go see for yourself if you want.' He goes to bed, feeling monumental, liberated. He is free—and so is his family at last."

It was vintage Ambrosio—told seemingly without pause to breathe, full of vivid details, even the shift in tenses, the subtle progression from "run" to "transport" to "fly"—and I could feel the goose bumps rise again. It was a story about transcendence, about the ancestors reaching from beyond and picking you up, giving you energy and peace. It was about burying the past once and for all, and doing the right thing when the universe had done you wrong. It was about these forgotten histories, about those forgotten by history, who heard the voices, and in them found their own final resolution.

It was a story that Ambrosio told us, but found necessary to tell to himself, too, for it was an allegory that pertained in part to the cheese. And, to my ears, it pertained in part to my book. (American takes a mystical walk in a Spanish village, sees a bunch of rabbits, gets swept away, lands, then has to figure out how to silence the voices and bury the bones.)

"Everyone in the village knows this story," he said, "but some believe it and others say, 'Yeah, Manuel's been drinking again. It's another one of his crazy things.'"

So which was it:

$1 + 1 = 2$? Or $1 + 1 = 1$?

I knew Ambrosio's answer, for every story he told was somehow meant to keep the village alive, and to keep himself alive in it. To send his voice echoing, so it might echo back over the ages. The beauty he saw, the ardor he felt for that disintegrating place, no matter what day or season, was so humbling and constant that it always caught me sideways, always left its stabbing pain. He kept adding magic to

Guzmán, as much as the vessel could reasonably hold. And although he loved the village as a parent, he always seemed to be seeing it for the first time, through the eyes of a child.

Perhaps this was his greatest accomplishment. He bent time until nothing was linear. So everything moved in circles, like the seasons. While clinging to the past, he always saw Guzmán as new and necessary. And he made you see it, too.

LET IT BE SUMMER one last time, then. Ambrosio has a delivery to make in his truck, and I volunteer to go with him. Just him and me, up in the spacious cab. We wake early and drive three hours north, near Santander, on the Atlantic coast. Ambrosio talks the whole time, and I seem to understand every fascinating word (though who knows?), as he tells the histories and stories of the towns we pass.

We make the delivery, a load of seeds exchanged for over 400 wooden pallets. It's very hot, tar-meltingly hot, and after reloading, Ambrosio's shirt is soaked through. Winded, he says, *"¡Puta madre, comamos!"* We walk to a truckers' restaurant nearby, a place with maybe eight tables, and he jokes with the waitress. He speaks to her in conspiratorial tones. "You go back and find the biggest container you can," he says, "then fill it to the brim with ice-cold beer."

Then we're driving back through Castile,* orange in the waning light, the moon over a bed of clouds, down past Burgos, Lerma, Aranda. He points out things on the Meseta, calling them by name, giving me yet another tutorial. Then we are off the highway, twisting through the villages of the Duero—Villafruela, Torresandino, Olmedillo—toward home. At Anguix, we take a right and climb up through Quintana-manvirgo until suddenly, at twilight, there it is: Guzmán, shining on its hill.

"¡Santos cojones!" Ambrosio mumbles quietly. His eyes moisten

---

* Writes Machado: "Castile, mystic and warlike / Castile, the genteel, humble and brave." And then, with the other hand: "Miserable Castile—a master yesterday— / wrapped in her rags, disdaining the unknown way."

and fill with light. *Holy balls, it's so beautiful!* We both gaze upon the vision of the church tower, the turrets of the *palacio,* the ocher houses cemented together against the world beyond. There are many different Guzmáns, but all I can see now is his. And so we ride, the Castilian and the *americano,* the storyteller and his apprentice, borne on some tide of our own. Add time and these stories repeat forever, never to end.

We enter the village just below Ambrosio's telling room in the hill, then bank left past Pinto's bar. We carry on past the stable where the cheese was first made (a sheep hand-painted on the wall, the words "Páramo de Guzmán" haloed overhead), past the house in which Ambrosio was born. We roll down a dirt track to the barn, and Ambrosio pulls the truck up alongside the barn that once held his sheep, facing out toward the *coterro* below and Mon Virgo, the fields and vineyards growing fat with their fruit, a sight that brings an overwhelming sense of peace and contentment. Ambrosio turns off the engine, playfully taps both hands on the wheel.

His eyes skitter over the rolling land, patchworked now in dabs of green, yellow, and crimson. He takes a deep breath. Then he smiles contentedly, saying nothing as he takes the notebook from my hand and scribbles: *acabar, terminar, finalizar, concluir.*

"Feen-eshed," he says in English, handing it back.

"Finished," I say, writing the word for him in my neatest hand— and then two more:

"The end."

FORGIVENESS (PART II)

"Remember it!"

THE END, NOT UNEXPECTEDLY, WAS ANOTHER BEGINNING. During my hiatus from Guzmán to finish the book, Ambrosio had been elected mayor, garnering over fifty votes and capping a miraculous comeback from the days twenty years earlier when he'd been run out of town. Among his first acts in that new position was to rename the streets, returning some of them to their nineteenth-century appellations: The Royal Road, The Castilian Way. Meanwhile, he'd moved again, to a house in the fields nearer the village. Both his sons had joined him full-time on the family lands, to make a life farming, while his daughter Asunita had moved to Egypt with a boyfriend, still making art.

By now it had been almost ten years since my own family had taken up residence in the concrete manse on Calle Francisco Franco, and I couldn't imagine finishing the book without returning once more with everyone in tow, especially our youngest, Nicholas, who was so pained not to have been present the first time around. Perhaps it was more selfish than that, too. If Guzmán had become this timeless kingdom on the hill in my mind, the place where Leo was forever three and May forever one, where everything was frozen (including my book) and no one could ever touch us, then it was important to add time to my own story to release it, to see my kids walking the streets, to break the false spell of everlastingness. I needed to acknowledge one certain reality—one I'd unconsciously worked hard to deny since becoming a father—primarily that my life would have its end, too. There was no magic Castilian village that could change that.

It was November 2012, and I flew over alone, for a last round of interviews before their arrival. I caught up with Julián at his office in Aranda. He'd just returned from a business trip to Brussels, and though it was a national holiday he wore a jacket, purple tie, and blue shirt. His practice was still thriving, with a busy schedule of arbitrations and trials. He had that same shy boyishness, despite a few added pounds. He'd been drinking wine with friends, and he reiterated his one regret: that he hadn't called Ambrosio when everything went sour. Otherwise, he knew of nothing else to apologize for, though by now he'd resigned himself to the fact that there'd be no reconciliation. "It's over. No chance," he said. "In Castile, part of keeping a grudge is that you never change your position. But if it's a real Castilian grudge, there should be blood. Ambrosio had a dozen chances to kill me. But I know him as a good man, and his bark was always worse than his bite."

All of this was history now, said Julián, but what made it particularly hard were the friends they shared in common. His wife was very close to Asun's brothers, while Julián's best friend was Nacho, Ambrosio's cousin. "Nacho has gone through a hard time recently, and normally, I'd just pick up the phone and talk to Ambrosio about him, but I can't. And that hurts."

Afterward, Julián wanted to go for a drink at a bar around the corner, gin and tonics served in huge goblets. Now he seemed to have all night, smoking his Gauloises, his phone silent, but I'd arranged to meet Ambrosio for *cena*. And there was nothing I could say that might console him. I'm not sure why but I found myself apologizing. "No," he said, "don't feel guilty. It's not necessary. This is very Castilian, these grudges and silences."

He took it as a matter of course, and yet there was something so lugubrious in his demeanor that it made leaving him all the more difficult. Crossing the street for the car, I spotted a liquor-store window display for Páramo de Guzmán wine in the window,* and I thought of Julián passing it each day on his way to work, another reminder of his losses.

Soon enough I was perched again at the cheesemaker's table. It felt as if I'd never been gone. A crackle of lines radiated from Ambrosio's eyes, his cough came and went with his cigarettes, sounding slightly more terminal. He was fifty-seven years old now. In conversation he would later say, "Though my childhood is always with me, I'm beginning to prepare for my death."

It no longer being necessary to tiptoe around the topic of Páramo de Guzmán, I asked Ambrosio where he stood on it these days, and he surprised me yet again. "It's been twenty years since I lost the cheese, and I think I've mellowed," he said. "In the beginning, I was crazy. The whole thing ate at my brain. First I was two hundred fifty pounds and strong as an ox; then I was two hundred fifty pounds, weak and bloated. I lost everything except the will to kill Julián." With Asun listening attentively, Ambrosio fell into another violent fantasy.

"I'd devised a machine that would break rocks," he started, "with very sharp rotors." He detailed a scenario in which he'd planned to

---

* Bearing a designer label, the wine was produced on the same grounds as the cheese at the original site in Roa. Páramo de Guzmán still made cheese, too, but the days of its international stardom seemed over. A quick trip to the Páramo de Guzmán website is a most curious experience, for the company that began in a stable in a tiny village greets the visitor with an Ibiza-like trance-track, creating a sexy groove while one peruses its lineup of wines, self-described as "unctuous," "very lingering with notes of toast," and "soft velvety of sufficient graduation." Meanwhile, the cheese is "the most prize-winning and well-known in the country." And the factory complex now includes a restaurant, hotel, and lounge.

douse Julián in gasoline, and while smoking, carry on "a transcenden-
tal conversation" with him. In this case, he didn't want Julián to suffer
in death, so eventually he'd light him on fire.

"Why not a gun?" said Asun.

"I wanted to torture him psychologically," Ambrosio said. And
then mash the body in the machine. "Nobody would have ever known
what happened because the burnt bone would have mixed with the
rocks," he said. Then he told about the revelatory moment, the one in
which he'd decided not to kill Julián, this time describing how he
went to his son, who'd awakened from a nightmare and needed his
father, which was different from the way he'd described the moment
as one in which he'd gazed upon his daughter's angelic, sleeping face.
Regardless, "I closed my mind door," he said, "and tried not to think
about it again. After a while, the violence went away. I came to be
more calm and meditative."*

With nothing to lose, I thought I'd try one more time: What would
happen now if Julián came to the door? Would they let him in?

Asun and Ambrosio blurted their answers at the same time, then
Asun deferred momentarily.

"After twenty years, I'd let him in," he said.

"And I would beat him," said Asun. "For everything he did to our
family."

Ambrosio clarified. "I'd let him tell his side of the story. After
twenty years, I'd like to hear his version."

"He's a really bad person, Ambro," said Asun. "An asshole. He
used to come here every Wednesday with Nacho, and I would prepare
the food for *comida*. After 1990, he never came again. Why? What
happened to Julián?"

"We knew each other from 1962," said Ambrosio, explaining to
his wife as much as to me. "It was an intense friendship, a gorgeous

---

* "The perfect narrative," writes Benjamin, "is revealed through the layers of a
variety of retellings." And I had a feeling that this one was still being aged and
perfected, even as I'd reached my end with it.

one, almost the same as mine with Angel. I saved thirty years of our pictures, letters, and cards in a box. All the arguments he's used so far aren't correct. I'd like to hear him explain it."

We'd been here before, to no end. As long as a meeting was hypothetical, it was conceivable and nonthreatening—but I guessed that if the issue were forced, as I'd forced it before, history suggested intractability. Still—who knew with this Ambrosio?

Asun turned to me. "As you can see," she said, "it's complicated. Money and these feelings—it's a very explosive mix."

All these years later, he and Asun still seemed to suffer from PTSD. The death threats, the *guardia civil* at the door to collect what they could, the rock-bottom loss of everything. It was only while discussing the cheese that I saw them bicker. When I asked how much debt they had left to pay, they engaged in a testy debate as Ambrosio tried to write down some numbers, then seemed overwhelmed by the math. *"Mira,"* he said, "I will *still* die without so much as owning this pen."

It was a profound realization, to know your lot like this, and in both their minds, Julián would be forever to blame. Acceptance, for them, was knowing they'd never accept another version, another telling, for what had been done to them.

There was one last thing we'd never discussed, and I brought it up abashedly. Why did they think it had taken me so long to finish Ambrosio's book?

They looked at each other as if they'd discussed the topic before, and then Asun blinked quickly and said, "I think you came here and found an incredible story, and that's what it was at first, a great story that you thought might make a book. But then you developed feelings, these feelings of friendship, and you found something here, in this friendship, more than you wanted a book."

Ambrosio was nodding now. "You were fascinated by *everything,* not just the cheese," he said. "The most important thing is that we met each other, the great satisfaction of meeting, and we're in this conversation. We've entered this big joy of being together."

How right they were! How divided I'd been! And how I'd feared the consequences of having to cross-check Ambrosio's story—and therefore reveal him for being less than a god—or of trading on various village secrets, asking so many intimate questions to reveal them to the world. What had made me feel queasy was this thought that the village, and Ambrosio, may not have wanted to have anything to do with me after reading this book of mine/his/theirs.

And yet this is what I'd come to do, tell a story. And if this was the cost, perhaps I'd be forgiven, if not by Guzmán, then by myself.

"The storyteller," wrote Benjamin in his infinite wisdom, "is the man who could let the wick of his life be consumed completely by the gentle flame of his story." But I'd take it out of the conditional: He *is* consumed by the flame, and it ain't gentle, friend. If everything around him catches fire, and he still owes England some sterling, then so be it: His arsonist's job is complete.

MY FAMILY CAME TUMBLING through customs at Barajas airport on the Monday afternoon before Thanksgiving. Leo, almost thirteen now, with a shaggy mane of hair, nearly reached nose-high on Sara, while May, wearing a stylish red hat as if she'd come directly from the Champs-Élysées (again!), emerged on the gangly legs of a ten-year-old. Nicholas, who was seven, rode on the cart stacked with luggage, then leaped off, sprinted ahead, spun around, ran back, and leaped on again, yelling, "Cowabunga!"

"We've already had some adventures," Sara said with a mirthful eye roll, delighted to have both feet planted in Spain again. "Where are the *jamón* sandwiches, anyway?"

It seemed surreal, the five of us . . . *here.*

The ride to Guzmán under cloudy skies, once the backseaters had survived some early motion sickness, was ecstatic. The questions came in overlapping waves: Who lives in that castle? How do you say "beautiful" in Spanish? Where's the king around here? Can you tell the story of that knight guy again? Does it snow in November? Will Real

Madrid play this week? What time is it back home? Would pigs and hogs live on this mountain?

We shot out through the last pass of the Guadarrama, and there was the Meseta below—again and again and again—and the kids all sucked in their breath at once, as if on a roller coaster. When we finally found the road leading to Guzmán, Leo said, "I think I remember this," and whether he did or not didn't matter, for it was a first act of repossession.

This belongs to us.

We came into the village just before twilight, the sun sinking beneath the ceiling of clouds to light the land, the thin green murk of day giving way to a brilliant golden glow. We drove to the *palacio,* where we were staying, and when we parked, the children went sprinting off in the direction of the fields and *frontón,* eager to explore and play soccer. Sara and I unloaded the bags and then went ambling along the road down to meet them, one we'd traveled many times that summer long ago.

I half expected to see Honorato watering his lawn or Clemente springing a surprise hello, Fernando the Mute under his tree or Carlos the Farmer in his tractor, but there was no one around for this particular homecoming. Not a soul. And perhaps this was most fitting of all. The houses were shuttered, and not a single window was lit from within. The air was cool and clean. The village was all ours, and we held hands, walking past Pinto's ruined house—he'd closed the bar and moved north, Ambrosio said, doing carpentry or something— until we came to the track that led to the *frontón* and the Molinos barn.

Which is when we heard a low rumble.

As we approached, a huge figure loomed over Nicholas, talking rapid-fire in that gravelly baritone. Nicholas was looking up at him, head cocked, laughing, uncertain what to make of the giant he'd just met in the twilight of a Castilian village five thousand miles from home.

Am-*bro*-zee-*oh.*

There were hugs, and that overwhelming pleasure of reacquaintance. Sara looked bewildered at the first onslaught of Ambrosio's high-octane Castellano, but she slowly started picking out the tune, responding as best she could. Already, the kids couldn't believe this place, the freedom and the sky and the colors, the miniature soccer goals set up at the *frontón*. "Awesome," they kept repeating. May, ever intrepid, took off running into the fields, flapping her arms, and the boys played soccer, Nicholas wearing a white Real Madrid jersey (#9, Ronaldo), while Leo, having graduated to the Premier League, wore his Chelsea blue (#9, the Spaniard, Torres), playing like the same little kid he'd once been, but now the ball coming off his foot soared, dipped, and clanked hard off the crossbar. Soon everything fell into shadow as the sun dropped beneath the earth's curvature, everything except the church tower as it caught the last errant rays of day and shone ivory. And if I had died on the spot with my children flapping and singing, kicking balls and running in those fields, and my wife with that smile, and Ambrosio with a tender hand on her shoulder, the mayor detailing plans for new, energy-saving lights in the village, I would have died a happy man.

A very happy man.

Soon we were all piled in Ambrosio's car, headed to his house for dinner. Asun met us at the door, having prepared a minor feast, oohing and aahing over the children. She remembered May as the wriggler and Leo as the boy who ate only white food. In no time Ambrosio had both his guitar and his *charango* out, singing for them, teaching them a song. And it went on—and on.

At midnight we piled back into the car, transecting the fields, in contentment, on our way to sleep in a palace, and as we climbed the hill to Guzmán, Ambrosio veered the car to the side of the road and abruptly leaped out. "*Sígame,*" he said. Follow me. And then we were out in the vineyard, in the dirt that filled our shoes, what had once been a field of sunflowers before Josué had replanted it. "His love," said Ambrosio, "is right here with us. In every vine."

He turned to the children. "*Escuchad,*" he said, in a hoarse whisper. *"El silencio."* He placed the wide-brim hat he wore on Nicholas's head, which had the effect of both settling him and provoking awe again. "Listen to the silence." We are not a quiet people, but there we stood in a loose circle around Ambrosio as he pointed a finger at the moon. Nicholas tilted the hat up so he could see the giant, and the universe beyond. Ambrosio paused a long moment, then said, "In the city, there are so many loud noises, and here in the country we have church bells. Church bells and this silence. It's the most important thing: Learn to listen to this silence, because it will tell you many things, unimaginable things, things of great beauty and meaning."

The kids were rapt as Sara and I tried to translate, but sinking together into that earth, I had a feeling I'd had at least a hundred times here. It was that feeling of being a child again, of being told the story that would never die. Ambrosio pointed up the hill to Guzmán and said, "I think there's something a little bit magical about this place."

And then we left the vineyard, picking our way back to the car. As we did, Ambrosio draped an arm around me, saying nothing. Maybe it was goodbye, or maybe what he said in silence was something he'd told me one September.

I had returned to Guzmán for the *cosecha,* the grape harvest, and on this day the whole Molinos brood—including Ambrosio's mother and father, his brothers and their families—could be found in the field, slicing bunches from the vine with their *garillos,* placing the grapes in cane baskets and dumping them into a trailer attached to the tractor. Everyone worked hard, in wordless rhythm. At one point Mika cut her finger, blood pooling darkly on the ground, and as she gasped, Ambrosio took a grape and squeezed it until the juice ran over the cut, sterilizing it. Then a bandage was applied, she held her hand above her head for a while, and eventually, with that bloody bandage, went back to work.

At the end of the day Ambrosio had leaped up on the tractor, gesturing for me to ride behind on the trailer, atop the overflowing pile of grapes, back to the barn. The first chill of fall brushed the air, and the sky was molten, burbling with dark oranges and reds, and my heart was racing. *So this is joy.* We parked at the barn, lingered, then said our goodbyes, and I started walking the dirt path back up to the village, where I'd parked my car. On my way I heard his voice calling me from behind. "My-kull," he boomed. When I turned, I saw his hulking figure standing atop those mountains of grapes. He was pointing—he was always pointing!—at all those invisible kingdoms in the sky, at all that life-giving land spread across the *coterro* below.

"*¡Recuérdalo!*" he was yelling.

"Remember it!"

ACKNOWLEDGMENTS

But for the energy, support, karma, and humbling generosity of those named here, this book would have remained a dream:

Sara Corbett, true north, *always*.

Andy Ward, the *majo* who made it happen.

Susan Kamil and Sloan Harris, believers.

Random Housers who brought it to life: Kaela Myers, London King, Benjamin Dreyer, Allison Pearl, Evan Camfield, Robbin Schiff, Anna Bauer, Noah Eaker, Giselle Roig, Poonam Mantha, Chris Jerome, and the rest of the team.

Huge thanks to my co-conspirators on the front line: Carlos "Sancho Panza" Gomez; Jeff Braverman; Gerry Hadden; Anne Cassuto.

Gratitude and indebtedness to those friends who read drafts and provided invaluable insights in key moments: Dan Coyle, Bill Lychack, Miles Harvey, Anja Hanson, Gibson Fay-Leblanc, Lily King, Tyler Clements, Brock Clarke, Cammie McGovern, and Laura Hohnhold.

Map and illustrations: the ridiculously clutch Benjamin Busch.

Fact-check: Trent McNamara.

Major thanks to Jim Nelson, for his support of this project. And to others in the *GQ* family: Devin Friedman, Dan Riley, Adam Rappaport, Fred Woodward, Michael Hainey, Mike Benoist, Will Welch, and Ben Bours.

Friends who gave sustenance, help, renewed faith, and enthusiasm when most needed: Wil "Cheese Fry" Hylton, Joel Lovell, Donovan Hohn, Jenny Rosenstrach, Charlie Baxter, Nicholas Delbanco, Kate Porterfield, Colin Harrison, Mark Bryant, Clare Hertel, Robert Draper, Doug Stanton, Melissa McStay, Derek Pierce, Lynn Sullivan, David Mclain, Andrea Hanson-Carr, Ned Flint, Hallie Gilman, Colin and Kate Snyder, Charlotte Bacon and Brad Choyt, Susan Conley, Tony Kieffer, Joel Antolini, Heidi Marble, Kim Wasco, Rick Lynch, Jeff Eckhouse, Lance Cromwell, Chris Bowe, Stuart Gerson, Moira Driscoll, Edward Lewine, Mark Adams, Paige Williams, the family dinner crew, the Darien posse, the Chatauqua element, the MacDowellers, and everyone at the other Telling Room in Portland, Maine.

Thank you to those who offered space in which I was privileged to write: Patty and Cyrus Hagge, Eliot and Melanie Cutler, and Mark and Aimee Bessire. As well, great thanks to Darien Library and Bowdoin College (to Anthony Walton and Liz Muther); Sampere in Salamanca; and the coffee shop on Forest, all of whom made a home for this book.

Scholars and experts: José David Sacristan, Gerry Dawes, Monica Linton, Patricia Michelson, Ari Weinzweig, Clara Estow. At the University of Burgos: Marta Navazo Ruiz and Ivan Garcia. In Madrid: Pascual Llopis and José Ignacio Casado of the Association for the Recovery of Historical Memory.

Support: David Granger and Peter Griffin for sending me to Spain in the first place; the incomparable MacDowell Colony and everyone there who encouraged this work, including David Macy, Kyle Oliver, and Courtney Bethel. And as well the NEA, for instrumental funding that kept this project alive at a crucial juncture.

This book also belongs, with love, to my children: Leo, May, and Nicholas, who lived it. And to my brothers (Paterniti and Corbett) and their families; Chris Corbett and Manny Morgan; Diane Bennekemper and Lorraine Martin; the Simmons-Corbett crew; and my extended family. And to the memory of Arne Heggen, David Stockwood, and Rose Ells, storyteller extraordinaire.

Finally, in Spain: My appreciation to Javier Supuerta, Honorado Escudero and family, Emilia del Rincon, and to the extended Molinos family, including Puri, Angel, Roberto, Mika, Asunita, Josué, and Kiké. To Ambrosio and Asun: an eternal debt of gratitude. *Un abrazo muy fuerte.*

To Guzmán, and its citizens: *Gracias por todo. Alla. Ta' lo . . . ¡Venga!* May you live forever, dear village on the hill!

MICHAEL PATERNITI is the *New York Times* bestselling author of *Driving Mr. Albert: A Trip Across America with Einstein's Brain.* His writing has appeared in many publications, including *The New York Times Magazine, National Geographic, Harper's, Outside, Esquire,* and *GQ,* where he works as a correspondent. Paterniti has been nominated eight times for the National Magazine Award and is the recipient of a NEA grant and two MacDowell Fellowships. He is the co-founder of a children's storytelling center (www.tellingroom.org) in Portland, Maine, where he lives with his wife and their three children.